CompartMENTALized

My Journey

from

Camptown

to the

National Security Agency

A Memoir by Tena Lawyer

Cover Design: Tashara Allen, Clare Carey, & Liane Larocque

This memoir is dedicated to my beautiful daughters, Tierra Sherelle and Tashara Burnett, and my heartbeat and favorite guy, Noah Ryan. I love you all. Thank you for allowing me to grow with you!

Disclaimers

1. "The views expressed in this memoir are those of the author and do not reflect the official policy or position of the National Security Agency, the Department of Defense, or the U.S. Government."

2. The National Security Agency (NSA) reviewed and determined the submitted book entitled "CompartMENTALized: My Journey from Camptown to the NSA," PP-21-0587, to be UNCLASSIFIED and APPROVED FOR PUBLIC RELEASE with no restriction on venue or medium. However, nothing in this notice of approval should be construed as verifying the accuracy of the information included. NSA is not responsible for "fact checking."

3. I fully embrace the notion and accept the gifts imperfection brings. Therefore, making this manuscript/memoir completely error-free, is left as an exercise for readers.

Preface & Caveats

Before I could release this memoir/book, it was approved through the National Security Agency's (NSA) Pre-Publication Review process. As a retiree, who possessed a Top Secret (TS) clearance, I agreed to a lifetime commitment, to basically have everything I publish reviewed by NSA to ensure it does not contain classified or sensitive information. Here's what they determined: "NSA reviewed and determined the submitted document titled "CompartMENTALized: My Journey from Camptown, VA to the NSA," PP-21-0587, to be *UNCLASSIFIED and APPROVED FOR PUBLIC RELEASE with no restriction on venue or medium.*"

I changed the names and used either a pseudo first name or last name of former or current NSA employees I mention in this memoir to adhere to requirements to protect personal identifying information (PII). I gained permission from non-NSA individuals, where I used actual names, and found it necessary enough to do so. I did not exclude anyone deliberately — I just let the relevant memories flow onto the pages. There are so many people I've encountered on my journey — the stories are endless.

The stories revealed in this book are my own. My observations, which some will believe/say are over generalized, my thoughts, knowledge of events, accomplishments, and blunders, from my point-of-view (POV) and perspective. First, as a woman, a black woman, a mother, veteran, and a former federal government employee.

Most notably, I'm a product of my grandmother's rearing and the community of Camptown, which greatly influenced who I am, even today. I dedicate Chapter 1 and 3 to my grandmother Novella and the community that raised me, Camptown.

Why I wrote a memoir? First question I always ask, is why not? During the height of the COVID-19 pandemic, I felt compelled to write my story as a testament and acknowledgement of my noteworthy existence and journey.

During the time, I came to the realization, my journey has been far from the ordinary and felt inclined to share it. My experiences as a soldier and a civilian employee, working in one of the most secretive intelligence agencies in the Intelligence Community (IC).

As a retired NSA employee and intelligence soldier, I've walked the halls of the Central Intelligence Agency (CIA), National Geo-Spatial Intelligence Agency (NGA), Defense Intelligence Agency (DIA), National Reconnaissance Office (NRO), Federal Bureau of Investigation (FBI), and every military service's intelligence commands. I wrote this memoir for people who may never find themselves in these spaces. It's a good glimpse behind the fence lines, the dark glass windows, the badge readers, and that "NSA Employees Only" exit on the Baltimore Washington (BW) Parkway.

I also felt obligated to share lessons I've learned, places I've travelled, personalities I encountered, while finally sharing all my truth — full of twists, turns, celebrations, losses, and revelations.

The title of this memoir is drawn from having a TS clearance with additional access to Sensitive Compartmented Information (SCI) while in the Army, and as a civilian. and my feeble attempts to compartmentalize my personal life from my career.

Like SCI, a program that separates already classified information into distinct compartments or buckets, never to be comingled, I compartmentalized my private life from my career What I mean is, even though I really dislike being put in a box or category, I strived to keep all aspects of my life outside of work, in a separate box, in the top of a closet, with an airtight lid.

Always aware and mindful of how women, particularly black women, are viewed, interpreted, and need I say, marginalized, unintentionally or intentionally — I was not going to give anyone at NSA yet another reason to make unjust or prejudicial judgements and distinctions about me (and others) based on my double minority status — race and gender.

Keep in mind, psychologist define the ability and the desire to compartmentalized as a "subconscious psychological defense mechanism" used to avoid mental discomfort and anxiety caused by a person's having conflicting values, emotions, and beliefs. My life and work were not aligned with my values and belief system. I was struggling mentally and eventually, physically.

I prefer to compartmentalize in a way — I like structure in my life. To me, there's nothing like organizing and prioritizing how I approach my work, life, and relationships. It makes sense to me. I believe there's a place and time to do everything — in their own swim lanes.

As a civilian leader, I led two Training Departments with over 150 staff members combined. I've traveled the world teaching and learning — Australia, Germany, Japan, and South Korea, and have been stationed or worked in several states across the U.S., including the beautiful islands of Hawaii. My career with NSA was successful as well. I advanced in grade from GG-13 to GG-15, and in ever-increasing responsibility, authority, and leadership positions, at multiple locations.

I would characterize my career in the Army and as a civilian employee as successful. I served honorably. I was never reprimanded for anything while in the Army, not as much as a single, negative, counseling. I achieved the rank of First Sergeant (1SG), an E-8 position, and in my opinion, the toughest and most rewarding job in the Army.

Chapters in this memoir describe memories, significant events, assignments, and positions chronologically from my college days, career as a soldier, then, as a civilian working in NSA. I provide glimpses into my otherwise private life — my relationships, marriages X 2, challenges, and family dynamics, because even with great effort and attempts to separate the personal from professional, I came the realization that I was indeed compartmentalizing and at what cost.

I have wonderful memories, particularly from traveling, but I also have endured great pain/loss, frustration, and anxiety, which prompted quite a few lessons and impactful, life-changing revelations and direction. This is my perspective, which, of course, is my reality

Part I – The Early Years in Camptown!

Chapter 1

Novella Means "A Short Novel"

Some of the world's best educators are grandparents.

- *Charles Shedd*

Born & Raised in Camptown

Her name is Novella Moore Lawyer. She was a distinguished looking black woman. High-cheek bones with bronze, light brown skin, which she contributed to having Native American in her DNA. She was of average height, about 5'5". Her hair was mingling grey and fell just shy of her shoulders. She usually wore her hair in about 4 big plaits, tucked so she could "slap a wig on and go."

From my first memory of my grandmother, she was round and soft, with huge, 44 double D breasts. She was loaded in the "bosom" department, as she called them. Her bras were amazingly enormous to me as a child. As you can imagine, she gave the best hugs and provided a soft pillow to snuggle or for quick naps. My grandmother had a beautiful smile. She was proud that she managed to keep all her own teeth, which was considered rare for older adults who grew up in the early 1900s.

Most people in our neighborhood called her Miss Novella. Although married to Abraham, aka "Ham" Lawyer, a common practice in our community was to use the prefix "Miss" and first names. Not Ms. But Miss, like Miss Bessie, Miss Stella, Miss Rena, and

Miss Isabelle. We, affectionately called her Gramma...pronounced like grammar, without the 'r on the end. Gramma!

Tragically, my gramma said she delivered nine babies in all, but only four survived - Ruth, Andrew aka Buddy, Reynold aka Teensy, and Ellouise, my mother. She then raised four grandchildren, Elvis Patricia aka Pat, Avon, Wendell aka Butch, and me - Tena, spelled with one "E" and not an "I."

Several wood-burning stoves adorned the old house. One in the slanted, creaky floor, front room (aka Living Room), one in the kitchen, where I recall my grandfather spent most of his nights, and one upstairs in a bedroom that was large enough for two queen size beds — one on each side of the stove. Each stove had a metal or wood box nearby, stacked neatly with kindling/wood. That meant a lot of chopping wood, especially during the winter months.

Speaking of chopping wood and keeping fires burning, she got blisters on both of her hands. Her parents were an older couple when she was born. Her parents owned the land and the two-story house with the peeling white paint, warped boards, and a screened-in front porch. She had two half-sisters born from her mother's first marriage, but both were grown and long gone.

Both her mother and father began to age and ail when she was just fifteen years old. She had to help around the house. She cooked and cleaned. She emptied and replaced every slop-jar, in every bedroom, daily. And...she chopped a lot of wood in the coldest winters and admitted life for her was tough then.

Gramma went to school until the seventh grade; I recall her telling us. Probably the one-room, Negro school located near what we call "the pines." It was referred to as "the school on Council's Farm" in Camptown by Isle of Wight (IOW) County education records. Given she only had a seventh-grade education, she was very articulate. She read and wrote well beyond her education. Her penmanship was remarkable. She quoted and read the bible flawlessly.

Wearing thin as a sixteen-year-old girl in the early 1930's, Gramma prayed to GOD to send her a "hardworking man" to help her maintain the house and take care of her parents — and he did. Her lesson to my cousins Avon, Carol Lynn, and me, was "Be careful and be specific when you pray because GOD might answer your prayer." I'll never forget that day. She then jokingly said, "I asked for a hardworking man, and that's exactly what I got. I didn't ask for a good husband, you see. I wasn't specific. Your grandfather was a hard worker." To this day, this lesson prevails in my mind when I have conversations with GOD – be specific in prayers.

We lived on Pocahontas Avenue in Camptown, Virginia (VA). My sister-cousin Pat and I lived with our grandparents while our mothers worked in Newark, New Jersey, and Williamsburg, VA, respectively. It was a common practice in black families in the 1950s and 1960s for the younger, able-bodied family members to move north for job opportunities and send money back to help support their parents and children.

This was especially true for young black women. My mother, Ellouise, lived and worked in New York City, Atlantic City, and Williamsburg all before I was in the second grade. The entire family couldn't afford to just pack-up and leave the South without resources and possibly support from a relative(s) in a northern destination.

Look Whos' Coming to Stay

I had just turned six years old, when my cousins, Julon, affectionately known as Gigi, her younger sister Avon, and brother Wendell, aka Butch, showed-up in Camptown from New York City on Halloween evening, 1969. Their beautiful mother, Dorothy, aka Aunt Dot, passed away unexpectedly in New York, so my Uncle Buddy, their father, brought them to Camptown for his mother to raise. Aunt Dot was young and beautiful when she died and left three beautiful children.

Gigi was the oldest at around 10. Avon was almost 8, and Butch was 6, like me. With a bedroom downstairs and two bedrooms upstairs, one big enough for two queen beds and a wood burning stove between them, this old house offered plenty of space for all of us. I don't remember their father visiting after that. Their maternal grandmother from Trinidad, who lived in New York, visited Camptown almost annually. Rest assured, when she came, we'd have money for candy and snacks. Pat and I were always included in her gift giving.

I was so excited to have them there and to play with them. Avon was the prettiest girl I had ever seen. Her sometimes green, sometimes hazel eyes, and golden-light brown hair was a sight for every country boy's eyes. I wanted her to be my sister, for real. She talked fast and with a strong New York accent that I could hardly understand at times. Avon was sensitive as a kid. She struggled to come to terms with the loss of both of their parents. I think of the three siblings, she was the most sensitive and affected by their parent's deaths — you could tell that gramma felt that way too. She kept a close eye on Avon.

Everybody loved Butch. He made friends easily, and he had a way of making his friends feel like they were his only "bestie." He was slightly below average height for a boy his age when we were kids. He had a late growth spurt in high school and the first few years that he was in the U.S. Army. It surprised all of us. Suddenly, Butch was taller than all of us. He looked down on my gramma — she loved it as along as the look was accompanied by a hug.

He had hazel eyes and smooth brown skin. Butch was incredibly attractive. He even tried his hand at modeling and acting for a bit. He held onto a slight New York accent that stood out from the rest of us. The southern twang in Camptown is undeniable. He was athletic, loved music and girls; and they loved him. Most of my friends had a crush on Butch, and he knew it. He'd flirt and "look into their eyes," he said. That's how he would "get them." Butch and I were the same age and in the same grade, we bonded and had spats like a brother and sister.

6

Unbeknownst to me during this time, there was a court custody case that separated the siblings, leaving Avon and Butch in Camptown. Streetwise and beautiful, Gigi was taken back to New York. I thought she was so cool, smart, and beautiful. Gigi was not my uncle's daughter; he was aware, but he wanted to keep the three siblings together.

Next thing I knew, I heard Uncle Buddy had been murdered in New York. I don't think my gramma ever got the complete story. Avon & Butch were solemn or just numb. As the story goes, he was playing cards. Gambling. Something about a woman. Stabbed. Dead. We'd also learn he was AWOL from the Army. Avon and Butch didn't benefit at all from his service. He had been dropped from the Army rolls. I tried to piece all of this together with my young mind. Bottom line, Avon and Butch lost both of their parents before they were in their teens. Unimaginable!

Gramma made sure Avon and Butch spent time with their sister and mother's family growing up. We'd all visited with their family in Harlem one summer when we were teens. New York was the biggest city I'd ever seen. For a kid from the country, riding the subways was amazing. When Gigi became an adult, she left Harlem and moved to Franklin, across the river from Camptown, to be near her sister Avon.

My oldest sister-cousin Pat's "government name" is Elvis Patricia Lawyer. Fact. My Aunt Ruth, Pat's mother, was a huge Elvis Presley fan. She loved his music and watched every Elvis movie there was. A lot of black women were Elvis' fans. He was the hit maker in the late 50s and 60s. They saw Elvis as a good-looking, white man, who could shake his hips.

He had a sizeable, black fan-base, from his musical movies. When Aunt Ruth was pregnant, she told my grandmother she would name the baby Elvis, boy or girl. She kept her word. Can you imagine a little black girl, growing up in VA in the 60s, named Elvis? Pat despised her name, and probably still does. Now she uses a simple E. in front of Patricia. E. Patricia Lawyer. It does have a ring to it.

Ironically, Pat was born to dance. With swagger and grace for a curvy woman, Pat is a dancing machine. "She started dancing before she could walk," Gramma would say. After watching Soul Train on Saturdays, she showed us the latest dance moves and ensured we were doing them right. We always practiced in the front room aka living room, where there was space.

In the late 70s, our cousin Preston and Pat entered the Soul Train dance contest held in Norfolk, VA., at the Scope, a concert/sports arena. The winners would head to Los Angeles and dance as guests on the hit TV show we watched every Saturday after chores. Pat and Preston danced their tails off but weren't tapped to move to the final round. Their consolation prizes were cases of Sprite sodas in the can — one of Soul Train's commercial sponsors.

They felt robbed. They said the other couples were way too choreographed to show skills and they shouldn't have been selected. We were proud just the same. I had never seen that many cans of sodas in my life; we drank Kool-Aid as kids. Those two cases slid around in the back of my mother's big Buick trunk, all the way to Camptown. I couldn't wait to have a cold one. In my mind, Pat and Preston won by showing-up and doing their thing on the stage. I was proud of them, and my mother was too. I could tell.

Our New Home

In the late 1960's I wasn't quite in the second grade when my grandmother, Novella, my mother Ellouise, and my cousins and I moved from a wooden, two-story house built on a crawl space foundation to a new four-bedroom, concrete slab rancher, constructed right behind the old house. The old two-story house's foundation provided a safe haven for dogs to have puppies or for snakes to keep cool during long, humid summers in southern Virginia.

Gramma was so happy to get that house for us. If it weren't for the government's Federal Housing Administration (FHA) insured loan program for low-income Americans, I don't believe she thought she could. The new home was perfect — a four-bedroom, one bath, lavender rancher. Yes, lavender as in the shade of purple. My grandmother, "inspired" by my cousin Butch's lavender Hot Wheels car, picked the color from the palette herself. Never had anyone in our neighborhood seen a lavender house. Not in Camptown or neighboring Franklin for that matter.

I desperately wanted siblings. Now I had three. I was thrilled. Until we were into adulthood, gramma reminded us of this new family concept, especially during our teen years when we formed new friendships, bonds with kids in the neighborhood or at school, and even boyfriends. At that age, we often preferred not to include each other in our plans or outings with our personal friends. We always wanted to go somewhere or do something without our "sister-cousins" or Butch in the picture — he was a friend stealer, for sure.

The challenge to hang out alone became incredibly frustrating for Pat, the oldest. She fumed at the revelation, "If Avon and Tena couldn't go, you can't go either," Gramma asked, "What are you going to be doing that she can't be around?" Concluding," if it's not a good environment for your younger cousin, then it's not a good environment for you either, so stay home!" Reluctantly, Pat gave in but not without a robust and secretive threat. "If you go home and tell anything, you ain't going NO MO."

Lessons from Gramma

Miss Novella didn't like gossip or contribute to Camptown's little "Peyton Place" tendencies. She listened to grunting or feuding neighbors and her girlfriends, but once they left the house, she quickly told us never to repeat what someone said about another person, especially if you don't know them. And if we heard ANY of her conversations, we were NEVER to repeat them. Her advice was two-fold. First, you don't know if it's true or not, and more importantly, "If a dog brings a bone, he will certainly carry one." I remember one of us asking her, "What does that mean?"

She regularly spoke and taught using parables or proverbs. She wanted us to learn that if someone is willing to bring gossip to you, they will take what you said with others. "A dog can't help but be a dog," she'd say. This lesson is a hard lesson for some to learn, even into adulthood. I believe we all struggle to keep juicy, chinwag to ourselves. Who doesn't like unbelievable gossip? It takes a concerted effort not to keep it to yourself, especially if asked by a friend or family member.

Another lesson and one of "Gramma's Commandments" were to always tell the truth, no matter the consequences or how difficult. I cannot count the number of times Butch learned the hard way. Gramma declared, "If you're willing to lie, you will cheat. If you can cheat, you will steal. If you can steal, especially if you can get away with it, you're capable of doing anything, which makes you completely untrustworthy in every regard."

As kids, you're a bit confused by this. Your imagination conjures up all kinds of things a liar does — kind of scary stuff. Of course, in adolescence, Butch's "storytelling" wasn't particularly good at all. He told unbelievable, "What had happened was, stories," to gramma. In jeopardy of getting a "whooping," mind you, he was an animated actor. Avon and I listened, and snickered under our breath, which he hated. Does he really think she's going to buy that? She wouldn't.

This lesson, by far, is one of the greatest lessons and gifts of my life. It's a condition or expectation of my children, Tierra and Tashara, and of those around me. Always tell the truth. What I've found in doing so, believe it or not, is peace! Yes, peace of mind that I don't have to worry about anyone discovering a lie and you don't have to tell other lies to "secure" the first lie. Over time, you become known as the colleague or friend who tells the truth, no matter how ugly that truth may be, and people want the truth. They will call you for it. It's amazing.

I've told the raw truth, when I knew it would be difficult for the person on the receiving end to swallow it. I've given what we call candid and honest performance feedback to struggling instructors even though it might hurt their well-developed egos and make them reconsider their career choice. Of course, I gave such feedback professionally. This type of truth, laced with specific actions and support to help them succeed, is given in a way that isn't embarrassing or a personal attack. It's the truth, and they know it. Nothing got my grandmother more upset than to learn or surmise anyone of us was telling a lie. I'm sure others have experienced this, but you'd get a "whooping" for telling a lie, not the infraction.

Another invaluable lesson she nailed home was, not everyone uses or even possesses common sense. *What on earth did she mean by that?* Well, as she described it, having common sense does not equate to formal learning. It's an awareness and the innate ability to make practical choices and make sound judgments. It's able to understand a situation and then act appropriately. Common sense to my grandmother was more valuable than any degree. She often reminded us that displaying common sense is not a given. I later defined and found what our grandmother was saying was also the gift of discernment, rare and considered a blessing.

Gramma taught us good manners — civility. Always say please and thank you because people are not obligated to do anything for you. We spoke to all adults, neighbors, and sometimes strangers. Saying the greeting of the day when you walk past someone within hearing distance was expected. When I started working at the NSA, I discovered not everyone was taught the same good manners. Giving the greeting of the day catches some people off guard. Don't expect your hello to be reciprocated, more about my observations at NSA and its culture in later chapters.

Growing up, my grandmother also taught us humility, modesty, and the ability to laugh at our own mistakes. She had a great sense of humor. This last attribute was revealed in unexpected ways. I wasn't going to include this story about gramma, but my family and a best friend found it unimaginable. To set the stage, our neighbors were my grandmother's best girlfriends. Miss Bessie and Miss Julia Jenkins lived next door — the sisters had for years. I found their names and their parents on census records from the early 1900s. They were longtime friends. I can smell Miss Bessie's cakes from across the yard right now. It looked like a single-layered cake without frosting or glaze — she called it sweet bread. It was made entirely from scratch. Regardless, this was the best cake/bread I'd ever had as a kid.

One Sunday afternoon, my grandmother's friend from next door, Miss Bessie, came to visit. This was a common practice for them to visit each other, especially if one of them wasn't feeling well and hadn't seen each other in a while. Now only Misses Bessie, Julia, and Rena could sit in her bedroom. This was black women's code, especially if married — other women were not allowed in the bedroom that a couple communed. Other visitors sat in the living room or dining room/family room. Gramma and her girlfriends always caught-up in there. Gramma's bedroom gave private sanctuary for "the girls" to catch-up, especially when we were teens doing our own thang around the house, like listening to music on the radio or watching TV. There was one family TV and one stereo component.

Well, Miss Bessie was sitting in my grandmother's room catching up, when "it" happened. They started to discuss the small handgun that my Uncle Teensy gave my grandmother to keep for protection. It was in her bloomer drawer, as she called it. You see bloomers, are panties. The guy was in a place so highly forbidden you dare not even poke with your index finger.

Back then, we didn't worry too much about break-ins. Most families in Camptown left their doors unlocked. Gramma got up and fished out her pretty, pearl-handled, cute .22 caliber handgun. We were milling about, oblivious until we heard a gunshot. In the house, no doubt! We ran to Gramma's bedroom door. She had the gun in her hand, pointing it toward the floor, shaking like a leaf. She didn't move. She was paralyzed with fear, initially.

Pat asked first, "What are you doing, Gramma? Did you shoot that gun? Why?" Gramma's shoulders started moving up and down. She began to chuckle. First softly, then louder with a huge grin. Miss Bessie started to laugh, and she rolled out of her chair onto the bedroom floor, still laughing. Mind you, these women are in their mid to late 60s. She couldn't contain herself.

Gramma says between laughs, "Lord have mercy! I didn't know it was loaded. I pointed it in the kitchen and shot. Jesus, I'm so glad none of you all walked past my door. Oh lord. Oh lord!" Miss Bessie chimed in, "Novella...you didn't know...it was loaded?" she cackled. "No-vel-la...no!" Gramma started laughing at herself slowly. Then, uncontrollably. She got up, still pointing the gun at the floor, and put the gun back in her bloomer drawer. I never saw it again.

And finally, gramma taught us to never stop learning and teaching. She believed you can train old dogs' new tricks. I'm grateful for Miss Novella. For her love, wisdom, stability, sense of humor, resourcefulness, and steadfastness. She was in her mid-fifties when she started raising four grandchildren. She was "on disability," which meant she received a minimal monthly check from the government because of heart disease, which didn't permit her to work. When I found out the amount of those checks, I could only shake my head in amazement at what she was able to do for so long. She raised four children and then four more who were never cold, hungry, or neglected to any extent.

Miss Novella undoubtedly was and is the greatest inspiration and teacher in my life, and I believe that of my cousins, who she raised to honor and treat like siblings, which we did. She taught us siblings don't have to come from the same birth mother or father. It's the way in which you love and support someone that makes them your sister or your brother. If you're ever around Pat, Avon, & me, it's evident; we have an unbreakable bond. My loving gramma passed away at 68 years young. The sibling bond she helped to create is a testament to Miss Novella's heart and wisdom which lives on within each of us.

Top: My grandmother Novella, aka Gramma, and her dog Tippy. Below: Gramma and her grandchildren. L-r, Avon, Butch, Gramma, and cousin Susan. I'm on the right lifting Susan's chin.

Chapter 2

Notorious Wheezy and Mysterious Duke

Honor thy father and thy mother; that thy days may be long upon the land which the Lord thy GOD giveth thee.

- Exodus 20:12

Notorious Ellouise aka Wheezy

It can't be denied back in the day, my mother, Ellouise Lawyer, was a "whole snack" as my daughters say. My mother had a gorgeous smile. She was smart, tough, career-driven, and an extreme extrovert, which made her very popular in Camptown -not in a bad way. She was desired by a lot of men, young and old. The kids all over the neighborhood knew my mother and revered her. I was proud of her and proud to be her daughter.

One of my first memories of her was before I went to first grade. She worked at a restaurant in Williamsburg, Virginia as a host. For my birthday, she picked me up from Camptown to spend the weekend in Williamsburg with her. After driving back to Williamsburg, we went directly to the restaurant where she worked — the Cascade.

The Chef came from the kitchen with the biggest, three-tiered, cake I had ever seen! It looked like an all-white wedding cake, and it was for me. Mind you, I was 6 years old. He and the kitchen staff sang Happy Birthday. I couldn't wait to show gramma. That cake lasted for weeks. My grandmother suggested we freeze some...so we did.

My grandmother bragged that the one thing Ellouise could get was a job. And she could. In the mid-60s and early 1970's, she worked in the restaurant industry, as a Teacher's Aide for Head Start in Camptown and moved to Atlantic City to work in the tourist and gambling industry there. Wheezy also drove one of the first school buses that transported children from our community school to Carrsville Elementary School.

There wasn't much my mother couldn't do. At a paper bag manufacturing plant in Franklin, called St. Regis, she was a supervisor when it wasn't very popular for a woman to do so. At St. Regis, she was trained and certified to run machinery and to drive a forklift that moved the huge palettes of large bags around. I believe she was the only woman driving forklifts at that time.

When my mother was just 17 years old, she got pregnant. Imagine being a young black girl, unmarried, and pregnant in 1961 — it couldn't have been easy. I was born on a Wednesday, October 25, 1961, at the hospital, downtown Franklin. My parents never got married. He married the mother of his three sons — the first one born almost five years after me. I don't know what caused their breakup, but it made my mother angry as hell and not just with Duke.

I never saw my parents together as a child. I just remember my gramma telling me about a neighbor across the street who insisted she confirm. "Novella, is that Ellouise and Duke's baby?" they'd asked her while she held my hand at the mailbox at the street. I was a toddler, squeezing my grandmothers' hand. She'd said, "Yes." The neighbor looked me over — at my soft, black, sparse hair, my light skin-tone, and advised my grandmother to "keep a hat on that baby's head so she won't get black."

In my mother's younger years, Wheezy was fit and athletic. She played softball on St. Regis's women's team for a couple of seasons — she played first base. I would join her in the outfield when I reached high school.

She went out on dates. She and her girlfriends, particularly my "Aunts," Audrey aka Jean, and Diane, from Camptown, would dress to the nines, to go to dances at the Franklin Armory, where they had to take their own "set-ups" of mixers, ice, cups, and spirits. They played card games like Bid Whist and hung out frequently. Wheezy and her girlfriends lived life to the fullest.

Mysterious Duke Reid

I was told I am the product of my mother's first relationship with her teenaged boyfriend, "Duke" Reid. His actual name is Robert Earl Reid, but his family and folks in Camptown and Franklin called him Duke, and so did I. Duke was mysteriously. legendary in our community and Franklin.

Picture this, an attractive, shy/introverted, light-skinned, black man, with a long, black, ponytail. Back in the day, "a high-yellow" or light-skinned black man, was considered more desirable than darker-skinned men. Not sure why. The limited number of light-skinned men made them noticeable, and distinguishable from other men, I suppose. To be attractive and "damn near white" gave Duke a license to sling — and you know what I mean by sling. But for Duke, he prescribed to the notion that the blacker the berry, the sweeter the juice! He loved dark-skinned women. I believe he loved women period.

My first memory of my father was when I was about 5 years old. It was late Christmas day, and his best friend gave him a ride to my grandmother's house to bring me a present. I don't believe Duke ever drove a car. He rode a bike to visit his buddies on the weekends at local shot houses in Franklin. I've never seen him behind the wheel of a car. Never. So, I remember hearing someone knock on the front door. We knew it wasn't a person who came to our house often, because only the life insurance man, white people, and special guests used the front door. Everyone else came through the side porch door.

Someone opened it. I ran to the hallway leading to the front door to see who it was. At that age, I ran everywhere. "Company" at our house on Christmas day?! We called guests, company, you see. I hoped whoever it was, had some children and toys. When I slid across the hall in the dining room with my socks on, I looked at the front door and directly in the face of a stranger. *Who is that white man?* I thought. I slid my ass back across the hall. It was definitely a Tom Cruise, "Risky Business," moment.

Then I heard my mom call me. "Tee-Nah." I said, "Yes, Ma'am!" "Come here." she said. They were weirdly cordial, chatting at the door. Mostly about work. This time I walked into the dining room, did a right turn, and headed to the door. There was a pink girl's bicycle with a white basket attached to the front. And right beside that bike was a white man with a long ponytail, staring at me. *Who is he?* I thought.

My grandmother was sitting so that she was facing the door with her arms and hands resting in her lap. She was completely silent. She observed. I heard the man speak to her when he came in. "How you doin' Miss Novella?" She responded with a short, "Fine," and a head nod toward the man.

My mom stood at the door with him. Before I reached her, she said, "This is your daddy, Duke...he brought you a bicycle for Christmas." I couldn't utter a word. I was speechless. My D-a-d-d-y? Did she say daddy? I looked at the shiny pink girl's bicycle. He'd taken the liberty of spray painting my name using stencils in black spray paint. T-I-N-A! Spelled the typical way. He bent down, so we were face-to-face. He looked in my eyes and asked, "Do you like pink?" I couldn't speak. I moved my head up and down, indicating yes. *He's a white man,* I said to myself.

He didn't stay long after that, nor did he move from the door. He left, explaining his friend, named Robert too, was outside in the car waiting for him. I walked over to my grandmother. I slowly did a 180 and sat in her lap. I was very shy then, especially with him. They said good-bye. He waved and said good night. I waved back.

I saw him intermittently. His visits were just like that — every two or three years, usually Christmas or my birthday. He'd almost always secretly and unannounced, show-up with money, a toy, a BBQ grill he made, or a stuffed animal. I would smile back at Duke and say thank you. Wheezy didn't seem to be angry with Duke for her plight with me. She was outraged with the woman he married some years after I was born. Oh, the rivalry was real; still is. They would act like they liked each other at times. I think this was for my and Duke's benefit, but as soon as the coast was clear, out of earshot of each other and Duke, the eye rolling, mouth popping, 'cussing started. And it usually started with, "Who does she think she is?" and ended with, "That black bitch!"

My parents. Ellouise Lawyer, top. Robert, aka Duke, below.

Chapter 3

"Over the River" - The Camptown Community

A common definition of community is a group of people with diverse characteristics who are linked by social ties, share common perspectives, and engage in joint actions in a geographical location.

- American Journal of Public Health

Camptown, Virginia (VA)

What's the definition of a community when the group of people have similar characteristics, perspectives, culture, and life experiences? I'm inclined to believe such a community develops a strong sense of identity. They become family.

I love my fellow "Camptown-ers!" I know how they think. How they operate. What is acceptable and what may cause "your tail" to get confronted, or 'cussed slam out! This was crystal clear when I was a child growing-up in Camptown.

As a kid, it was nothing to see an adult in our community correct a child when they were away from their mama and 'dem. If you were in the streets of Camptown showing off, adults had no problem calling your parents or walking "your fast tail" home to straight snitch on "your grown tail." We were raised by the village.

The small community of Camptown in southwest IOW county, is where I spent my formative years. It's about a mile or so, east of the Blackwater River and the town of Franklin, VA and 50 miles from the west of Hampton Roads. When asked, most people from Camptown say they're from Franklin. We're not, but if you know where Franklin is on Route 58, then more than likely you will know where Camptown is.

Welcome to Camptown sign that welcomes visitors to our community.

Camptown is/was surrounded by the mill, miles of timber/forestry, railroad tracks, and the Black Water river which divides Franklin from this little community, locals call, "Over the River." The paper and timber strategically located along the river, combined to form Union Camp in 1937. With four paper machines and a bag plant then, it turned out 1,100 tons of paper products per day. As a point of reference, Union Camp was later acquired by International Paper in 1999. Regardless of the ownership change, most people still called the mill Union Camp.[1]

If you've visited or driven through Camptown in the 60s – 80s, you will never forget the smell. For years, especially when I was a kid, Camp's paper mill reeked of what smelled like rotten eggs for miles. We couldn't smell it. We were used to it. It wasn't until we left Camptown and came back, that you got a good whiff.

The 2010 population census of Camptown was 766 residents. Unfortunately, 2020 data is not yet available due to the Pandemic. I suspect at the height of Camptown's population in the early 1970 and 80's, there were approximately 900, mostly black people.

According to the same census (2010), Camptown had a total area of 6.3 square miles, most of which is owned by the mill. There are four major streets with families – Pocahontas Ave., Council Rd., Washington Ave., and Lear Place. A single cross street connected three streets. Two streets were across the bridge and

---

[1] https://en.wikipedia.org/wiki/Union_Camp_Corporation

railroad tracks below, that went through the mill supplying needed supplies; one was Church St. Multiple walking paths and trails crisscrossed Camptown and created our world.

Living in Camptown in the 1960's, we could use the mill's steam whistle as a personal alarm. There were four distinct alerts that I remember. It sounded like a train whistle but with more organization — the whistle started low and short. By the third pull of the whistle, it was louder, much longer, and stronger. The mill's whistle blared across Camptown where most of its black workers lived.

The earliest whistle was to start the workday. The next whistle we'd hear was for lunch break. When we got old enough and weren't in school, we'd take my granddaddy's fresh, hot lunch to the door of the timber-side of the factory. The next whistle that always seemed shorter, was the alert to return to work after lunch. The final whistle of the day was quitting time. We could set our clocks to Camp's work schedule. Fathers, granddads, uncles, and brothers came walking down the streets of Camptown from work, lunch pail in hand, going home.

Camptown was a mixed pod of houses, mobile trailers, prefabricated houses, and small black businesses. Our little community had an entrepreneurial vibe. I recall five churches and four barbershops. There were shot houses, mostly in a small cluster. These houses were a part of the social fabric of the community. They sold alcohol, mostly shots from a single fifth (bottle size) and beers. Scotch and water, a mixed drink, was popular. This was a haven for black men to socialize and show themselves as men among men. Rarely were women present, except for the lady who owned and ran the shot house. Just look for the woman serving up shots, cold beers, and stuffing cash in her big bosom.

There were at least four family-owned convenient stores that sold necessities like toilet paper, sugar, flour, cheese, bologna, etc. My grandmother Novella owned one of these stores for a while, which eventually became one of the barbershops in the community. Countless ladies sold penny candy or freeze pops out of their kitchens.

Before I went to elementary school, during a time my mother was visiting, and she took me to a cinderblock place in Camptown on Council Rd, where the road curved past the school. This place had vintage, five-cent Jukeboxes with push buttons to make song selections on every table. I don't recall the name of the place, but it was black and locally owned. They sold food, cold beer, and spirits. I felt like I was in another world. Black people smiling. Smoking. Flirting. Dancing. The smell of fried food lingered inside and outside.

We had our very own community car wash courtesy of Union Camp. It was a simple, push button and drive through sprinklers. It was free to use for both Camp's employees and the community because of snowflake-like particles that spewed from the mill almost weekly. There were reports that if "the snow" wasn't removed in a timely manner, it left rust spots on the hood of cars.

I don't know if this substance was ash or paper. Not to mention, the bubbly mustard color, flow just beyond Camp's fence line on Council Rd, that people in the community said was hot acid. A few boys that I knew, claimed to have thrown a cat or two in there. Bolstering boys. Of note, the Environmental Protection Agency (EPA) did not exist. It wasn't until July 1970 that the EPA, under President Nixon, was born.

Granddaddy Long Legs

When the lumber mill, established in the late 1880's, expanded in the late1930s, it hired black men from all over VA and the south. The mill even built homes to attract even more families, complete with rent control for employees. If you lived in a Camp house, more than likely your father or a male in your household worked for Camp.

My maternal grandfather, Abraham Lawyer, moved from Silver, South Carolina to Franklin for work. He ended up getting a job at Camp's Mill. He was 10 years older than my grandmother. It wasn't until I found my grandparent's marriage certificate on Ancestry that we learned our Granddaddy was a widow when he married gramma. His first wife, Annie, died at just 19 years old from an ectopic pregnancy. Neither my grandfather nor my grandmother mentioned this tragedy to us, or that he had been married, but it certainly explained the pain he seemed to be trying to soothe with alcohol.

I think in a way, my grandfather was so unsettled and haunted by things that happened in S.C., he didn't talk much at all. It was only when he returned from the shot houses that we heard his deep, rattly voice. He worked and slept Monday–Friday. He drank liquor and "raised hell" come Friday evening through Sunday afternoon," my grandmother would say. He was tall at six feet, four inches, and dark.

We all called him Granddaddy. When I called him, I'd say under my breath, "long legs," like the insect. That was who he was to me – Grandaddy Long Legs! He was missing several teeth, both top and bottom. If he didn't smile, he was attractive. He spoke broken English, which is associated with the enslaved Gullah-Geechee people who lived on the sea islands of S.C. (Actually, the sea islands are from the coast of N.C. to northern FL). He couldn't read or write, so he relied on my grandmother to read correspondence to him. He used an "X" to sign his paychecks from Camp's mill.

He drove a unique vehicle to transport long wood logs across the street from the timber side of the factory to the processing plant to make pulp. This almost 7 feet tall contraption, complete with wheels and a driver's seat where my grandfather sat, allowed logs to be stacked underneath the high driver's compartment in an area of about 6 feet wide by 6 feet tall, filled with logs.

Come hell or high water, weekdays, Granddaddy was atop of his Dr. Seuss-looking log carrier, waiting for the light to change, driving back and forth across Route 58, between the processing plants. A traffic light

31

signaled them to go. Then one or more of these vehicles would come careening out of the huge, long wooden buildings to travel across the road (Route 58) to go inside yet another long wooden building for processing. The vehicles were so tall and awkward, I was told an employee ran over a fellow employee and didn't even know it.

My mother and her siblings caught holy hell from what I was told. My gramma described him as an abusive, weekend, alcoholic. The stories gramma told - about running and moving temporarily to New York and with family, with her four children in tow, were hard to believe. He barely said good morning to his grandchildren. I remember an incident where he "raised hell" and woke up the entire house. I had to be four or five years old. It was before Avon & Butch moved to Camptown.

Granddaddy came home from one of the shot houses on Washington Rd., drunk and very talkative. He looked in the refrigerator where he found crooked-neck yellow squash. At the time, I slept with my gramma downstairs in the old house. Pat slept upstairs. We were all in bed. He stuck his head in the bedroom where we were, yelling at my grandmother, claiming she was cheating with our neighbor, Mr. Aaron, the man that gave her the squash earlier that day.

We all knew Mr. Aaron. Hell, he knew Mr. Aaron. She would never cheat with Mr. Aaron or anyone. Mr. Aaron used a portion of my grandmother's land, left to her by her parents, for a vegetable garden. He used another section of her land towards the far-back, which was almost 2 acres, for a pig pen. Yes, pigs and hogs in our backyard.

In exchange, we got vegetables and pork. My grandmother was free to pick whatever she wanted from the garden. She usually just waited for Mr. Aaron to pick and bring his white plastic bucket of vegetables to the porch. She never wanted people to think she was taking advantage. When he slaughtered, we had pork for the freezer.

My granddaddy "popped-on" the light. He stepped down into the bedroom and raised a squash to hit my grandmother. He held onto it by the neck. I sat up in the bed, scared to death. My gramma was still laying there. As he was getting ready to swing the yellow boomerang like weapon, my gramma sat up and in one fell swoop, picked up one of those old fashioned, long-handled, drum sprayer for mosquitos and hit him in the middle of his forehead.

Blood spewed across the room from the inch long gash. I gasped. Gramma, cool as ever, now standing, told him sternly, "If you don't get your drunk tail out of here, I will hit you again." He grabbed his head and ran. He yelled, "Um-men (Gullah for woman), you is crazy!"

Granddaddy worked at Union Camp until the day he died. That's when gramma discovered he was really 13 years older than her, not 10. She laughed it off and mentioned he probably didn't know what year he was born. I didn't understand my grandparent's marriage. I never saw them being affectionate — never saw them kiss or hug. They didn't sleep together by the time we came along. My grandmother mostly prepared meals for him — a hot lunch and hot dinner. Rarely did I see them communicate. She always yelled for him, "Abraham...come and eat!" That was the extent of their communications. She did pray for a hardworking man. That he was.

Camptown Elementary School

Back in the old wooden house, we didn't know we were poor, but by government standards, we were. An outhouse and smokehouse adorned the backyard. There was plastic on the windows in the winter to keep the cold wind from coming in and fans in windows during the summer months.

I remember having a couple of short-lived pets — a goat and a duck, appropriately named Billy Goat and Donald Duck. No Shit. My grandmother's intentions were that both would be supper one evening.

My cousin Avon refused to eat either. She folded her arms across her chest and cried. "I am not going to eat Donald, she proclaimed. He's our pet," she cried. She probably went to bed hungry that night, excited to get breakfast on the way out the door for school. I tried not to think about it. I knew I could pass whatever I could not stomach under the table to Pat; that was our secret.

In 1967, I loved the song "You Make Me Feel Like A Natural Woman," by Arthea Franklin. I sung the lyrics best I could until I got to the part...

"You make me feel"

"You make me feel like a natural woman (woman)!"

"You make feel..." which I would nail.

This was one of the only times, I recall my gramma popping me in my mouth, after she promised she would, the first time she heard me sing it. Apparently, I forgot, because I was completely shocked when her hand made contact with my mouth, making a loud "pop" sound.

This song was on the local radio at least three times a day. I didn't know what Ms. Arthea was singing about that was so bad. I just liked the music. To this day, this song brings a smile to my face. Lord help, if my grandmother heard some of the sexual content in today's lyrics. I'm sure she would cringe.

As it was, 1968 was a tumultuous year in history and in my own life — a time when innocence was lost for our country. First Martin Luther King Jr. was shot in Memphis, Tennessee in April. I watched his funeral on television with my grandmother. I watched tears stream down her face. It wasn't until years later that I got it. I understood the gravity of this Civil Rights leader's death and what his assassination meant to so many with dreams of a better life.

Then Robert F. Kennedy in Dallas, Texas. I felt my grandmother's sadness. At six years old, I felt the hopelessness shared by black people. Gone too soon. Events like this took the wind of out of black people's sails. Deflated. Hopeless. Frustrated. And angry, which is often a result of fear. Most resolved things might never change for the better. Once again, our parents and grandparents in this little black community felt both deflated and defeated.

In September of 1968, I started first grade at our neighborhood elementary school — Camptown Elementary. The new construction on Council Rd was a result of a $250K grant approved by Isle of Wight County (IOW) around 1959 for improvements to "negro schools" in Camptown and Carrsville. At the time they were far from equal to white schools in the IWC.

The Camptown school moved from the "Pines" near the fork in road to Pocahontas Ave. and Washington Ave. The newly constructed elementary school opened in 1964 on Council Rd. Our new school housed grades 1-5, complete with a Library/Audio Visual room, a cafeteria with lunchroom and stage. It was a sky blue, single-story, cinderblock constructed with classrooms and restrooms along a long hallway. Outside the school was a basketball court, two playgrounds, with a flagpole centered on the front doors, along the long circular drive.[2]

Camptown is the perfect example of how school integration went down in the late 1960's into the 70s. Keep in mind, VA was a hold-out state that intentionally drug their feet in implementing the Supreme Court decision in the 1954 Brown v. Board of Education.

---

[2] www.theschoolhousemuseum.org

In doing so, additional cases cropped-up across the U.S., in attempts to foil integration throughout the South. It wasn't until the Supreme Court, again ruled on integration of schools that eliminated dual systems in some states like VA, that claimed separate was equal. Of course, this isn't and wasn't true, then or now. See Green v. Kent County, 1968.

It was a short five-minute walk to school from our house, through a path to Council Rd. We walked. Lots of laughs. I can see children running through the paths to get there. Playing chase. Screaming. Laughter again. Dropping jackets. Books. Papers. Running. I was coming up on 7 years old when I started. Since my birthday is in October, I had to wait an entire year after turning 6.

My grandmother volunteered at the school my first year, especially after Avon and Butch started school there. Butch was in first grade with me. Avon was in second grade, just down the hall from us, and Pat, in the fifth grade. Gramma and the principal, Miss Elouise D. Berry were friends; they were on first name bases. Miss Berry had the deepest voice of any woman I have ever heard. To a first grader, this was scary. Bizarre. *Is she a man, gramma?* Miss Berry was known as the no-nonsense principal, with an automatic paddle. I never saw it, but I have cousins who did.

Our school was the pride and joy of the neighborhood though. Quite a few adults/parents in neighborhood worked at the school in some form or fashion. The ladies in the kitchen were grandmothers and mothers of students. We got our little red, plastic chip in the classroom to get lunch.

The smell of a delicious hot lunch coming down the school's hallway was intense. Mouthwatering. After running at recess before lunch each day, my stomach usually ached for a meal on those sectional trays that were washed over and over until the color faded from them. The janitors were from Camptown too. Gramma knew them all.

Some of fondest memories of that year at Camptown Elementary was the annual May Day Celebration. I will never forget it — complete with a Maypole. May Day is the first day of May, traditionally a celebration or festival to mark the beginning of Spring and resurrection of nature after the winter months. It's normally associated with flowers, dancing around Maypoles with celebrations including crowning of a Mayday King and Queen.

We made so many tissues paper flowers to stick in the fence around the basketball court that our fingers hurt from twisting green pipe cleaners. Rolls and rolls of streams were available to decorate the court with fake Maypoles. It was done, it was beautiful. I'll never forget the on May Day at Camptown Elementary.

Carrsville Elementary School

Early September, one evening in 1969, my grandmother made an announcement that was more like a caution. She gathered all of us together in the family/dining room. She told us that we wouldn't be going back to Camptown Elementary. We were going to a new school. My mother was our school bus driver. Butch & I were going into the second grade at Carrsville Elementary. Avon, third. Pat would be bused to Windsor Elementary School where she attended for 6th and 7th grade, then onto Windsor High School. We matriculated via the same path. We rode a humpback yellow bus to Carrsville, VA, about 6 miles from Camptown.

The county decided which schools to keep and which to close. Even in good condition, it was selected for closure. It remained open until the new government program Head Start, opened there. Head Start was created in 1965 to provide low-income children educational services to foster growth in social, emotional, cognitive, and physical development and to ensure children were well prepared for kindergarten. Camptown Elementary became a Head Start/kindergarten school. [3] My mother, Wheezy, moved back from Williamsburg to work as a Teacher's Aide.

Gramma warned us at the new schools we would be in classes with white children and teachers for the very first time ever! She told us to keep our hands to ourselves. Don't talk back or be disrespectful. "Do what you are told. And most important, don't do anything to any of them white children!" She told us if we did, we'd be wrong even if we were right, looking directly at Butch. Like most boys at age 7, he needed plenty of reminders.

---

[3] https://obamawhitehouse.archive.gov; May 18, 2015

It wasn't long before gramma's warning would be tested. Butch and a little white boy named Tracy Bradshaw got in a scuffle in the boys' bathroom. Butch exited and was encircled by a bunch of 2nd grade boys, covering a bloody twisted nose with one hand; a student holding his other hand. Another rubbing his back. Flailing hands and arms. Pointing. Yelling. Demonstrations. The kids all talking at once; they attempted to tell Ms. Bradshaw (no relation to Tracy), our second-grade teacher, what happened in the boy's bathroom.

The dust settled and everyone returned to class. I was reminded of my grandmother's speech. Boy she would be mad, I thought. She'd be so disappointed, certainly. And she worried knowing exactly what could happen if any of us so much as laid a finger on Tracy Bradshaw or any other white student. "Didn't I tell yawl," I could hear her. Butch quickly disappeared with the white nurse dressed in an all-white nurse's dress to include her nurse hat, stockings, and shoes. The next I saw Butch, he was with my mother on the school bus, sitting in the front row, ready to go home.

I was told when my mother got to school to pick us up with the bus, the short, bow-legged, white principal, Mr. Thomas, who was "sweet on my mother," went out to her bus to tell my mother what happened. Butch was still in the nurse's office. Mr. Thomas didn't want my mother to be alarmed when she saw the blood stains on Butch's shirt and his busted nose — according to the nurse, it wasn't broken. When I got on the bus, Butch was sitting in the front seat behind my mother. I looked at him and rolled my eyes. I kept walking and found a seat. The swelling in his nose had gone down considerably. He still had an ice pack though.

I adjusted well... I suppose. I got good grades. I was never sent to the office for disciplinary reasons and in the 2nd grade, my new best friend was a white classmate named Peggy Lankford. Peggy and I were inseparable. We held hands in line. We skipped and played. If she were in front of me in line, I played with her long brunette hair. It felt like corn silk. I was completely fascinated with her hair. She wore a single barrette on the side of her head near her temple to hold her hair out of her face. She let me take it off and put it back every chance we got away from our teacher.

I think we were all fascinated by white people's hair — yet they never seemed to look at or mention our hair. My hair was usually in plats. It was in the quite common 4 plat-style. Imagine, a plat the size of a slice of toast on each side of the head. For example, one plat on top, about the same size and a final plat in the back of the child's head...back and center. Plain plats. Initially, we didn't have barrettes, rubber bands, or those cute two-ball, or colored elastic ties. We wore ribbons with bows.

It was school picture day. We took them in the old, cold gym. Our teacher passed out little black combs from a small cardboard box, just as our class was getting ready to take individual shots. Since I had a comb, I combed my hair as fast as I could just before sitting in front of the camera. When the pictures came back, my mother and grandmother were shocked to see my hair. I had torn it up! The plats were no longer in place. I tried to comb it down, all around, like Peggy. I was stuck with that 2nd grade, disastrous picture.

As a second grader, Carrsville was fun and different than Camptown Elementary. I remember recesses and playing with new black and white friends on the beautiful, green playground behind the school. We had plays and assemblies with students and grades intermingled. Students just weren't friends outside of school. We weren't going to a white classmate's house, that's for sure. We'd go back to our community and they to theirs. Rarely did we see any of our classmates in Camptown until we were in high school.

The cafeteria and food at Carrsville, now regulated a bit by the state, was okay. The kitchen staff was all white, except for one black lady. They cooked and baked from scratch, down to the hamburger and hotdog buns. The school was in good condition. It was first through fifth. Two brick structures connected by a walkway.

The gymnasium was also a separate, cold, large building. I believe it was the original Carrsville Elementary. We froze in that place. Running around was your best option to warm up, and boy did we run. We played everything in that gym in winter months — kickball, dodgeball, basketball, and volleyball. I really missed seeing my gramma during the day. I knew if she felt welcomed and had a ride to Carrsville, she would have been there.

My 3rd grade teacher was Miss Wells. Miss Wells was a well-groomed, fashionable, black teacher from Franklin. Her classroom management skills were exceptional — you did not talk out of turn in Miss Wells classroom. You did not get out of your seat without permission, and you did your work. She was demanding academically and challenged every student regardless of color. The best thing to happen to me in formative education was to be in Miss Wells' class and not with Butch, who was in the other 3rd grade class.

Miss Wells ensured students learned. She was a stickler for penmanship, completing assignments, and proper grammar. She had a noticeable tick, where she'd lift the corner of one side of her mouth, in a half-smile. The angrier she got, the faster the tick. Years later, I learned that Miss Wells was a member of Alpha Kappa Alpha Sorority (AKA), Inc. I became her sorority sister.

When I was in the 3rd grade, my granddaddy Abraham passed away. He didn't get to move to the new rancher with us. I was just shy of 10 years old. His dying was my first experience with death, up close. One summer afternoon, he jumped up from the sofa by the wood stove that he slept on. He ran toward the front door as if he needed air. He grabbed the knob but didn't turn it or open it. Then he spun around and collapsed and died in front all of us, at the front door. Years later, I was told he had emphysema. He was a very heavy smoker — unfiltered Camel's cigarettes.

Our 4th grade teacher, Miss Butler, let us listen to vinyl records on rainy days when we had indoor recess. I memorized every word of "Leader of the Pack" by The Shangri-Las. Ms. Butler was kind. She wore a huge southern bouffant hairstyle. I loved when she read Charlotte's Web to us each day after lunch and recess. I could visualize Wilbert the pig and the spider Charlotte. Her soft, southern voice would often lull me to sleep.

I became close friends with a black girl from Carrsville, named Manya. She was a bit small, or skinny I should say, brown, and but beautiful. She, her sister Vickie, mother, and grandmother lived on a corner of a huge farm in Carrsville, in a small 2-bedroom house, which wasn't much to look at. Manya and I agreed to do a class project together. That meant we needed to visit each other's homes over the weekends to work on it. I was excited. This was my very first visit to a house outside of Camptown.

My mother was home and dropped me off and left. She picked me up a few hours later. Manya came to Camptown too. You would have thought the Queen was coming. All our neighbor knew thanks to Butch, and we were surrounded by the boys — Bow T, Andre' and Greg (brothers), Alex and Larry (brothers), and Timmy and Billy (brothers) — our close friends and neighbors. They were our Pocahontas Ave. tribe when we were growing up. We went to the same schools and were often classmates. They were sure to come over to the yard to see Butch that day.

Now in the 5th grade with Butch and my neighbor Andre, I developed a sense of humor right along with them. We laughed at everything, probably like most 5th graders. Our teacher, Miss Car, was a young, tall, white teacher with teased, big hair like Peggy from the television show "Married with Children." She wore what was considered way too short skirts and low-cut blouses. She was constantly flirting with construction workers at the school building working on another wing. She'd smile and look out the window — they could see her. I watched her. Then she'd sit her tight skirt in the window seal with her back to them, teaching us.

Miss Carr asked us to write a poem related to holidays, seasons of the year, and anything else she could think of. Andre would stand in front of the class to recite his poem. "Beans, beans, in the pot, the more you eat, the more you fart." Miss Carr tried to interrupt him before he got to "fart," unsuccessfully every time. We'd fall out of our chairs. Miss Carr laughed too.

Four years at Carrsville Elementary school went by fast. I consider myself and my cousins extremely fortunate. I was never aware of any blatant racism, discrimination, or mistreatment of any student. The incident with Tracy Bradshaw and Butch was squashed. Tracy apologized profusely. Said he didn't mean to hurt Butch. He just shoved him too hard, and Butch lost his balance — Butch agreed. His nose hit a urinal. He and Butch became friends. His family owned a gas station and car repair shop. We'd see Tracy during summer months at the family gas station in Franklin. The person I now contribute the positive environment at Carrsville Elementary is the principal. I don't know what his staff thought of him, but he was friendly and respectful to black parents and bus drivers. We were off to Windsor Elementary for the 6th and 7th grade.

Piney Grove Baptist Church

At home in Camptown, we lived comfortably in our lavender rancher. I slept with my gramma if my mother was there. Otherwise, I had my own room down the hall and across from Pat and Avon's room. Butch's room was across from gramma. I never recall being hungry or cold. The deep freezer was always full. We had three meals a day. My grandmother made sure of that. She'd hit every grocery store in the Franklin, and Winn-Dixie in Camptown, for sales. If A&P had whole chickens for .30 cent a pound and they were .27 cent at Winn-Dixie, guess where she was going? Winn-Dixie. My mother would say, Momma, you lost the savings in gas, driving from store to store.

We attended our community's Baptist church — Piney Grove Baptist Church or Piney Grove for short. As far back as my memory allows, I remember walking to church each Sunday for Sunday school and then church service immediately following. We'd walk to church across the railroad tracks, under the bridge to our church, situated on Route 58 and Church St.

Sometimes, we'd walk over the bridge to church when crossing the train tracks became too dangerous. We finished church around mid-day. You either go to church or you were sick in bed – that was the rule in our house. We didn't have an option growing up. If you could not go to church, you could not go out, period. You were banished to the house the entire Sunday.

Now Sundays after church were our walking and visiting hours, and we'd walk for hours. We would stand in the streets and talk. We'd sit on neighbor's porches socializing with our gramma. We'd walk to a neighborhood store for candy and cookies or to the two fast food places across the railroad tracks, Tastee Freeze and eventually a McDonald's. We visited family, like our grandfather's brother, Uncle Mitch, and our cousins. Before we'd leave, Uncle Mitch allowed us to rub his completely bald and smooth head. We loved it.

I remember we were on our way to Sunday school one morning when Avon found a little brown lizard crossing the street in front of us, right there under the huge old oak going up the slight hill on Pocahontas. She ran after him and grabbed his tail to catch him. When she did, his tail pulled off and he kept running. She finally grabbed it and put it in her purse in her little white purse. We took the lizard to Sunday school. Being from New York, Avon intended to take him home and keep him for her very own pet.

The lizard survived Sunday school. When we joined our grandmother on the pew for church, she noticed Avon peeking into her purse. At first, she tried to ignore her, then she raised an eyebrow and gave her the "what's in that purse look? without saying. Only a head nod toward Avon's white, straw, latch-lock, purse. Avon mouthed, "A lizard." My grandmother, trying to play it cool, said, "A what?" Avon replied with "a LIZARD!"

At this point, my grandmother slid to the right, and leaned down to Avon's ear. She told her, "If you don't get that Lizard out of here, you had better." Avon, looking completely disheartened. She stood-up and marched out of the doors of the church facing Route 58 looking disgusted. My grandmother couldn't believe it. She told her friends the story repeatedly between giggling. "The girl took a lizard to church. Yes, she did. My lord." She laughed and laughed.

The first beach I remember was an all-black beach called Buckroe Beach in Hampton, VA, just north of Fort (Ft.) Monroe on the Chesapeake Bay. Our church sponsored an annual trip to the beach. I fell in love with the ocean and everything about it. It was so peaceful and beautiful. Endless miles of "blue ocean," as far as the eye can see, extends to meet the blue sky and white puffy clouds. The crashing waves coming one after another. It's meditative. To this day, I draw energy and peace from looking at the ocean and listening to crashing waves.

Windsor Elementary School

Avon, Butch, & I, headed from Camptown to Windsor Elementary, 15 miles away for 6th and 7th grades. We met other black students from the surrounding areas of Zuni, near-by Windsor, and Central Hill. Sixth grade was the first time we physically changed classes to attend multiple subjects, taught by different teachers. A 1960's and 70's practice we've continued in the U.S. to this day.

It was in the 6th grade that we all expressed an interest in playing a musical instrument. Somehow, someway, gramma was able to get us exactly what we wanted to play from a shop in Norfolk, VA. that sold used instruments. Butch, a second-hand trombone. Avon and I played used Clarinets. This was our introduction to reading music.

I believe it was during this time I developed a love for music, of any genre. We participated in every school concert — Spring and Christmas — usually wearing long gowns that our grandmother made for us. We played for two years until we got to high school, where all of us signed up for marching band.

The one and only school "fight" had occurred at Windsor Elementary when I was in the 7th grade. In class, I watched one of my friends, Renee, being harassed by a boy named DeAngelo Boone. He kicked her desk, grabbed the back of the seat, and slid her around. I wasn't feeling well that day. I guess my patience was thin, as gramma would say. It was probably one the many times I had strep throat and went to school. I had a thick bottle of medicine in my purse with a long shoulder strap. It was the pink stuff — liquid amoxicillin. I watched him and didn't flinch. Didn't say a word.

As soon as the bell rang to change classes, he pointed to Renee and said, "Wait till we get in the hall." Still silent, I walked out the door with Renee. DeAngelo was outside already, grinning like a bully. He turned and faced us. As soon as he shoved Renee's shoulder, I started swinging my navy-blue purse, holding on to the long shoulder strap. I swung hard. I made contact with his shoulder, next his arm, as he put it up in defense. The glass medicine bottle inside, made good contact with his shoulder again, since he was taller than us. He yelled, "Girl, are you crazy?!" He ran down the hall. I exhaled. This was the one and only scuffle I'd get in to at school.

At home, we lived a simple life. We did chores around the house and in the yard. We cut a lot of grass. With almost 2 acre, girls and boys cut grass in our house. Gramma taught us to do everything from washing dishes, ironing, cooking, laundry, and general house cleaning. She insisted we act as her Sous Chef to teach us how to cook and bake. We loved to. We had a schedule for washing dishes; each of us took an entire week. After dishes, you might get another chore like sweeping and mopping, or cleaning the one bathroom we all shared. When our schedule conflicted or we needed a break, we negotiated with each other to get someone to do your chore for a day or two. We used food and toys, or whatever we had, to barter with each other.

With one bathroom — it was a busy spot for my grandmother, sometime my mother, three teenage girls, and one boy. We needed a schedule and timer for everything, as in, you have 5 minutes in there!

The morning ritual was yelled frequently, so it stuck. Pee. Brush your teeth. And get out! In the evening, you could leisurely use the restroom or take a hot bath, but not in the mornings. "No ma'am!" Talk about dancing around to hold morning pee. I'd cross my legs, skip down the hall and almost cry. "Pat, I'm going to pee on myself right now if you don't open the door!" I'd bang on the door till she felt sorry for me.

Although Butch and I bonded like sister and brother, we also fought like a cat and a dog. When we were just teenagers, we had a love-hate relationship, especially when gramma wasn't around. As soon as she'd leave the house, Butch and I would find a reason to squabble and scrap aka fight. I was usually the slick one who got in the first hit, then I'd take-off and run to my room and lock the door. He would run down the hall screaming, "I'm going to kill you, Tena! I'm going to kill you. You better not come out of that room. I swear!"

I would laugh out loud behind my locked door. I'd hold the handle to make sure Butch couldn't open it until it was locked. Then, I'd slide down the door with my back on it until my butt hit the floor. I'd sit there, heaving, breathing hard, until my gramma returned. I knew I couldn't go out without a fight. He huffed, puffed and paced-up and down the hall until he gave up.

"Tussling," as my gramma would say, one day Butch pushed me into her old-fashioned China Cabinet, and we broke one of the doors' long pane glasses. Shoot! We had to fess-up that we were fighting. Avon and Pat were not going to take the blame.

'm also reminded of a fight Butch, and I had, but this time we were in the backyard with what could have been deadly consequences. Butch got the first lick-in. My gramma had an old frog gig, which looks like a long cane fishing pole, with a miniature pitchfork on the end to poke through frogs. Yes frogs. Frog legs are delicious — taste like chicken. It was laying behind the house just underneath the back steps. Butch punched me in my arm as hard as he could and took off running, so did I. Right after him.

We ran from the back of the house to the front. He took the hard left toward the back edge of the house again, nearly running into the back steps. I was catching-up with him. When I took the left, I reached down and grabbed the frog gig, switched it to my right hand like General Okoye in the movie Black Panther, and threw it at Butch like a javelin.

It caught him and stuck in his right heel about an inch up from the bottom of his foot and in a half-inch deep. It stopped him in his tracks. He pulled-up short; the gig was sticking out of his heel. He dropped and rolled on his left side and looked at his foot, then his heel, with the frog gig sticking up in the air. He let out a loud yelp! I instantly froze. Wow. That was...amazing! "I'm sorry Butch!" I didn't think I would hit him. "Please don't tell gramma! Please!"

Avon and I were able to pull the gig out that went through his Chucks — Converse Chuck Taylor, tennis shoe. Surprisingly, his injury didn't bleed much. There were three perfectly round holes in his heel, like a wide fork. Bright red blood filled each circle. It was astounding to see. The next evening, Butch couldn't put any weight on his right foot. Oh shoot! He's gonna tell gramma. I know it.

It was obvious something was wrong. Gramma would notice or he would have to tell her because of the pain. He did. And they quickly packed-up to get Butch to the Emergency Room. His heel was swollen and turning a nasty bruised red and dark green color. I was so afraid and sorry that I hurt Butch.

When he and gramma returned, his foot was bandaged up and he was walking better; probably because he returned with a snack and soda. He had a tetanus shot and came home with the pink liquid-antibiotic. We stopped fighting. I learned to just go along to get along with Butch. I ignored his antics and shenanigans, and he ignored mine. As we matured, we learned to appreciate each other's company. I would see him in California (CA) — he and his family — after I joined the Army.

Windsor High School (WHS) Class of 1979

Windsor High School (WHS) started in the eighth grade and at that time, 8th graders could participate in H.S. sports. As a student athlete, I was busy. I played basketball, ran track, was in the concert and marching bands. Avon, Butch and I, marched in every invited parade, played at every home football game, concert, graduation, and the like. We were real band geeks.

I remember trying out for the cheerleading squad for football season my sophomore year. I made the team with little effort. I was surprised. I cheered for first home football game. During that game, I did a quick Superwoman change in the band room into my

53

band uniform. I changed just in time to take my first-chair, Clarinet position on the field for the half-time show.

Our band and school had such a small population of students that one clarinet out of ranks of a 50-piece band made a difference. WHS competed in sports with schools in our district/league that were twice our size, until the school and district moved to a different, smaller, league. I didn't cheer again. I turned-in my uniform to the coach. Band had my heart, and I didn't have to wear those short skirts with pantyhose in 30-degree weather. I thought they were ridiculous.

I ran track for three years, from the eighth grade until my sophomore year. I completely skipped my junior year in high school because I had enough credits that all I needed to take was English 11 during the summer. Once successfully completed, I went straight from the 10th grade to being a Senior — yes, 12th grade.

After three years as a stand-out sprinter on the track team, I promised my basketball coach I would play softball since she coached and asked me to play every year. My senior year, I kept my promise — this was a poorly thought-out decision. I regretted it as soon as my former track coach and history teacher, informed me that she would no longer communicate with her former alma mater, Cornell University's track coach, about a scholarship for me, if I played softball.

In hindsight, after placing at the regional and state AA track meet, in the 100-yard dash and the 200-yard race (note, not in meters) as a sophomore, I had great potential for another successful year, and possibly a track scholarship had I ran and possibly, not skip my junior year. I didn't consult anyone about my decision, I just did it and no one seemed to have any insights as what I was doing and giving up. But as they say, hindsight is 20/20.

During this time, we did a lot of travelling by chartered buses with our Youth Choir, H.S. band and for other events. We went to roller skating in Norfolk. We took a bus to Kings Dominion Amusement Park in Richmond, VA. And our marching band, got to travel to march in parades.

Our H.S. senior field trip was an evening at Busch Gardens in Williamsburg, VA., complete with a concert. We jammed to Evelyn Champagne King's hit "Shame." I enjoyed our senior night at Busch Gardens with my then HS boyfriend, Reginald (Reggie) Harden. He was tall, handsome, and a lettered athlete. He played basketball, football, and ran track and he was good at all of them.

Reggie adored me. I didn't understand why. I hadn't always treated him like a priority. If he had his way, we'd go off to college together, marry right after, and have enough babies for a starting five on a basketball team. He was sweet and kind. He also became a stand-out Wide Receiver who played at East Carolina University.

Years after he stopped playing football, Reggie was hit by a drunk driver on a Sunday morning. I'll never forget the call I got. He was apparently out for a morning jog and was struck by a drunk driver. I could not believe it. Tragic. I was in the Army at Ft. Gordon.

I thank GOD, I'd seen him and had a chance to talk with him at our 10-year high school reunion. I admitted to him that I knew he was way more dedicated to the relationship than I was. He was a good boyfriend. We were both young, but now over 30 years old, I recognized how I took his feelings for granted. He smiled with his gorgeous pink lips. He said it was okay. I'll never forget that smile, complete with a beautiful dimple. He gave me a gentle hug.

When we were in high school, my grandmother converted to a Jehovah Witness. It just kind of happened. I knew she was attending bible study with a woman that did not attend Piney Grove, but there were quite a few people in Camptown that attended bible studies. It wasn't a big deal, but I didn't see it coming.

Then she quietly stopped going to Piney Grove and started going to "the Hall." She also started witnessing — like knocking on strangers' doors, asking if they wanted one of those colorful Watch Tower magazines and if they believed in hell. The Watchtower covers really drew kids in, but in my opinion, if you read the story about a fiery pit in hell, the magazines scared a kid.

We didn't have a car most times. I say most times because if my mother was living with us at my grandmother's, we had transportation. My mother kept a car. If she moved out, which happened way too often, we walked. On a regular basis, we walked to get daily needs — things like bread, milk, eggs, and orange juice. Boy did we go through some milk and orange juice. With four developing teens, I guess it's quite understandable.

When my mother lived with us, she didn't play with foolishness — she was stern and firm. Yes, I was afraid of her, but I quickly learned how NOT to piss her off — by NOT causing any trouble. That meant I had better mind my grandmother, get good grades in school, and NOT be a "hot, fast tail."

I distinctly remember the last whooping I got. She beat my butt and legs with a belt for lying on my sister-cousin Avon. My grandmother stepped in the hallway of the lavender house and said, "Ellouise, that's enough!" My cousins and often Wheezy's boyfriends or husbands, three in total, seemed to learn the hard way. With each failed relationship and disappointment, Wheezy seemed to become sterner, or just angry.

In the late 70s, disco and funk music were in full effect. We walked to the Franklin Recreation Center (Rec. Center) on Banks Street, across the river in Franklin. Most Saturday nights, there were teen dances with Disc Jockeys (DJs) that came from Portsmouth and Norfolk radio stations. We loved those dances — especially as teens. It was an opportunity to hang out with friends from Franklin H.S. and to dress in our bell-bottom jeans, crop tops, stacks, and afros. We'd walk home at 2 a.m. from those dances. Things were different then. If we were together, my grandmother wasn't worried about us walking.

Mrs. Otelia J. Rainey

As teenagers now, we continued to attend Piney Grove, but with less pressure and more freedom to "visit" or walk the streets of Camptown on Sunday evenings. We were all members of the Piney Grove Youth Choir and Organization. My best friend's mother, Mrs. Otelia J. Rainey aka Ms. Otelia, was our leader, choir mom, community leader, travel guide, advisor, comedian and second Mom. I was her "Tena Mae."

I learned so much from Ms. Otelia about being a mother and leader. She had no pretense...none. She was her authentic self, day-in and day-out. Attractive. Educated. God-fearing. A registered nurse and a very present mother, who took groups of youth/teens from Camptown and Piney Grove on summer trips, starting in the early 70s. I'm sure the conditions for black church groups traveling Interstate 95 south toward Miami, Daytona, or Orlando, FL. was not an effortless feat. Imagine. Planning. Safety. Chaperones to make the long trips on Franklin's black-owned, Blount's Chartered buses.

We would leave Camptown after 11 p.m. or so. We slept the night away to shorten the trip and time. We would wake-up and find ourselves close to South Carolina and the first stop, South of the Border; a mandatory stop. We'd countdown the miles, right along with Pedro and those huge, colorful, exciting, billboards along 95, until we pulled-up to stretch out.

To this day, I contribute my love of travel to Ms. Otelia. The more we travelled locally or long-distance, the more I wanted to travel. I wanted to see the world. Sometimes I travelled alone with the Rainey family and my BFF - to Luray Caverns, Monticello, Mount Vernon, and black beaches. I'm probably forgetting a place or two. This amount of travel for a black girl in her formative years and teens, from a small southern community in VA, was highly impactful. It opened my mind, which expanded beyond my small hometown.

I think I was 14 or 15 when Ms. Otelia came up with a plan to hold the 1st Miss Camptown Pageant, and she wanted me in it. This wasn't anything new — she was always coming up with ideas to expose the community youth to different things and to help us off-set the cost of the annual Youth Group trip. We had community cleanup days. Car washes. We'd take a bus to the skating rink in Portsmouth for a nominal fee and we'd have fundraisers like this — and now a Miss Camptown pageant.

Ms. Otelia probably believed the neighborhood would think the pageant was rigged if her daughter, Della, my BFF, were to compete and win. Another challenge was, Della with her beautiful golden skin and golden hair to match, absolutely hated getting her hair combed or professionally done for any reason.

I was all in, and so was gramma when she learned this would reduce the cost for my summer trip. There were about 3 other girls, all whose goals were to raise as much money as possible and/or solicit donations to off-set the cost of the Youth Group's summer trip, participate/volunteer for community and church events, and be selected by a panel of judges the evening of the pageant.

I agreed to compete. Each year my grandmother saved and scrunched for months to get the money together for all four of us — Pat, Avon, Butch, and me, to go with Ms. Otelia. So, for the pageant, we all sold things like homemade donuts out of my Gramma's kitchen — ones with a ton of confectionary sugar on each one. We sold freeze cups, freeze pops, and popsicles. We sold candy apples door-to-door in Camptown. I volunteered to help clean an empty lot of paper, cans, plastics, and other debris down at the end of Washington Ave.

I raised the most money and for the talent competition, I played a solo piece on my clarinet. The judges loved it. We even had an evening gown portion of the pageant where I wore my old sky-blue prom gown. At the end, I was crowned Miss Camptown complete with a Tiara and a bouquet of flowers. Only Ms. Otelia made a big deal out of my new title. She loved it and wanted me to be recognized by Union Camp as the first Miss Camptown. I don't believe they were interested. She couldn't get me a photo op in the front office with the Camps.

The Meeting – Three Brothers!

I didn't meet my three half-brothers until I was 15 years old. I had seen them and their mother around town/Franklin once or twice. Undetected, my grandmother pointed them out. She'd say calmly, "Those are supposed to be your brothers." I'd sneak a look at them. They were cute boys with soft curly black hair. I didn't respond to my grandmother. She knew I read her loud and clear. We had a connection in that way.

I was working at my Uncle Peter's convenience store in Franklin, located on the corner of South and Thomas Streets went I met my oldest brother. Uncle Peter was one of my father's older brothers. He lived next door to us in Camptown and always treated me as his niece — well before I was formally introduced to Duke's family. He provided and gifted me with periodic school clothing and shoes, often providing more concern, care, and support, than Duke.

Well, he offered me a part-time job for that summer, and I accepted. I was at work one mid-day, when Pop (age 10, then), walked in the store to purchase cigarettes for his mother. My cousin Marc, Uncle Peter's son, who was usually with me at the store, introduced us quite matter-of-factly. "Pop, this is your Sus-ter," Marc said. "Her name is Tena, and she lives beside me."

Pop stopped in his tracks and stared at me. He looked me in my eyes and asked, "Are you, my sister?" I said calmy, "I think so. You're Duke's son, right?" He stuttered Yyyyes... yes!" He made his purchase and ran out of the store.

Before I knew it, Pop was back in the store, asking me to come home with him. His mother said it was okay, he said out of breath. He smiled from ear to ear. He wanted me to meet my other brothers.

Introductions to Tony, then age 8 and Kiminey, 6, went fast that afternoon. They were the cutest little boys. Beautiful curly black hair, smooth skin, and great smiles; all of them. The next weekend, all three spent the weekend with me at my gramma's house in Camptown. They loved being with their big sister.

I couldn't get rid of them that summer or the next. The next summer I landed a job at Camptown Rec. Center, in the former Camptown Elementary School building; this was my very first, tax-paying job at the age of 15. My supervisor, Mr. Herman, was respectful, organized, knew how he wanted to run things, and would shut the entire operation down, if kids were misbehaving. My brothers spent several afternoons, in the dark, cool, sitting in the one hallway of Camptown Rec., waiting until it was time for me to go home.

Top: Welcome to Franklin sign on Route 58/258, Franklin, Va.Below: We lived on Pocahontas Ave. in Camptown.

Top: L-r, back row: My mother Ellouise, Pat, then me. Front row, grandma Novella, Avon and Butch. Below: My senior photograph – Class of 1979, Windsor High School, Windsor, VA.

Chapter 4

University of Maryland Baltimore County (U Must be Crazy)!

Education's purpose is to replace an empty mind with an open one.

- Malcolm Forbes

I graduated from Windsor High School in 1979. Since my SAT scores were accidentally sent to the wrong University of Maryland, they mailed me a catalog and an application to apply, so I did. I also applied to in-state schools like Virginia State, Old Dominion University (ODU), and Virginia Union. I was accepted at all but going out of state was different — not a lot of my classmates were heading out of state.

I was familiar with "the" University Maryland (UMD) Terrapins, who wasn't. I learned UMBC was a smaller, newer campus, just north of UMD and where Uncle Teensy lived in Landover, MD. He assured my mother and grandmother that he wasn't far, and I could visit him on weekends. He'd keep me fed, and I could do laundry, he assured them.

Once accepted at ODU, I sent a letter to their Women's Basketball Coach, soliciting a full or partial scholarship to play basketball. I wanted desperately to play for Coach Marianne Stanley, and play with three-time All-American, and two-time women's college basketball Player of the Year, Nancy Lieberman. She was the best women's college player, and she was about an hour away from me. She would be the slower

2 guard, and I the faster, point guard. 30 years later, my two nieces graduated from ODU. How ironic is that? One of them is an Art Professor there, today. I did get a letter signed by Coach Stanley suggesting I attend try-outs once enrolled. Without a sure thing, I decided on out-of-state.

University of Maryland Baltimore County (UMBC = U Must be Crazy) is in Catonsville, MD, just southwest of the city of Baltimore and about 4 hours away north from Camptown. When I attended, it was the newest brick and mortar institution under the University of Maryland's system of colleges. UMBC opened in 1966; was considered the baby of the bunch.

I stepped foot on the campus of UMBC for the first time in late July 1979, to attend the Black Student Union's (BSU) orientation, I hadn't been on the campus. I didn't conduct any college visits. Not sure why, now. I don't recall a lot of students who weren't getting a sports scholarship, visiting college campuses to help decide whether they should attend — especially out-of-state colleges.

Freshman Year (1979-80) – Go Retrievers!

My mother drove me from Camptown to Catonsville, MD for freshman orientation. She spent the weekend with her brother, Uncle Teensy. She was pleased to learn the campus was a straight shot — 95 North to Route 166 Catonsville; follow signs to UMBC. It was a beautiful and spacious campus. There was nothing historic or old about it. All the buildings looked new. The three dormitories (Dorms 1-3) were built in the early 70s. They were modern with central air and heat, controlled in individual rooms.

O is for Obren

The first serious relationship or love of my life, as he calls it, came in college. He was the smartest boy...I mean, young man, I had ever met. It was his casual conversations and his smile that drew me in. His smile with perfectly, straight white teeth, was magical.

I met O at the Black Student Union (BSU) orientation for students entering as a freshman or as transfer students. Yes, a separate orientation for new black students. I thought I looked cute. I was standing on the steps of Dorm 1 with my orientation roommate, Andrea.

We were waiting to walk to the dining hall for the orientation party with another freshman. I had on a new blue jean vest and matching tight jeans. I thought my outfit was on point — new shoes from Branch's Shoes in Franklin to boot. A sky blue, short sleeve t-shirt under my vest. Starched. Creased. Clean.

O walked out the front door of Dorm 1 and stepped down to the first landing. And like other black students who had walked out, his group stopped and said hello. He'd met Andrea earlier that day, so he acknowledged her by name, but looked at me. He said, "Where are you ladies from?"

We were encouraged during one of our sessions to, say hello to your brothers and sisters! We are all we have here, said one of the Counselors. I remember O distinctly calling us ladies. It did not leave my mind for weeks. I had never been called a lady, and I felt like one. He was smooth. An extrovert. Smart. Double majors — Political Science and Economics. My country ass responded, "*hay!*"

The first letter I got in the mail from O after orientation included "Esq." after his last name in his return address. I remember thinking, what does that mean? Is he someone special? After conferring with my grandmother, esquire denotes a lawyer, an attorney. His parents had encouraged him to use the Esquire abbreviation after his last name. He had a plan, and they had a prophecy.

When I returned to UMBC the next month to stay, I learned my dorm room was at the St. Mary's Seminary, an all-girl facility, and 2 miles off-campus. St. Mary's Seminary in Catonsville is a division of the Seminary and University, in Baltimore, established in 1791 and recognized as the first Roman Catholic seminary in the United States.

UMBC leased dormitory space at their Catonsville location to accommodate an overflow of resident students. The freshman girls there became known as the "Belles of St. Mary's" — a reference to the famous movie with old-school comedian, Bing Crosby!

Regular shuttle buses transported students back and forth to UMBC campus daily. O and I knew the schedule by heart. He was either visiting me at St. Mary's or I was with him in Dorm 1.

There were a few surprises and benefits to staying at the Seminary. First, it was a small group of girls.

We were all freshman, so most of the black girls gravitated toward each other. Most of us became life-long friends.

The area surrounding St. Mary's dormitory was incredibly quiet. It was also very creepy with its Chapel next to a cemetery. Oh yes, we ran through there Halloween night.

A huge benefit was being able to watch the Baltimore Colts practice in the huge fields just outside. I couldn't believe it when one of the girls I knew asked if I wanted to go outside to watch. She grabbed a blanket and snacks. The Colts! Right there. They were forbidden from fraternizing with us, but a few of them crept up the steps to play cards with one of the sisters down the hall — several of us got a good peep.

I befriended two biological sisters from Baltimore, the Bells, who introduced me to the club scene in Baltimore and rap music with "Rappers Delight," by the Sugar Hill Gang. They were proud Western H.S. graduates. One was a true freshman, the other a transfer student who wanted to attend and room with her little sister.

The Bells showed me how to behave at a nightclub. I had never been to one, just Rec. Centers and school dances. They had a car and knew their way around Baltimore. We would leave St. Mary's around 11pm, careen through the streets of Baltimore going from club to club to see which one was hopping. We'd return with the rising sun. Clubs in Baltimore played the best music in the early 80s and I knew I belonged in legendary Odell's on North Ave.

I dated O my freshman and sophomore years. We were inseparable. We navigated the campus and surrounding area of Catonsville together. We ate in the dining hall together and bought an occasional pizza or sub from Sorrento's.

He was so different than any boy I knew — he had well thought out opinions. He and his family were cultured and educated black people. I learned something new every day from him. I mimicked his study habits. I studied when he studied. We wrote and typed papers together. He had attended a private school until he convinced his parents to allow him to attend public high school at DuVal High School in Lanham, Maryland. His parents agreed.

As a freshman, I tried out and made the Women's basketball team. I couldn't believe it. At the time, everyone was a walk-on player and had to tryout. I'm sure it was the 3-point shot that I selfishly took at the top of the key, playing #2 guard during a short scrimmage, that did the trick — nothing but net. It wasn't until my junior year that UMBC, offered its first two Women's basketball scholarships — it was 1982.

Academically, college was way more demanding than my high school studies. High school was a piece of cake in comparison to UMBC. After graduating #11 in my class, I was an average student my first semester – just average. I got a C in three courses for a total of 9 credit hours because I decided to drop a course after attending it once or twice – not sure why.

Now this changed my status from a full-time student (minimum of 12 credits) to a part-time student. Who knew?

As a result, I was placed on Academic probation, not because of the flat 2.0 but because as a full-time student, I didn't have enough "quality points." A letter from UMBC was sent home that explained this resulting situation and my status as a student. My mother decided to open and read it. *Shiiiiiittt!*

As basketball players, both the men and women's teams returned to school in early January, well before the spring semesters started, to practice and finish our scheduled games. As an option, athletes took winter session courses for 1-2 credit hours, to stay on top of things. It was the advantage I needed and took my first winter session. With free room and board until the spring semester started, student athletes were required to pay for a single course and typical winter school fees. It was worth it, and I had a portion of my student loan to use.

The spring was uneventful. I was able to move on-campus to Dorm 1. My roommate, we shall call Cee, played basketball too. Cee was cool. Didn't see her too much. She was from Cherry Hill, a suburb of Baltimore which meant, she was rarely in the dorm. She was usually at home, unless she was meeting up with a girl; she liked girls. Mostly white girls.

They came and went. Lacrosse players. Soccer players. When she was in, we had an unspoken code. I'd just say hello to her and her friend, start packing-up my books and toothbrush, and I was out to O's.

Every now and then I'd wake up to find a girl asleep in Cee Cee's bed without Cee. If I woke them up, I'd politely say, "*hello,*" and go about my business. I had stopped saying, "*Hay!*"

I took 17 semester hours to catch-up. I still hadn't declared a major, and no one seemed to care. I picked my own courses and registered before the fall concluded. That semester, following O's lead, I pulled my GPA up significantly. I also got a part-time job as a Student Marshall.

Marshalls worked directly with Campus Police. They monitored campus parties, mixers, and school-sponsored events to ensure the orderly conduct and the safety of students. Armed with a special Marshall logo golf shirt, walkie-talkie, and assigned Marshall number to communicate with the police station, I watched these intelligent students get belligerent — shit-faced, throwing-up, drunk, week after week. It was entertaining and mind blowing at the same time, especially the chapter 5on-campus frat parties.

I made about $20 an event, which was a huge help. School supplies, hair relaxers, and toiletries weren't free. I spent the summer working at St. Regis Paper Company, where my mother was a supervisor, making 50-pound bags for dog food. I made the most money I had ever made. I returned to school with some book money.

Sophomore Year (1989-81) – Crossing the Burning Sands to AKALand

In the Fall of 1980, I was so happy to be back in school. I worked hard that summer, and I was missing

O. I tried-out and made the basketball team again —
this time with much less anxiety about it and less
effort. My new roommate, Phyllis Curry, was from
Annapolis and had become friends with O. As a result,
we became friends. She asked me to room with her
when we returned for our 2nd year, so I did.

Things were going great with O and I. I spent the
Christmas holiday with him and his family in Lanham,
MD. His parents were cordial and inquisitive about
me, my family and where I came from. Eventually,
they relaxed with thoughts of me being a country girl
from the south who adored their O. I was the first
serious relationship they were aware of. For
Christmas, O gave me a promise ring. It was cute with
a small diamond and gold band. I wore it with pride.

O and I, of course, had talked about pledging a
fraternity and sorority since we talked about
everything. His mother was an Alpha Kappa Alpha,
Sorority (AKA), and her expectation was O would
become an "Alpha Man," a member of Alpha Phi Alpha
Fraternity — the brothers to AKAs. So naturally O
hadn't considered any other fraternity than "Alpha Phi
Alpha" at that point.

I didn't know very much about sororities and
fraternities, so I was learning, observing, and forming
my own opinion. I remembered Uncle Teensy wacked
me across my bottom with an Alpha Phi Alpha paddle
he brought home from St. Paul's College in
Lawrenceville, VA. He left circles on my butt where
his paddle had holes. My tail was bruised! This

thoroughly pissed off my grandmother. She let him have it right in front of his college buddies.

Phyllis was interested in pledging AKA – that was no secret. Her aunt, an AKA, was her inspiration. She asked if I was interested in pledging a sorority. At the time, I was still considering. I shyly told Phyllis, yes and hoped she didn't ask me why I was interested.

At the time, my closest friends, besides O and Phyllis, were my teammates on the Women's Basketball team, Lisa, and Tina with an "i." We had bonded over two winter sessions. I wondered if they were interested in AKA or were they leaning toward Delta Sigma Theta Sorority. So, I asked. They had seen the flyers announcing the AKA's Rush. Lisa planned to attend. She was interested. Tina, with her usual laid back, go with the flow attitude, said, "Well, I'm down to go if you guys are going. What da hell," in typical Tina fashion. We went to the AKA's RUSH together.

I believe the small minority population at UMBC drew black students to groups like fraternities and sororities. UMBC was "so white" that most black students needed a support group. Black students who didn't pledge were still supportive of black Greeks and their events. It was nothing to have what we called "independents" as best friends, roommates, and students our sorority relied on.

I had zero expectations. We walked in the room, and it was covered in salmon pink and apple green. AKA paraphernalia was everywhere! To include their clothing and shoes! The smiles around the room were electrifying. This place was lit with Pink & Green magic. I remember thinking, what a good-looking group of women. *Do I fit in with these women?* I was country. Awkward. And a tomboy! The rush was fun. Lots of games that centered around AKA, its history, and UMBC's chapter — Lambda Phi. A party with good snacks and sweets, which is always a nice treat for a college athlete on a meal plan.

Days after the rush, I started thinking about whether I should pledge. I thought of my Uncle Teensy's first wife, Aunt Shirley. She was an AKA; it dawned on me. She became an educator – a high school principal, I believe. I could honestly say, I have a relative that I knew and admired, and she was an AKA. I made the commitment to Phyllis and my teammates that I would move forward with the next step – we all did.

Now, I just had to break the news to my mother and find the money to pledge. *Where in the world would I get the money?* As it stood, I wasn't getting an allowance or anything. I got small money orders here and there, but not near enough to pledge a sorority. *Why was I doing this again?* Somehow or another, I was able to scrounge up the initiation fees with the help of my mom, uncle, and a loan from my teammate, Lisa. Lisa always seemed to have money. I was happy when I had $5. She also had a car and was never out of rum. Yup, Bacardi. I had my very first mixed drink of rum and coke, courtesy of Lisa.

After being notified of AKA's acceptance and paying fees and miscellaneous expenses, we gathered needed clothing, supplies, and waited. We started the pledge process early February of Spring 1981.

O ended up pledging Omega Psi Phi Fraternity. They started a new chapter at UMBC and drummed-up quite an interest. He started pledging a few weeks before we did. I was missing him like crazy. After I started pledging, I didn't have time to really think about it.

Somehow or another, O got word to me to meet him in a new, unopened, academic building during the weeks we were both pledging. Like most dating pledgees, we were forbidden to see each other. Sometimes, we'd go days without even passing each other on campus. When we saw each other in our secret location, it was comforting to get a hug and kiss. He appeared to be doing well even though I knew it was hard for him. I heard him sing a portion of a solo for the first time at their probate show. My AKA "big sisters" made me leave as soon as it occurred to them, those two are dating, and she is looking at him. Damn. To the hallway I went.

On April 11, 1981, we "crossed the burning sands in AKALand." We finished. We pledged for 8 weeks; I believe. 8 out of 10 pledgees who started, became members of the first black sorority, AKA! I was exhausted but I was also ecstatic to "go over." I couldn't wait to see O. We'd flaunt our colors. Party together. Travel to see pledgees. Support our sorority/fraternity, respectively. And finally have sex in our dorm room and not an academic building.

He finished pledging approximately a week prior to me. He was free. Chilling. Stepping. And getting massive attention from the ladies, especially now that he was a singing, barking, Que. He had Que Psi Phi swag. I couldn't find him that night. He was probably celebrating too. I opted to put on some tight-ass jeans since I'd lost weight pledging, and one of my brand-new AKA t-shirts, and party with my line sisters. We went downtown Baltimore, clubbing.

O broke up with me shortly after the summer break started for a "cute twin" at near-by Towson State. I spent the rest summer trying to get over O, by celebrating with my line sister and road dog, Isha Alexander. I didn't want to sulk about O. For what? He made his decision; I was stuck with it. Isha and I planned overnight trips to Ocean City, Baltimore, back home to Camptown, and lots of fraternity parties, BBQs, pool parties, representing in our salmon pink and apple green.

Junior Year (1981-82) - A New Relationship

In my junior year, I started to see my second so-called "boyfriend" at UMBC. I had never had anyone break-up with me – it was usually the other way around. This was tough; especially when O asked for his promise ring back. *Really.* Eventually, I moved on from O. I say eventually because it took a minute to get over him—to stop trying to see him and sleep with him. He was familiar.

DJ Michael was a brother I knew from UMBC's men's basketball team. I didn't know him all that well until both teams were housed in Dorm 1 during the second winter break, January 1982. Staying on-campus during winter break allowed us to continue to practice and play, especially if we made the conference playoffs. When we were not on the road for away games, the dorm was a lively place to be – an entire wing of hot, semi-intelligent, athletes.

The men's basketball team gravitated towards the women's teams, of course. We played cards a lot and Michael played music. He would become my Sorority's go-to-DJ for campus parties. He had his own equipment and kept-up with the latest hits. At the end of the winter session, we didn't see each other much. Basketball was almost over. I was completely single and feeling myself.

It was late into the spring when Michael asked me if I wanted to go the Inner Harbor, downtown Baltimore. Of course, I said yes. It was a beautiful, balmy, Baltimore day. I had never been to the Inner Harbor. It was amazing! I had never seen an area on the water quite like the Inner Harbor. The smells of the seafood, waffle cones, fudge, and an occasional whiff of his cologne stayed with me until I returned to the harbor years later as a soldier. The impromptu date was light, fun, yet a bit romantic.

During the summer months, I spent time with Michael and his family in White Oak, MD. His older sister, Peaches, and I became friends. His family taught me how to have a real Maryland blue crab feast complete with beer, lemons, and lots of hot butter. Michael and I always made the run from White Oak/Silver Springs to the D.C. Wharf — rows of boats and bushels of blue crabs to choose from. Haggling for the best price. Yelling. Blue crabs everywhere.

We'd rush to get back to his aunt's house. Anticipating the feast, she'd prepped for our return. The stack of newspaper spread across the table, a roll of paper towels on the table, and a few crab claw crackers for the inexperienced. The beer was usually Miller High Life Ponies – the perfect size for a crab feast. Ice cold. The butter was piping hot in small dipping bowls. This IS how you eat blue crabs.

I'd sit there and eat crabs until I became paranoid about having an allergic reaction to iodine. I'd observed my now Soror and teammate, Lisa, have a reaction one evening at basketball practice. We'd just left the Dining Hall for practice from their occasional seafood night complete with shrimp!

About 30 minutes into practice, Lisa's face began to itch and turn red. Before anyone could intervene, her face had taken on a new shape altogether. I'd never seen that before then. It was unbelievable — watching her eye lids, nose, lips, her entire face, swell till her eyes were slanted. Tina and I watched in amazement. Lisa recovered and was fine the next day.

Back to DJ Michael. Initially, I had a great time with him. We had a lot in common, particularly our humble beginnings and sports. Being raised by someone other than our mothers. He was very sociable. Michael and I got close quickly. He went home with me to Camptown. My family really liked him, especially after they witnessed him give me a boxed, hair relaxer during our visit. Having an older sister with a relaxer helped. He knew what he was doing. He gave me the best perms/relaxers during those times.

4th Year (1982-83) - Consequences and Repercussions

I was going through the steps of registering and taking courses. By now, I had self-declared my major as African American Studies (AFRAM). It was the only major that interested me. I took several AFRAM courses that were eye-opening.

I was learning and discovering so much about Africa, Africans, and African American history. None of which I was exposed to in primary and H.S. I never wanted to skip an AFRAM class. Rain or shine, I was in class to be enlightened by a mostly male, highly educated, cadre of professors, who wore being black on their sleeves. They wore Afros and Dashikis. A few had changed their names. Real cool shit.

For a drama class that fall, I spit 8 bars and my sorority sister Wanda, did the other 8, flawlessly, of "The Message" by Grand Master Flash & the Furious Five, to an almost, all-white student audience, at a multi-arts exhibit at UMBC's only theater. This would begin my appreciation for Rap and Hip Hop as an art form, and the hard work that goes into a performance.

Shortly after the semester started, a Phi Beta Sigma brother that I had two AFRAM courses with, offered me a job. In his mid-twenties, he'd become the night manager at the International House of Pancakes (IHop) on Route 40. I accepted. I needed the cash flow badly. I lived in an on-campus apartment with a full kitchen and three roommates. I was no longer on a meal plan at the dining hall down the hill. I had to purchase my own food and cook if I wanted to eat. Not to mention the need for essentials.

I worked the graveyard shift from 11:30 pm to 7:30 am, Thursday night through Sunday morning. Whatever tips I made on a shift; I took home. I also got a paycheck at an hourly rate of $2.35; minimum wage in 1982 was $3.35.[4] Tips were expected to close the gap between minimum wage and IHop's hourly rate.

Working at IHop late night and early mornings was an experience of a lifetime, especially dealing with intoxicated patrons at 2 and 3am, and young, H.S. prom dates that did not tip, yet demanded the kitchen sink. These were the highlights of this short-lived job. Believe it or not, I still enjoy IHop's buttermilk pancakes, which I took home hot and fresh each morning.

I believe it was in the Fall semester of my last year that I became aware that DJ Michael and one of my sorority sisters were much more than friends. I found myself in a real-life scandal, of sorts. Michael's apartment "on the hill" at UMBC was directly across from mine. I could see his car when he was there. When it was not, he was usually off-campus with her.

Ironically, I knew they hung out. Hell, I'd hung out with them both one evening, just chilling, listening to music. They were just friends, so I thought. They got each other – he understood her, he explained. She

---

[4] Department of Labor (.gov), History of Federal Minimum Wage Rates

didn't have a lot of close friends, since she was a transfer student. Mature. Introverted. I had empathy for her. I imagined their friendship, right along with my budding feelings for Michael, shifted. I felt vested. What started as a casual, rebound of sorts, turned difficult, and forbidden.

In the spring semester, I began to accept the time I was getting. I compartmentalized Michael's other relationship. But this didn't exactly go well with my AKA sisters. One evening, after the official business at our chapter meeting, my sisters confronted both of us about Michael. They wanted us to "stop seeing him immediately." This entanglement was "not a good look" for the chapter. They were concerned, and rightly so.

Two of three of my roommates were sorority sisters and in attendance at the meeting. They knew my day-to-day activities and certainly who was visiting our apartment in the evenings/nights. I recall one of my sisters say, they didn't care if either of us dated Godzilla, as long as we did not date DJ Michael! I had no words.

I started crying like a damn baby. After the meeting, I went directly to the restroom to get myself together. I was standing in front of the sinks and mirrors, wetting a paper towel to put on my now red face and nose. My sorority sister, in the triangle with me, opened the door to the restroom and came in. She walked directly towards me. We hugged. She said she knew I was pregnant and planning an abortion. She was sorry. She left. I tried to get myself together. I walked back to my apartment alone.

I learned so much from this relationship in a course, I entitled, Self-Worth 101. I decided what I would and could not tolerate. How I wanted to be treated. The level of commitment I would demand, or I would be out. After this mess, patience was not my virtue in relationships.

The chemistry and connection with Michael happened so casually like a lot of relationships. Before you know it, you're in way too deep. I never thought about what the outcome might be. From 17-20 or so, I didn't do a great deal of thinking about outcomes. The next time I was in a committed relationship was with my first husband, and the father of both of my daughters, Michael Allen. I guess I had a thing for Michaels back then.

After waffling at UMBC for four years, without direction and without a degree, I faced a massive student loan debt. I left UMBC at the end of the spring semester 1983 with 91 semester hours: short of the required 120 credits to graduate. I didn't know what to do, how to finish, or even if I could in a reasonable amount of time.

I didn't want to be the guy we met at orientation named Buddy, who happily admitted he was on year six. I couldn't do it. I had never failed at anything in my life. Six years at one college and no degree - not me. Why weren't we shown a positive example of someone who was graduating after three, hell four years? Would that have changed my outcome?

I will never forget the final drive off UMBC's campus, deep in thought. Would I return for year 5? Buddy, I recalled. What a damn negative example. What would I major in? It would take me another two years to piece together a degree. Do I really want to major in African American Studies? What will I do with that? Damn. Michael won't be returning, I'm sure. His basketball scholarship was over. He was looking to play basketball overseas. O would graduate with two degrees in a few weeks. He stuck with the plan. *Who or what was I going back to?*

I thought of my AKA line sisters. I didn't spend a lot of time with them after the chapter meeting about DJ Michael and me. I honestly couldn't face them. I was also trying to figure out how to replace that loan I personally lent myself as the chapter's treasurer to pay late tuition and fees. The semester was ending. *Shit.* How and where in the hell would I get that? I was in debt to Sears too – damn them with their on-campus applications for unemployed students. *I have royally F*'ed – Up!*

In the hallway of Dorm 1, in my UMBC Women's Basketball uniform.

Pledging AKA with my Line Sisters. L-R, Tina Dowhite, Phyllis C. Spencer, Me (#4), Kim Jackson, Genia Loving-Clash, and Isha Alexander-Farewell. Not shown: Lisa Shannon and Pamela S. Hutcherson.

Part II– Standing in a Foxhole

Chapter 5

You're in the Army Now!

"You're too pretty to be going in the Army?" "Huh, why do you say that." "Well, I was told women went into the Army when they are ugly & looking for a huz-bun or theys dikes."

- Confidential

The Army and Not the Navy

When I got home to Camptown for the summer, my dear Uncle Teensy came to visit. Uncle Teensy was always more like an older brother since he was my gramma's youngest son and the last to leave home. We talked through my circumstances. He wasn't as disappointed as I was. I felt like a failure. He ensured me that my credits were not a waste of time or effort. He knew I could finish my degree and knew exactly how—I should join the U.S. Army.

Now, my uncle had served in the U.S. Navy, so initially, his push was confusing. For days, he encouraged me little, by little, to explore the Army because, based on his experience, I would get promotions faster in the Army than he experienced in the Navy. In his mind, promotions meant more money and that was ultimately what I needed—more money!

I remembered when Uncle Teensy left college before graduating to join the Navy. He had gotten his girlfriend "P.G." That's what old black people called pregnant women around children when I was growing up. In those days, being P.G, was not so "P.C.," especially if the couple was unmarried.

As a result, gramma gave Uncle Teensy two options. 1) volunteer and go into the service of his choice or 2) be drafted to go in the Army or Marines and straight to Vietnam. He married my Aunt Shirley before he shipped out for Navy boot camp. They had a beautiful baby girl and named her Susan. Aunt Shirley went on to get her bachelor's degree and pledge AKA!

My gramma believed, rightly so, with him out of college, he would surely be drafted. She preferred he volunteered for the Navy to reduce the chances of him being on the ground in Vietnam. The reality was, black soldiers made up 16.3% of draftees and 23% of all combat troops in Vietnam, despite being 11% of the population in the mid-60s.[5]

Uncle Teensy completed a three-year, shore-tour enlistment in telecommunications, as opposed to any ship-duty, and got out. Ultimately, he regretted his early departure from the Navy, and he wished he'd retired with 20 years. I knew he secretly wanted someone in his family to make a career of the military. Little did I know, I would.

Before Uncle Teensy was to leave to go back to MD, he drove me to the Army's Recruiting Office in Suffolk, VA. I felt like my uncle and the Army Recruiter were truly in cahoots. The recruiter repeated pretty much everything my uncle told me. The Army would allow

---

[5] Time Magazine: Black Vietnam Veterans on Injustices They Faced; June 2020

me to go back to college while on active duty to complete my degree. With tuition assistance, the Army would also pay for it. He failed to mention that more than likely I would have to attend college courses during my lunch hour, evenings/nights, and a few weekends – all non-duty hours. The most exciting pitch, if I enlisted for four years, I would be entitled to the Student Loan Forgiveness program. My uncle beamed. I was a bit skeptical.

The recruiter told us with over 90 college credits, I could go to basic training as an E-3 (Private First Class) not as an E-1/Private. After 6 months, I would automatically be promoted to E-4 or Specialist. Wow. This was sounding better and better. A promotion too? The only condition, I would have to enlist for four years.

Then the recruiter quickly and vaguely mentioned Officer Candidate School (OCS). He suggested I wait until after boot camp to see if I was "interested" in becoming an Officer. I was interested but I took him for his word. I didn't learn until I was stationed in Germany that as a recruit, I could have applied immediately for OCS with the number of college credits and an Armed Services Vocational Aptitude Battery (ASVAB) score of 110.

Recruiters are forever trying to get just one more recruit! In all fairness, monthly and quarterly quotas, tied to their performance evaluations, pressure them; failure to meet your quota could greatly impact recruiters' careers, well past their recruiting assignment. He excitedly talked about the Army's

Buddy program – known as a "2-fer" in the recruiting world. He said if I could get a friend or relative to enlist, we could attend basic training together and possibly be stationed together for our first assignment. Carol Lynn, aka Carolyn, was my first thought.

I was scheduled to take the ASVB in neighboring Franklin at the Armory, at the next scheduled offering. I convinced my cousin Carol Lynn, who just happened to be one my cousin and best friend, high school basketball teammate, and Spanish 1 & 2 classmate.

She surprisingly scheduled herself for the ASVB too. She was athletic and her fiancé was in the Army at that time. It was perfect. I wanted Carol Lynn to join the Army with me. Short version of this brilliant idea – Carol took t h ASVB. And announced "Girrrl, I ain't going in NO Army, you go head!" Good news! I had scored high enough on the ASVAB for a job in the premiere Military Intelligence

Analyst. These jobs required a Top-Secret clearance and offered an Enlistment Bonus of $4K! All I needed to do was to successfully complete the Advanced Individual Training (AIT) after boot camp, and a portion of the bonus would be mine right away, with the rest at the end of each year completed. With the Army, there are always conditions! With the student loan repayment AND the enlistment bonus, I raised my hand as quickly as I could, which was June. My report date for boot camp was October 17, 1983. My uncle was right, joining the Army did pay off...big as shit!

Gramma, Please Don't Go!

In August of 1983, two months before I was scheduled to go to boot camp, my gramma passed away. She had her third or fourth heart attack. I honestly lost count. It happened so quickly that no one was prepared. Yes, she was older and slower. She had been in the hospital for her heart disease before I got home for the summer. Like most black woman her age, she took a ton of prescription medications before she passed away – one or two to control blood pressure, one or two for heart-related illnesses, one or two to protect her organs from all the meds she had to take.

It was a quiet weekday afternoon. Pat and I were there with her. Pat lived with my gramma since I was in college. Butch was in California and Avon was married with a beautiful little girl, Julvonne. We nicknamed her Vonne. I was getting ready to go in the Army. I had gone for a run that day. To get in shape, I usually went for a run around Camptown or played basketball at the new Otelia Rainey Rec. Center. I had just taken a shower and laid down for a nap. My cousin-sister Pat, yelled for me. "Tea-Nah, come look at gramma!"

I ran to her bedroom. I looked at her. She was sweating profusely. I had never seen her sweat like that. She was still. Eyes closed.

"Gramma!" I yelled.

"I'm so sick. I don't know what to do," she said.

I went to get a cold, wet washcloth. I ran back to her room. I put it on her forehead, folded neatly so she could see. Pat stood at the door. She started calling 911. I went into the kitchen and got her a glass of water. I poured it from a glass gallon, old Tropicana jar. I went back in my grandmother's room, and she was repeating over and over, "Lord have mercy. Oh lord, have mercy. I am so sick. Lord, I'm so sick. Have mercy."

Tears streamed from my eyes. I looked at Pat. She was crying and talking to the 911 operator. "Yes, she's had a heart attack before." Pat said. I grabbed my gramma's hand and held it close to her chest. The ambulance arrived and she was transported to the hospital in Franklin, VA. We called my mother and my Uncle Teensy. My mother came that afternoon. Uncle Teensy lived in Maryland.

The next evening when my uncle arrived, he and my mother went to visit gramma at the hospital. I stayed home with Pat and her baby girl, Resheema; we call her Sheema. She was just six months old. When my mother and Uncle Teensy returned, they reported she was feeling better and was in good spirits. She was quite talkative, but loopy. She had gone into cardiac arrest earlier that day and was resuscitated. She complained about her chest being sore. She said it felt like someone had been punching her in her chest; unfortunately, they had.

They both laughed at how, because of low oxygen levels, she saw things and people that were not there. They reported that she told Pat, who was at home with me, to get "that baby" off the foot of her bed. She didn't want her to fall. Her newest, great grandbaby, Sheema, clearly on her mind. My gramma also mentioned our neighbor, we called her Sissy. My grandmother loved Sissy like a daughter, and worried about her. She asked Sissy to fold clothes on her hospital bed that night. Of course, there weren't any clothes on her hospital bed, neither was Sissy. I'm sure if Sissy were there, she would have gone along with gramma's request with a quiet, "Yes, ma'am." That was her beloved Sissy.

Around 2 am, the phone rang. It was the hospital. They advised my mother and Uncle Teensy that my gramma's condition had changed – she'd taken a turn for the worse. When they arrived, they were informed she passed away. Her heart stopped again. They could not revive her. This was the saddest morning of my life. I couldn't believe it. She had purchased or got "on-time" all my toiletries from Parker Drug in downtown Franklin. She had an account there; they knew her by name. Who would see me off to boot camp? My plan was to start an allotment to send her money each month. "Every little bit adds up," gramma said.

Farewell for Now

DJ Michael showed up for Gramma's funeral. It was good to see him; I could feel he cared and supported me. The very next month, I was in MD with his sister, throwing him a farewell party. Michael was on his way to England to play professional basketball for the Nottingham Knights. His scholarship at UMBC had ended with his fourth year. Like a lot of college players, playing ball "overseas" wasn't a bad option; with lodging arranged and pay, players made decent money. We had fun that night — he was very affectionate. He was heading to the U.K. and I, off to the Army. We had no idea if we'd ever see each other again.

The next morning, his sister and I drove him to Baltimore Washington International (BWI) Airport for his flight to London. We were all standing at his gate, chatting it up when my sorority sister walked-up, gave him a gift box, hugged him, and did an about-face and walked away. I didn't open my mouth. No one did. We all just stood there. He smirked and batted his eyes which was his normal sign of discomfort. He pulled me into his chest for an awkward hug and a, "I'll see you soon."

Boot Camp, Where?

All I could do was count the weeks, then the days until I left for boot camp. I was so ready to go. I needed every distraction I could get to not think – think about never hugging gramma again. Thinking about Michael in England. Thinking about all the resources wasted at UMBC – time, money, and my heart. Not to mention the debt I owed to my sorority's chapter.

I spent the rest of the time in Camptown running and working out to keep my mind off things and to prepare for a physically grueling boot camp. My sister-cousin Carol Lynn ensured I had spending money and that I stayed entertained with lots of laughs until I shipped out.

I optimistically headed to boot camp in October of 1983, but I was not at all excited to be honest. I didn't feel overly patriotic, and I wasn't looking forward to boot camp – not any of it. I waved at my watery-eyed mom from inside the bus just before it pulled out of the station in Portsmouth, heading to Richmond, VA.

After a bit of processing at the Military Entrance Processing Station or MEPS, six or seven other recruits and I headed south via AMTRAC train to Ft. McClellan, Alabama (AL) for boot camp. On the train, we all had our own sleeper cars and meal tickets for the overnight ride. This was the first time I had ever been on a train. I sat there, looking out the window, thinking for hours. I kept going back to, "what have I gotten myself into?"

We arrived in Anniston, AL the next morning. By mid-day, we were scattered to different platoons, separated male and female soldiers, and marching everywhere in our civilian clothes. We in-processed medical, dental and were issued two duffel bags of uniforms and boots. I spent my 21st birthday practicing Drill and Ceremony (D&C) at Ft. McClellan's reception station. The entire company sang happy birthday to me. I never thought I would be in the Army, AND on my 21st birthday. I always saw myself having a rum & coke, legally, for the first time.

Just as we were settling-in and ready to start boot camp, we were told only the females who would become Military Police (MP), would stay at Ft McClellan for boot camp. The rest of us would be "shipped" to good old Ft. Jackson in Columbia, South

Carolina. The Ft McClellan reception personnel created our records, placed them in large brown envelopes with just our last name written in black felt tip for us to hand-carry to Ft. Jackson. After a single, impromptu class on "how to wear your Class A uniform," we put them on and boarded a Trailways bus for the ride to South Carolina. We were shipped.

Old Fort Jackson

We arrived at Ft. Jackson's Reception Station late the same night to two grumpy Drill Sergeants (DS) who assigned us a bunk and left us alone. We were up for breakfast at 0600. They integrated us with the female platoon already there. That morning, they began processing medical and dental. With shot records in hand, the Ft. McClellan crew was waved-on from station-to-station, except one! Flu Shots! I was first in line of the crew. I tried to convince the Specialist there that we had our flu shots at Ft. McClellan while holding up my record. His response, "You're in this line. You get a shot!" Damn.

Leaving the Reception station to start training is always an exciting day. Most are anxious to get out of the Reception station, while others are excited to just get it over with. My thoughts were the latter – just get this over with. That morning, we were loaded onto trucks for the 15-minute ride to Tank Hill.

I was sick as a dog with flu symptoms. Chills. Body Ache. Exhausted. And a runny nose now. I dared not go to medical, otherwise known as sick call. That might delay my departure from the Reception station. I was so ready to start and get it over. There were still two of us together from Ft. McClellan. We had hoped to stay together for boot camp. I didn't want to be left behind, waiting for the next group to finish in-processing.

When the trucks stopped at the end of our Company's street, about six Drill DSs were waiting – waiting to yell. "Get your sorry behinds off this truck! Get yo stuff! Grab a duffel bag and run – DON'T you dare walk! Do not walk on this street ever, Privates!" I could barely get myself off the truck. I managed to jump down and grab a duffel bag which was piled high on the shoulder of the road, beside the trucks. *Shit - this is heavy. This isn't mine. Did he say run?*

I dropped off the first bag in front of our barracks door as instructed. I ran back for another one. I grabbed a bag, DS still yelling and in people's face. I heaved up a bag and ran back. This time slower than the first; I wasn't sure I could make it without walking and doing the duffel bag drag. *Shit. I'm so sick. What a way to start.*

Once in front of the old, wooden, two-story, open-bays, white buildings, built to house soldiers during World War II, I dropped the second duffel bag and collapsed on top of it, exhausted. DS Calloway kneeled in front of me. He looked like the black Incredible Hulk – muscles everywhere. His brown round hat was touching my forehead.

In my face, he asked, "What's wrong with you, Private?"

Voice trembling and out of breath, "I...don't...feel...good. I think I have the flu. I got two flu shots." Tears were running down my face.

He said a simple, "Okay. Sit right there, Private."

With that, he got walked away, and immediately started yelling at another soldier. That night after chow, a few of my platoon-mates walked over to my bunk with whatever cold meds they had or were willing to share, since a couple of them drank cough syrup to get drunk. Who knew? They were not sharing shit. I slept like a baby until 0430hrs when the DSs came in and turned on the bay lights for us to get dressed for Physical Training (PT).

For the first time in a long time, I was eating three square meals a day, losing fat, gaining muscles, and developing a six-pack. We did PT Monday – Friday and we marched everywhere. I was hungry for every meal. Lights out by 2100hrs and up at 0430hrs.

An older sister from South Carolina cornrowed my hair in two tight braids to the back, whenever I'd ask; one on each side, ends tucked. I washed it in the shower. She'd put hair oil on my scalp, brush it, and braid it. It was shoulder length when I finally got a relaxer 12 weeks later, a few days before graduation.

The physical demands of boot camp weren't surprising or challenging for me. As a H.S. and college athlete, I had worked much harder. Neither was the mental training to instill Army values. Boot camp was indoctrination to the Army where soldiers learn the traditions, tactics, and customs. I pledged AKA back when the pledge program wasn't prescribed; and in some instances, it felt like boot camp. Truth be told, someone screaming, spitting, and otherwise in my face didn't faze me at all. At least I knew the DS weren't supposed to touch us.

In basic, I learned how to work as a member of a military team — like the many sports teams I had been on before, minus the obvious importance and danger. We learned to march, how to properly wear each uniform, and grooming standard. What I paid close attention to was basic rifle marksmanship qualification, and mastery of common soldier tasks.

I didn't think I'd have a problem handling a rifle. I'd done that before with my brother's pellet guns and Butch's BB gun. I beat each of my brothers, one at a time, in an impromptu shooting competition in Duke's backyard. Duke loved when I'd beat them in anything – basketball, horseshoes, badminton, and marksmanship.

Early in boot camp, I learned that I needed to fix my face, so it did not look like I had an "attitude." About a week or so after we started boot camp, I was called out of the breakfast chow line by DS Calloway.

DS Calloway was a Staff Sergeant (E-6), who called himself "checking-on" the black female soldiers. I quickly figured out Calloway really wanted to see if he could flirt with soldiers, to see if it would be reciprocated. He asked how I was doing. I stood there at parade rest. Half awake, half sleep, and half annoyed. "Okay," I said, "hungry."

The Company's Senior Drill (Sr. Drill) was a Sergeant First Class (SFC), E-7, and a much older white man. I saw him out of the corner of my eye, walking toward the chow hall line, looking at Calloway and me talking.

He seemed to pick-up his pace. He aggressively walked directly up to me and put his brown round hat, right on my forehead. I looked into his eyes. I could smell his coffee breath. He said, still staring at me, "Is there a problem here DS? What's this Pri-vate's problem?" He said "Pri-vet" with his southern twang like it was a nasty word. Looking like he was gritting his teeth and rolling tobacco in his jaw, he stared. I stared back, probably a bit too bold for his taste. He didn't move.

DS Calloway replied quickly. "No Senior. There's no problem. Lawyer is a good soldier." Calloway, in a stern voice now, looking at me, said, "Get back in formation, Private."

My expression did not change but I did. I processed what happened. Why did the Sr. Drill react to me that way? What did I do or not do? I knew my unfazed demeanor and the second-too-long stare down pissed him off. He had turned red in the face. I just needed to figure out how to prevent that from happening again.

This same Sr. Drill denied my first helicopter ride after I qualified "Expert" at the weapons range. Soldiers who qualified expert were given rides back to Tank Hill in a Boeing CH-47, Chinook — an actual helicopter ride. At that point, I hadn't flown on an airplane yet, let alone a helicopter. After the "K" last names, he just skipped over "Lawyer," looking me in the face. I knew I qualified expert. Damn. I couldn't wait to tell DS Calloway to see what he had to say.

That lesson proved to be highly beneficial for years to come. I needed to be "mindful of my face," particularly when dealing with the unfamiliar. I told myself, "Don't appear angry or threatening." I thought of my gramma's advice again — "You can catch more flies with honey than vinegar."

Mind you, a helicopter ride meant avoiding the 2–3-mile march back with your full rucksack, Load Bearing Equipment (LBE) canteen and weapon, through little Egypt. Little Egypt was a portion of a dirt road we had to take back to Tank Hill. It was so sandy and hard to walk through, the DSs called "route step mark." Which basically means to get through the rough terrain the best way you can. We'd form-up again once we got through Little Egypt.

My mother, her long-term boyfriend Sonny, and my little cousin Julvonne attended my boot camp graduation ceremony. They drove down from Portsmouth, VA. I was beaming with pride and happy to see all of them.

After graduation, I went home for the Christmas and New Year holidays. I had a 2 January 1984 report date to Corry Station, Pensacola, FL. I had no earthly idea what my training entailed. All I knew was I'd be trained at a Navy base in Pensacola, which my DSs thought was hilarious! They snickered and laughed and shortly before we headed out for graduation, DS

Calloway said, "Lawyer, watch out for the Sea-Men down there in Florida. Okay?" I shook my head at him and smiled. "Okay, Drill Sergeant!"

FORT JACKSON S.C.
E CO 1 BN 1 BDE
2 PLT
3   NOV   1983

Top: Close up of me in boot camp.
Below: My entire platoon and Drill Sergeants, front and center.

I arrived on time for Advanced Individual Training (AIT) at Corry Station in Pensacola. I finally got my first plane ride/flight from Norfolk, VA to Pensacola with a layover in Charlotte, NC. What a rush. I was dressed to the nines in civilian attire. I don't know where I thought I was going, but back then, you got "clean" to travel, especially on an airplane. I wasn't afraid to take an airplane to Pensacola at all. I love to fly, and to this day, I still marvel at the engineering of aircraft — the know-how to takeoff and keep all that metal airborne is amazing.

AIT was, and still is, required training for soldiers after boot camp. This training teaches soldiers the job skills they will perform during their enlistment or career. This is called a soldier's M-O-S. MOS equates to a job like Helicopter Pilot, MP, Cook, Driver, or Signal Interceptor. My MOS was initially 05K – code for Electronic Warfare, Non-Morse Signal Interceptor.

While other soldiers were attending AIT on Army bases with additional Army training requirements, we were chilling with the Navy in Pensacola, FL., but our world has completely changed from 1984. Corry Station is the very training base that on the morning of December 6, 2019, Mohammed Saeed Alshamrani, an aviation student from Saudi Arabia, killed three and injured eight other students/staff. motivated by his "jihadist" ideology and al-Qaeda of the Arabian Peninsula.

I reached out to two buddies who worked at Corry Station to make sure they were safe and watched as mainstream media tried to piece together why

Mohammed Saeed was at Corry Station in the first place. In a reference, pentagon officials confirmed that the over 5,000 foreign students from 153 countries were in the U.S for security cooperation training and that DOD vets' these students. On January 13, 2020, the Department of Justice (DOJ) said they officially classified the incident as an act of terrorism.

With the U.S. Navy as executive agent for Signal Collectors and Analysts, we had instructors from all branches of the services and joint service classes. At this time, I didn't know later in life, I would play a role in determining what this school taught in the form of training standards.

AIT was relatively easy for me apart from learning and copying Morse Code. I'm what you call a Code Rock (CR). To graduate from AIT, we had to copy Morse Code at a rate of 18 groups or words, per minute. This is an objective that required listening to distorted Morse Code tapes, via headphones, and using a pencil, writing letters and numbers on a pre-stamped piece of paper of blocks or groups.

When you successfully complete a rate or speed, you move to the next level at your own pace. The amount of time in AIT could be significantly reduced by weeks, if the start of phase II is perfectly timed AND you don't become a CR. Not me — I got stuck on what felt like every other speed, for some strange, bizarre, CR, reason.

Some students completed this training in a couple of weeks, while others, like me, took a couple of months. Students who failed to make progress according to an expected rate, are required to attend remedial training for an additional two-hours per school day. The pressure was on. If by twelve weeks, students have not passed 18 groups, they are subject to reclassification. This may result in a new job/MOS, a new school, more than likely not your first choice, and at an Army base. This alone motivated soldiers to master code. No one wanted to be shipped out to Army training. In the early 80's, Corry Station was like being in college and living in the dormitory.

I found the second phase of the training after Morse Code, which was basic signals acquisition, tuning, measurements, and tear-line paper printer, and reporting, much easier. Rote memorization was easy for me, but I found turning knobs and tuning to detect, acquire, and identification of foreign electronic intelligence by taking signal measurements miserably unexciting. It was nothing like I imagined at all.

Early military communications advanced from visual and audible signals to electronic communications that included text, audio, facsimile, tactical ground-based communications, microwave, and satellite communications. The US Army kept up with communications and technology advancement. I had no idea of the critical importance of these skills in predicting adversarial plans and actions. What we provided was valuable intelligence to decision makers at every level.

Pensacola was beautiful. I loved the white-sand beaches. On weekends, we'd rent a car to get to the beach, out to dinner on payday weekends, and off-post parties. Since I was 21 years old, I rented the cars in my name for 'trusted classmates.' We'd arrange to go to "Rent-a-Wreck" together. I'd put the rental in my name using my MD driver's license. I drove the car back to post and handed over the keys for the weekend. Even though I insisted on insurance, that was about the dumbest thing I could do. I just thank goodness that no one crashed a rental car.

My best friend and road dog in AIT was a white soldier named Dara Lanier. She hailed from Alabama – you could tell by her accent, yet she loved to call everyone "dude" like a hippy from California. Dara was from a family of means. I wasn't sure why she was even in the Army. Dara showed me what to do at fancy restaurants - how to, and when to use each utensil and to place the napkin in your lap. I studied her.

Before I left home for the Army, Piccadilly's at the mall in Portsmouth, VA was probably as fancy a restaurant as I'd seen. I followed her lead. Watched her eat a lobster tail and shrimp cocktail with those little forks. Listened to her communicate with waiters and waitresses. She was blond, pretty, and pleasant — she got exactly what she wanted. She preferred a privately owned restaurant instead of a chain—fresher seafood she'd say. On payday weekends, we ate well, hung out at the beach, and drank rum and cokes. It was nothing for us to stay on the beach at a hotel, drive to Mobile, Alabama or party with our squid (Navy) classmates.

I successfully graduated from AIT before Memorial Day weekend, May 1984. Not everyone in my class did.

Even though the academic attrition rate after Morse Code was less than 10%, other military requirements and a tragedy, lowered the rate of graduation at about 80%. My mother came to Pensacola a few days before the graduation. We hung out with some my new friends and comrades at a near-by hotel, went to Red Lobster for the very first time, and drove back to Portsmouth, VA, where my mother lived, together.

Chapter 6

Specialist, You're Going to Munich Germany!

Home is where the Army sends you!

-Unknown

Munich or Bust

In June of 1984, I flew solo from John F. Kennedy Airport in NY, non-stop to Munich, Germany. My orders from Pensacola assigned me to the 66th Military Intelligence Group (66th MI Gp), with its headquarters in Munich. When announced in class, my classmates cheered! How did I get so lucky, I thought? Soldiers with orders stateside to places like Ft. Bragg, Ft. Meade, and Ft. Huachuca, jeered. They wanted to go "overseas." It appeared the worst-case scenario back then, were orders to Korea. The tears and pleading ensued...soldiers asked if they could trade with someone—with soldiers going to Ft. Bragg, any place but Korea.

There's always the one exception. I will never forget the soldier's face. She clapped, smiled, jumped up and down when our instructor called her last name, and said Korea! This soldier was excited to go to Korea or should have won an Academy award! She was ecstatic. Hell, the only thing I knew about Germany was that every military person I knew in my family had been stationed in Germany.

I arrived at the 66th MI Gp on a Friday afternoon. I was assigned an "in-transit room" in their barracks and told I would not be staying in Munich, except for that weekend. What? Where I was headed was a small village town on the Rhein River called Worms, pronounced Vorms. On Monday, I'd take a 4-hour train ride from Munich to Worms to the 527th Military Intelligence Battalion (527th MI Bn), Security Detachment – Europe (SDEUR).

The weekend seemed long — I was anxious. I couldn't wait to get settled in and unpack my bags in the place I would be for two years. I didn't adventure too far from the barracks that weekend. Armed Forces Network (AFN) fascinated me, and I couldn't stop watching their low-budget infomercials about soldiers completing high-value inventory sheets and just because you have checks, doesn't mean you have money in your bank account warnings. Yes, that was an AFN infomercial.

Sunday, I attended church with two sisters that I was sharing the suite in the barracks with. When we got to church, I learned the service was Pentecostal. Who knew I would attend a "laying of hands and sprinkling of holy water," service in Munich? The church did not feel like we were in Germany. It was similar to what we called "sanctified churches," I had visited at home.

Worms, Germany (1984-1987)

Monday morning, I reported back to the Orderly Room. The directions the Sergeant gave were brief and vague. No small talk for him. "Don't get off the train till you see WORMS HBF." He circled it on my ticket. "Here are your tickets and meal vouchers to use in the train's dining car.

I responded when I could with, "Yes, Sergeant." "Wear your uniform appropriately. If you take your jacket off, make sure you have a nameplate on your shirt. When you get to Worms, ask for directions to the Army Kaserne or take a cab. There's only one and it's not far from the train station."

I was terrified, but I had to do it. "Yes, Sergeant." I didn't have a choice. I had to travel alone from Munich, to Worms by train, and find an Army what? Kaserne? GOD, please go with me. I bought myself a map of Germany at the train station. The old school, fold-type; fold twenty-five times to get the top page on the top and bottom on the bottom, kinda map.

When I boarded the train, I quickly oriented the map and myself. We were heading north and west. Cool. I was oriented. I spotted the name of the first town we stopped in…it was on the map. Good. It was Dachau HBF. *Why does that sound familiar?* I asked myself. I returned years later from Berlin. I visited Dachau for a guided tour of this World War II concentration camp. The eeriest parts of the tour were the barracks and crematorium. The barracks configurations and bunk beds reminded me of photographs of the hull of slave ships, packed in.

If my map reading was on point, the next town was Augsburg. *It's really close to Munich,* I thought. A couple of my classmates from Corry Station were headed to Field Station Augsburg. The train ride was pleasant. There wasn't much to see once we got out and into the countryside of Bavaria. I couldn't get a good nap for tracking the progress by each city, all the way to Worms. GOD don't let me miss my stop, please! I had my very first schnitzel and pomme frites (french fries) on that train ride. I pointed to a picture. The plain schnitzel looked and tasted like a fried pork chop; the ketchup was a bit sweeter than American brands but the pomme frites were hot and delish.

I arrived at Worms Hauptbahnhof (Hbf) early afternoon. I asked for directions from the first person I saw in uniform. He extended his arm and pointed with his fingers and told me the Kaserne was a half-mile, straight down the cobblestone street that ran parallel to the train tracks. I walked with my duffel bag on my back and large suitcase in one hand. This small, one square block, post, with a parade field and flagpole in the middle, was my home for the next three years.

Our unit, Security Detachment – Europe, travelled all over Germany to military kasernes to conduct TEMPEST Security Testing. I wasn't trained in Pensacola to do this but was assured the job was part of our MOS – 05K. I didn't mind it all. This job taught me how to travel in a Temporary Duty (TDY) status.

We drafted, processed, and completed TDY orders to travel, selected hotels to stay in, teams to perform the testing, report writers, and drivers for each trip. I quickly got my license to drive. I couldn't wait to feel the speed on the Autobahn. I ended up driving all over Germany for work and play. I earned my first Army Driver's Badge, with 8K safe miles, after my first year in the unit.

Duty in Germany in the 80s were the best of times and the worst. The Cold War was in full force. The U.S. and its allies, distrust for the antagonistic Soviet Union, played out for over 40 years without a direct military campaign. In my humble opinion, this war was fought mostly by intelligence and all the INTs, played a part. My job or MOS, brought me and other soldiers right up against the Eastern bloc fence line, conducting test.

The more we knew about the former U.S.S.R.'s and communist East Germany's intentions, the better. Our work enabled U.S. decision-makers to create the lengthy standoff with the Soviet Union – without armed engagement. Both sides fought the Cold War using psychological warfare, electronic surveillance, embargos, and arms races. The Soviets retaliated with propaganda campaigns and blatant espionage. Security briefings provided a glimpse into spy tactics and operations security measures.

As soon as I checked-in, a fellow O5K/98K (my MOS) met me in the office. Her name was Belinda and she left Pensacola just before graduation to attend her father's funeral. I was excited to see her and know at least one person there. We would be roommates.

Belinda was gorgeous. Half black, half Puerto Rican, adopted by great black parents, from North Carolina. She wasn't interested in college and decided to "try" the Army for 4 years. Belinda was the first to tell you, "I'm no soldier." Her passion was fashion and make-up. She wanted to be a model but wasn't quite tall or thin enough, but exceptionally talented in the department. She directed and modelled several well-attended fashion shows in Berlin.

Thankfully, we weren't on the same team at work. We got a little bit of a break from each other, especially when we travelled for work. As weekend road dogs, we partied all over Germany with R&B group, Ray Goodman, and Brown (RGB). Yes, the original RGB. We saw them in concert in Mannheim at the NCO Club. Belinda caught the attention of one of the singers. He wanted to meet her after the show – he sent his tour manager for her, and she dragged me backstage with her. They invited her, I mean us, on the road in Germany.

They had another month or so of shows in Germany. We probably saw about ten RGB's shows, yet every time they sang "Special Lady," I swear it felt like they were singing to us/me for the first time. We swayed and rocked at every show. After the show, like disgraceful R. Kelly suggested, it was literally the hotel lobby for late night drinks and dinner. If the hotel didn't have a restaurant, someone went out for food for the entire crew, including Belinda & me.

They'd unwind and we'd reap the benefits of free drinks and meals. Afterwards, we'd crash in their hotel rooms. If they had a Sunday night show, we'd drive back to Worms early Monday morning for PT, then work. Then back on the road with RGB, come Friday evening. I was an official groupie & didn't care! We had a blast!

I'll never forget Clarence Oliver and the singer Kevin Owens, who later sang backup for Luther

Vandross, came to Worms to hang out and play basketball. They loved coming on post, seeing all the Americans, especially the black ones – "Brothers & Sisters! What's up!" they said. We played a quick 3-on-3, pick-up game in the gym. My homeboy Clarence, from Richmond, VA was on my team. He played drums for them and other artists. We blew their eyes out! RGB finished their tour and returned home to the U.S. To this day, whenever I hear a RGB song, I smile and think about my groupie days.

Life in Germany in the 80s in general, was cool. The dollar exchange rate was excellent. At one point, it was $1 to over 3.50 deutsche marks. I played basketball and softball on the post women's teams, which allowed me to travel all over Germany. I enjoyed seeing other Kasernes, the German countryside, shopping at larger Post Exchanges (PX), and seeing where and how other soldiers lived. soldiers.

Playing softball took me and my team on the infamous Berlin duty train — what a concept. The duty train departed from Frankfurt, Germany, at night, to travel though East Germany and into Berlin. Its mission was to deliver U.S. passengers and cargo from West Germany through then communist East Germany.

MPs rode the train back and forth from Frankfurt to Berlin to enforce regulations governing behavior of U.S. passengers and to protect them while they slept in sleepers' cars. When we woke up, we were just outside of Berlin. I slide the train window shade up. The sun was bright as I looked out the window at an approaching train, going in the opposite direction. A young man, East German I assumed, looking out of his window, flipped me a bird – he held it until he was out of site.

Berlin was huge, especially coming from Worms. It was the New York of Germany. We didn't win the European Women's softball tourney but the experience of traveling to Berlin on the duty train has never left me.

I saw DJ Michael again while I was stationed in Worms. He was still playing basketball in England when I arrived in Germany. He came to visit me for a short stay. We spent a few noticeably quiet evenings in Frankfurt together. I was there on TDY for a week. I'd work, and he chilled at the hotel until I returned each evening. In early1985, I took a flight from Germany to London for a week of leave in Nottingham, known for its role in the fabled Robin Hood legend. Complete with a Sherwood Forest Park, Nottingham is approximately an hour and half drive north of London. We had a great tourist-type day in London before the drive to Nottingham. Michael seemed acclimated to his new home, his team, and his role there. He'd even picked-up a bit of a British accent, I teased. I didn't see him again until well after I was out of the Army, working as a civilian for NSA.

My First Marriage

After enjoying the single life, a bit, along came Michael Allen and the July 1985 addition of the Worms Germany military community newspaper read,

"This Marriage Was Made on the Court!" We were featured on page 7. Here's how our romance started.

We were the hottest basketball players in our community and league. Both of us played in college and our skills were evident. It was after a double home game against Kaiserslautern, where the Women's team played first, followed by the Men's team, that we were introduced by another one of my teammates, Tanya.

On the rare occasion when this happened, you could count on a packed after-party at the Noncommissioned Officers club, aka the NCO Club, with out-of-towners. I scored over 20 points that game. I was hot and the gym was packed. The men's team encouraged us from the bleachers.

When the men's team was up, Michael, aka Microwave, shot his usual 20+, double-figured in rebounds, complete with a couple of dunks, and a smile at the foul line that melted the panties off the ladies in the stands, and one of my very married, teammates. Yes, I was aware. Unfortunately for her, her husband was Michael's homeboy from Memphis, which made the Mrs., off limits in that regard, he would tell me later. He also had an ex-girlfriend who lived down the hall from me in the barracks. Rumor had it, he broke it off with her, and she was not over him.

That night at the NCO club, I was hanging with my teammates, looking very fit and very hot. Tanya and I were standing at the back wall, I had a drink in my hand. He walked up to Tanya and said, "What's up Shorty?" he said so casually. I was intrigued.

Michael and I became the community's basketball sweethearts. He, 6 feet 4, attractive, muscular, smooth skin, nice fade, who affectionately called all women, "Shorty." He was a country boy. Born in Mississippi. Family moved to Memphis when he was young for better opportunities. They lived in the same house on Glenwood St., not far from Elvis Presley Boulevard, from childhood into his adulthood.

His mother, a sweet, highly Christian woman that I respected by never saying *Shit* around her. The first time we visited as a couple, I'd sneak outside and walk down the street for a quick smoke.

Top: Newspaper article that appeared in the Worms Community paper.

Below: Michael and I, at our wedding reception at the Worms NCO Club.

Life with Michael produced my greatest blessings; two beautiful girls. Tierra Sherell came along the year after her father, and I got married — 1986. I was pregnant a few months later. It was quick. I remember Michael tossed my birth control pills right along with a pack of cigarettes in the toilet.

It was in Worms that I met my dear friend and confidante, SSG Anastasia White - Stacey for short. On weekends and holidays, we hung out and played cards with the old heads (older in age soldiers), BBQed, or I'd sit at the bar in the club where she worked part-time as a bartender, just to get a good laugh. She was a country girl, just like me. She was my escape, when I needed girl time – which included her cooking my favorite grilled liver and onions, and a German Chocolate cake from scratch. Michael didn't mind our friendship at all. He and Stacey went head-to-head, round-for-round, "country clowning" each other.

Welcome Baby Girl

Tierra was born in Heidelberg, Germany after the most intense 24-hours of labor pains imaginable. This was the mid-eighties, when military hospitals and probably civilian ones too, had a reputation for not performing epidurals or providing pain meds out of fear it'd slow and/or halt the dilation process. Well, I was one of the women who delivered completely naturally but not by choice. My mother and Stacey were there with me. My mother flew to Germany from VA to help me for the first few weeks. I greatly appreciated it – she was such a help.

The day after Tierra was born, I re-enlisted right there in the hospital for another four years. My commander came to the hospital to administer the Oath of Enlistment and to see our new bundle of joy — Tierra Sherelle. Now that I had a family, it made sense to re-enlist. Another four, then I'd get out, I thought.

I returned to the States with a baby girl and a husband in August of 1987; we took leave in VA. My mother was still in Portsmouth. After breaking-up with a long-term boyfriend that she lived with, she moved to a clean, nice two-bedroom apartment. She was working in Portsmouth as a Data Entry Clerk and doing well. We spent time with family in Camptown, Franklin, and relaxed at Virginia Beach. Michael met my father Duke and my three brothers for the first time during this leave.

902nd Military Intelligence Group
Ft. Meade, Maryland (1987-1990)

Before our leave ended officially, we drove from VA to MD for my next assignment with the 902nd Military Intelligence Group (902nd MI Gp). Michael worked in the telecommunications center at the Hoffman building in Northern VA. We stayed with my Uncle Teensy and his wife, Audrey, in Silver Springs, MD until we found an apartment in Greenbelt. They had two little girls: Lynzee and Jaleesa.

Living in Greenbelt, which seemed logical and almost halfway for Michael's commute to VA., and mine to Ft. Meade. The apartment on Greenbelt Rd.

allowed easy access to both 495/95S and the BW Parkway.

In the 902nd MI Gp, I became a part of a unique Army analysis team that came with a fat civilian clothing allowance. We wore our Army uniforms while at work at Ft. Meade, and civilian clothes on missions. We were told it was to blend-in with civilians and to prevent our Army rank/grades from being a distraction. There was no way to blend with the big white elephant we drove around.

We travelled all over the U.S., driving our custom-made, 2.5-ton truck. It was called the Special Purpose Mobile Signal Surveillance System (SPMS3) or Spasm. Back then, the truck was considered high-tech with two Captain's chairs for Analysts, two racks of receivers, o-scopes, patch panels, and an IBM computer in the middle. The antennas that deployed were given celebrity names like the Jimmy Durante, because of his long knobbed, directional nose.

Our team leader, SSG Robert Kitchen, aka Bob, was a tall, thick, white guy from New Jersey. He had to constantly monitor his weight to avoid being placed on the Army's Weight Control program. Bob's father had been in the Army and met and married his mother in Germany; she was of German descent. They loved their big baby Bob.

A diehard NY Giants fan who couldn't wait to play Monday morning QB - Bob talk junk to anyone who would entertain him. Never in a bad mood and always the jokester, Bob kept us motivated and supported. He was the kind of leader who got his hands dirty –

literally. Our team was the envy of the Counter-SIGINT Detachment. To others, we were SSG Tena Lawyer-Allen, SGT Guy Collinsworth, PFC Kelly Sherwood, and PFC Denys Smith. To Bob, we were his family; Tena Beana, Guy, Kelly, and Pumpkin Head (Denys Smith). Bob gave her that nickname and boy, did it stick.

It was the coolest technical/intel jobs I had in the Army. One of the most exciting missions required us to drive across country to Stockton, CA. It took us about 4 days to reach Las Vegas, where we set-up to do a "dog and pony" demonstration for small MI unit there.

This was my first time in Vegas. I had never seen so many lights in my life. The strip was magical. We spent the weekend before heading to Stockton, eating, gambling, and keeping Bob out of innocent trouble. After our mission, we'd take the truck to the company that designed and built it for its maintenance and recalibrations.

During the week the truck was being recalibrated, we stayed just outside Anaheim, not far from Walt Disney Land. It just made sense to go. We had a blast, trying to keep up with the biggest kid in the group - Bob. We relaxed around the pool, laughing about our comrades in cold temps in late March in MD. We were the envy of our close-knit unit.

One morning while there, we got up at 0500hrs to get in line outside of Paramount Studios in Los Angeles for tickets to see the Arsenio Hall Show – we made the cut. Before the show started, we were given green t-shirts to wear to celebrate "Earth Day." I couldn't believe we were in the studio audience of the Arsenio Hall Show that very afternoon, watching Arsenio interview Whoopie Goldberg. Jackson Brown was the musical guest.

The best part of this trip was when Bob agreed we could drive south of San Diego to Chula Vista to see my cousin Butch and his family. My entire team went with me and was welcomed with open arms and a BBQ. Butch had gotten out of the Army and now lived in Southern CA where his wife Collette was from.

He met Collette, a beautiful, white girl from CA, while he was in the Army. They were married when she came with him to visit my grandmother in Camptown for the first time. They had two beautiful children, Tiger and Sheena. During this time, Butch and his family, in my eyes, were the picture of love and happiness. Butch bonded with the soldiers with me; Lisa, Pumpkin Head, Kelly and of course, Bob.

Rest In Peace Bob...We Miss You!

After I left the 902nd MI Gp, I didn't see Bob Kitchen again until I was a 1SG with 742nd MI Bn. He just happened to attend one of our Hail and Farewell dinners at a local restaurant. It was wonderful to see him. Bob hugged and squeezed me, while he announced to his entire table that I was his Army wife, and he hadn't seen me in years. His new wife, who I had never met, looked quite inquisitive about this Army wife business. She stared.

About 2 years later in 2003, our leader and friend Robert "Bob" Kitchen died suddenly, serving our country in the Middle East during Operation Iraqi Freedom.

SPASM- the 2 ton-truck we drove across country from Ft. Meade, Md.

L-r, SSG Robert "Bob" Kitchen and PFC Kelly Sherwood, in Las Vegas during our cross-country trip.

My friend Stacey was stationed with me again, now at Ft. Meade. She helped me prepare for the E-6/Staff Sergeant promotion board. I will never forget how she explained each answer and then demanded I repeat the book answer verbatim. She wanted me to be able to explain a response if asked instead of providing the canned answer in the study guide. I rocked it – I was 2 points from maxing the board at 198; 2 points were deducted for a current event question that I was clueless about.

I was proud of my performance – so was Stacey. A few months later, I was promoted to Staff Sergeant (E-6). Stacey was at the ceremony like a proud big sister. Michael and I were advancing in rank and responsibilities which required both of us to attend leadership courses away from home.

Home in Greenbelt, MD

Most evenings and weekends, my life in Greenbelt was quiet and uneventful. We did a bit of traveling to Atlantic City, Memphis, and, of course, to Camptown to visit family. We'd hang out with other soldiers and their families in the surrounding area and bases. We also spent time with Uncle Teensy and his family and, of course, Michael got in his gym time. Michael was a laid-back husband and father. He watched a lot of sports on television and offered to hold and entertained Tierra for me to cook and clean. When I could, I'd hang with my dear friend Stacey. We hit the road for somewhere. I was bored and I enjoyed my girlfriend time.

After a year or so at Ft. Meade, I wanted to get pregnant again. I saw Michael and I married for a long time, and I didn't want Tierra to be an only-child. So, we got pregnant with Tashara, affectionately known as Shara. The Army pregnancy uniform in the late 80s was hideous. I looked like a pregnant Girl Scout with the Army green pants, light green smock top, with nametag. It was1989 and the Army didn't have a battle dress pregnancy uniform. So, while everyone in the unit was in BDUs, pregnant soldiers stuck out like green thumbs or fat, green, clovers or something, wearing mint green smocks.

I was having contractions every 5-4 minutes when Michael drove me to Bethesda Naval Hospital around 7pm, on the 2nd of June 1989. Tashara Burnett was delivered much less dramatically than Tierra. The weekend prior, I walked and prayed for her to start making her way. I didn't want to get dressed Monday morning like a pregnant Girl Scout again, drive to Ft. Meade, waddle to my desk to sit most of the day. Just sit.

Shara was delivered at the premiere Naval Hospital in Bethesda, Maryland, now known as Walter Reed Medical Center; the medical center that treats POTUS. Since Ft. Meade didn't have a maternity ward at Kimbrough Army hospital, Bethesda was in best in the area. Shara came in the world kicking and screaming. My mother was there to help us with Tierra. I must admit, she stood in the gap several times.

Now a mom of two on active duty, made life challenging and tiring; to do well at everything, I needed to get organized and stay organized both mentally and physically. I had two kids to pack up for daycare and school; two little girls to bathe, to feed; two minds to mold; to protect. This could be a full-time job alone. I was a soldier and on weekends, a mom. Being organized looked like labels, containers, schedules, sharpies, tote bags, snacks, and packing lists, which I use to this day. I love a good packing list. What it didn't look like was kisses, snuggling, hugs, asking funny questions, being a funny mom, saying "you are enough," or asking, "how do you feel about x, y, z?"

My daughters Tierra and Shara.

The Toughest Challenge of Our Lives

My mother was the source of my inspiration until I was in my mid-twenties. I'll never forget. I had re-enlisted in the Army and was stationed at Ft. Meade for the first time. She called and asked if she could come live with Michael and me. At that point in my life, I had never said, "No," to her, or anyone for that matter, even if I thought it, was a horrible idea. I'd be uncomfortable and inconvenienced, which became the story of my life with her. No big deal. My mother had been there for me since my grandmother died. She was there when Tierra was born and again when Shara was born. What could I say but yes?

What I realized when she arrived in Maryland, would be the toughest and longest challenge of her life and mine. She was addicted to drugs — cocaine. She lost her car and her apartment in Portsmouth, VA. Her then-boyfriend dropped her off at our apartment in Greenbelt, looked at me and said, "Watch your mother, she likes to smoke cocaine too much," and walked out the door, never to be heard from again. I was speechless. I didn't know what to say. I immediately asked her about what he meant. She denied it. Said I didn't know him, and I didn't. I believed her, initially.

She stayed with us for a few weeks before she suggested she move to Newark, New Jersey with her sister, my Aunt Ruth. There she'd have access to public transportation, she proclaimed. As it stood in Maryland, she didn't have a car because both Michael and I commuted to work — Michael to the Hoffman building in Alexandria and me to Ft. Meade near Laurel, Maryland. I was all for it. My dear friend Stacey drove her to New Jersey.

My army buddy and "Road Dog" in Germany, Stacey, and I were close as ever. Her mother just so happened to live in New Jersey, not far from my Aunt

Ruth. After discussing the situation with her, like a dear friend, she was willing to take my mother to N.J. She came early and helped Ma and me load the things she brought with her from VA. Basically, her clothes and her prized floor-model television I got her before I left for Germany the first time.

My mother's move to N.J. was the worst move ever for an addict. It was 1989 and drug use in Newark was making the national news. During this time, I saw my mother about twice a year. She landed a job with the Internal Revenue Service (IRS) and quickly got her own place in Newark, away from her sister Ruth. They had started complaining about each other. I knew it was a matter of time before either my mother left on her own, or Aunt Ruth would put her out.

Each time I saw my mother, it became more and more apparent that she was using drugs. She had guests come in and take turns going into her bathroom to smoke crack or cocaine or something. Ellouise was in the rotation too. Then the calls started for money, even with her "good government job" with the IRS. My mother had never asked me for a dime before.

Michael and I became disconnected somehow. We just lived together. It was boring. I was soldiering and mothering, and he was commuting and soldiering. There was little communication and zero affection. The straw that broke the camel's back with Michael was to find a letter addressed to my husband from a female soldier in one of his leadership courses he attended; I believe it was Basic Noncommissioned

Officers course or BNCOC. In his letter, she mentioned knowing he was a married man, yet she wanted to keep in touch with Michael.

The icing on the cake was Tierra telling me her "daddy's girlfriend" lived in a high-rise apartment on Route 1 South, just across the Potomac River. I will never forget the pain that pierced my heart, driving down Route 1 in Alexandria, when she pointed and said that. I asked her to repeat it. "What did you say Tiera?" She said it again. Did she just say what I know she said? OMG. "What baby?" A third time. I wanted to ask her so many questions – but it wasn't fair. She was just 4 or 5 years old. I did clarify she said, "my...daddy's... girlfriend."

A few months before I came down on assignment for Berlin, Michael moved out, after I insisted, he did. He was just there — very independent and distracted. He had little to do with the girls or me. He had service obligations like Charge-of-Quarters (CQ) in Northern VA and I, at Ft. Meade. His commute was hellish and mine was no joke either. I dropped both girls off at two locations – Odenton Christian School and a home daycare, which made my commute even longer. I was left completely alone with two kids. I felt like a single mom already

He didn't try to stay. He didn't fight for the girls or me – he just left. Uneventful. I didn't believe he would move-out, but he came home with keys for a barrack's room in Northern VA and a plan to pack and leave that coming weekend. He didn't want any of the furniture or anything. He just left. I was in Greenbelt on weeknights and weekends with two kids, alone. I missed him, but I needed to stay focused, I was headed to Berlin in a few months. If he wanted to be with us, he'd have to put forth some real effort to get the Army to assign him to Berlin.

Chapter 7

A New Lifestyle

Sexual fluidity refers to the idea that a person's attractions, and therefore their sexual identity— lesbian, gay, bisexual, heterosexual—can change over time and that change depends on the person's situational, environmental or relationship conditions."6

Off to Berlin, Germany (1990-1992)

On December 30th, 1989, the girls and I left Ft. Meade for Berlin, Germany. Traveling now was completely different than the first time. I had to pack for three — two little girls and me. Tierra was age 3 and Shara, just over a year old. Snacks. Change of clothes for each. Juice boxes. Pull-ups. Wipes. Small toys. And passports. Except, I packed Tierra's passport in my Household Goods (HHG). *Shit!*

Now to get the full impact of this mistake, HHGs are shipped early and separate from the soldier. They're usually delivered after the soldier finds adequate quarters — a home. We're talking furniture, seasonal clothing, books, linen, and kitchenware – about 10K pounds of goods. Tierra's passport was in there! GOD only knew where my HHGs were!

I didn't discover this until we were going through Immigrations and Customs in Heathrow Airport, London. I can still see the look on the Immigration Officer's face now. We had a truly short layover before our flight to Berlin. When the officer waved us forward and asked for passports, I pulled out two passports,

---

my military ID and assignment orders. It was at this point, when the officer started flipping through the two passports, that I realized I had included my passport, and packed Tierra's. *Oh GOD.*

Looking at Tierra, the Officer initially asked, "Where's her passport?" I was confused. I thought I gave it to him. I hadn't looked at them after packing them in MD. *"You don't have her passport,"* he said nodding toward Tierra. I thought I packed it. "Oh GOD, it must be with my HHG."

He looked confused when I attempted to explain HHGs. He looked at my assignment orders and then back at my ID and the two passports. He looked again. He handed everything back and waved me through without stamping anything. He was just as frustrated as I was. Imagining what might happen when I got to Berlin's Immigration checkpoint, I prayed *Lord help!*

We arrived in Berlin the next day — New Year's Eve. With my PCS orders in and two passports in hand, we were waved through Immigration and Customs – we probably looked as pitiful and tired as I felt, and I was sure the girls looked the same. Tired. Hungry. In need of a hot shower and bed.

We stayed in guest lodging for a few weeks until I was offered quarters in the Berlin Brigade housing area, aka "BB," with temporary furniture, linen, and dishes. It was now February 1990. It seemed like as soon as I got settled and could exhale, I got the call my Aunt Ruth, who still lived in Newark, NJ., Pat's mother, died. *What!*

I knew she was in the hospital, but I had no idea her condition was so severe. For years, she struggled with managing Type 1 diabetes and alcoholism. She'd been hospitalized before, but this time she was diagnosed with pneumonia—she didn't make it.

Farewell Aunt Ruth

Aunt Ruth visited Camptown only rarely after she left – but when she did, we bonded. I was crushed. Not having Tierra's passport prevented me from returning to the states for Ruth's funeral service. I couldn't believe it. I probably didn't need to go. It was quite expensive for flights for three, and I had just arrived. I spent a few solemn days with my girls, thinking about my aunt. The passport issue was resolved as soon as I got my HHGs delivered.

The unified city of Berlin was ripe with excitement. With the wall down just a month prior, East Berliners were finding all kinds of freedoms on the West side. The iconic East German car, the Trabant, were everywhere – often, just abandoned. After unification, the city was chaotic with new art, anarchy, and techno music, along with new problems, like housing shortages in West Berlin and squatters in the East.

Living in Berlin was exciting, demanding, and uncertain. As soon as we arrived, I was told I would be working shiftwork; 6 days on and 3 days off. Even with the mission and site closing, we'd continue working until the official notification. Other soldiers and I, who had recently arrived, could expect to be curtailed to a shorter than 3-year tour. Resolved and thankful, leaving Berlin earlier freed us from some of the chaos of this new unified city.

I worked at the famed Teufelsberg aka T-berg - a man-made hill, 120 meters above sea level, built over a scrapped plan to build a Nazi Military training school in West Berlin. The facility, with its giant "golf balls," was converted into an American field station after WWII.

Recently, it was featured on one of my favorite television shows, The Amazing Race, and multiple news outlets, like 60 Minutes, which described T-berg as a Cold War "listening post." In the early 1990s, T-berg was operational 24/7, 365 days a year. As a Staff Sergeant (SSG), I was put straight to work as a shift leader for a mission and subsystem whose cover name was "Newspaper."

The first day I went to work, it was snowing like crazy. I think there were 3 inches on the ground with more to come. I dropped the girls off at the sitter's quarters in BB and caught the dedicated bus to T-berg. The bus pushed through the snow like a champ. It climbed the curvy road to the top of the hill to drop off soldiers, airmen, marines, and navy personnel, for an 8-hour shift.

I completed training and certification quickly after learning I could not take leave or travel with the post softball team until I did. I was soon reminded of why I didn't like my MOS or find the training in Pensacola rewarding. I did well as a shift lead, but I was bored to tears at work. I hated copying Morse Code, measuring sine waves, and busting bauds. It was not my cup of tea. Most shifts, days/swings/mids, I counted the hours until breakfast, lunch, or dinner, and then I'd start counting hours till shift change.

With a new city and new people, my entire life was primed for big changes. My husband Michael took leave to travel to Berlin to visit with us. He stayed 2 weeks. We never talked about our future together. I took full advantage of him being there and not having to use child-care while I worked. When I got home or was on break, he played basketball, spent time at the gym and Post Exchange (PX). He didn't seem interested in much else and definitely not interested in staying in Berlin.

As a matter of fact, he was contacted about an assignment in Berlin. With the help of my supervisors and NCOs at T-berg, the Army (assignments branch) agreed to station him in Berlin, but he declined. He made it clear he did not want to be stationed there. Instead, he proceeded on orders to Korea, unaccompanied for one year. It was probably best. I hadn't noticed much of a change in his attitude — being a father and husband was never his priority, in my opinion.

For the next two years, our only means of communication were rare international phone calls and letters. He sent the girls personalized things made in Korea, like sweatsuits, but that was about it. I was anxious to end the marriage as soon as we were both stateside and the Soldiers and Sailors Act, no longer applied. I vowed to never marry again...declaring marriage as "overrated."

Talking with my Uncle Teensy while he was in Newark for my aunt's funeral, he suggested that I ask my mom to come to Germany to keep my girls while I worked shifts. He seemed to think she needed to get out of Newark. I didn't need to ask him why. I was reminded of what the guy from Portsmouth said when he dropped her off in Greenbelt. I knew I needed help. What would I do when Tierra started kindergarten in the fall? I was exhausted all 6 days. The babysitter/child-care situation wasn't ideal. I had to pick-up Tierra and Shara immediately after each shift- at 0730 after mids and around midnight when I got-off swings. It was almost impossible to get the proper rest.

As much as I didn't want to, I asked my mother to join us in Berlin and she did. She kept the girls while I worked shifts and mostly slept. It was a huge help. And yes, there was one incident where my mother was questioned about looking for drugs while she was hanging out at the community bowling alley, not far from our quarters in BB. I warned her. I was not going to allow her to stay in Berlin, and she was not going to ruin my career by being associated with anything to do with drugs, period. It never happened again.

I worked shift work for a year or so before I heard about a day job in Protocol. I didn't mind being called a "day hoe." I was asked if I was interested. Absolutely! I didn't feel like I was abandoning the mission or the troops who worked for me. The mission would soon be over. I landed the job in protocol for a short six months before we received orders to leave Berlin. I was going back to Ft. Meade, but this time in support of the

National Security Agency (NSA) – with the 704th Military Intelligence Brigade (704th MI Bde) on the other side of post.

Are you a Switch Hitter?

I have never believed that I'm gorgeous or even beautiful. I think I'm quite average looking. I've been told I have a beautiful and welcoming smile. I can see that sometimes. I'm average height at 5'5" with broad shoulders – broad enough to carry the weight of what often feels like the world. I'm not particularly curvy. I don't have protruding buttocks. Honestly, I have never had much of an ass to speak of. My bosom seems to be my greatest asset. They've managed to stay north of the Mason-Dixon line, so to speak.

I've always appreciated beautiful women and have never found myself jealous of another woman's appearance. Equally, an attractive man is an attractive man. What can I say? To be clear, that does not mean I'm attracted to every woman or every man I encounter – quite the contrary.

But looks are just that – looks. As I've matured, I've come to realized that good looks, whether man or woman, does not equate to having intelligence, common sense, integrity, a good conversation, loyalty, a loving hug, a great sense of humor, and an adventurous spirit. Let's be clear. All those attributes are more important than physical attraction, right.

My dear friend and comrade Teart, who was stationed in the 902d MI Gp with me, mentioned her friend Linda, stationed in Berlin. Since I was going to be a single-parent with two girls in Germany, Teart said she'd reach-out to Linda to let her know I was there, and to lend a hand, if needed. That's what Army buddies and friends do – and more. Teart also gave the girls' their first pet. A domestic short-haired, kitten named Tiger for Christmas, just before we left. Teart sent Tiger, complete with shots and paperwork, on a solo flight to Berlin after we moved into quarters. Tiger made it safe and sound.

In the summer of 1990, I started dating a single, senior Non-Commissioned Officer (NCO), a brother who was an operational supervisor at T-berg. He worked day shift, commonly referred to as being a "day wh*re or hoe." It's field station lingo; I didn't come-up with it.

Anyways, I was both mentally and physically attracted to him. He was smart, tall, brown, and handsome. I didn't think this casual affair would last – it was something to do. He was divorced and very career oriented. My children and I didn't fit into his long-term goals and I wasn't looking for anything serious or long term.

Honestly, we were committing fraternization, which, of course, is against Army regulations. Technically, he was one of my superiors, but I wasn't concerned. Most black heterosexual relationships/affairs seemed overlooked or ignored by our white, Army leaders, down the hill at Andrews.

Unless it occurred during a formal training setting, where leaders, could be held responsible, like boot camp, they usually looked away. Our leadership team at Andrews Barracks in Berlin were white and physically distanced from troops fully engaged in the intelligence missions to end the longest cold war ever – about 45 years.

The first softball practice I attended, I met Teart's elusive friend Linda. Teart's plan was to call me early on with Linda's number, but that didn't happen until after our meeting. She played outfield. I introduced myself and mentioned Teart. *"Finally!"* she said. I was relieved to know a trusted friend's friend. Linda was a signal soldier who worked in the busy and demanding Berlin Brigade Telecommunications Center. This message center was responsible for the transmission, receipt, acceptance, processing, and distribution of incoming outgoing electronic messages.

Linda was tall for a woman, with an athletic body; she was very authentic. She knew who she was. A lesbian. She had no pretense about her, but she was also kind, considerate, and supportive. She made it clear, after getting up the nerve, that she was attracted to me.

Don't get me wrong now, Linda was not the first lesbian drawn to me. This was not my first rodeo. It happened in Pensacola and Germany, too. But in the past, I would have said, humbly, "Sorry, I'm straight. Sorry, I'm married, or I'm not like that, I'm sorry." But not this time, she was a friend of friends – Teart, and I would soon learn, she was friends with Sylvia, who was in the same company with me during boot camp, and Sandra aka Sandy. I thought, if nothing more, we would all be friends. And we were, but Linda and I became more than friends; we became committed partners and parents.

Sandy, a German-national, who I previously met during a TDY to Berlin. She was our sponsor in a sense. Sandy showed us Berlin - all of it! We ate at high-end restaurants, went on boat rides, travelled to play softball, we BBQed often, and enjoyed the city.

My new life with my friends, was great. My girls were my primary responsibility. I never forget that. They were usually in tow and absolutely loved the outings and all the attention. They were young and hanging with my teammates at softball fields and exploring Berlin broaden their little minds and made them happy.

My mother wasn't happy or pleased with this new relationship at all. She thought I was naïve, and I was taking a dip in the lady pond to drown my sorrows of a failed marriage. Quite the contrary – I was attracted to this lifestyle. We had a family in Berlin.

The handsome brother I was messing around with, asked me at work one day, off in a corner, if I was a "switch hitter." Confused initially, then thinking he was referring to my softball skills, I responded, *"I try, but I'm not very good at it."* He laughed. *Asshole!*

Don't Ask, Don't Tell

I didn't reveal the true nature of my relationship with Linda to very many. I had to feel comfortable and believe I could completely trust the person(s) that I told. This lifestyle was not as accepted in the early 90s as it is today. Certainly, not in the military!

Specifically, if the Army became aware, (having evidence) of homosexual acts by any soldiers, they were "kicked out" with an Undesirable Discharge.

During this timeframe, homosexuals, particularly lesbians, seemed to be experiencing what they called "witch hunts." I heard stories of unauthorized and totally inappropriate, barracks rooms inspections/raids conducted in the middle of the night in attempts to catch same-sex soldiers in bed together — that or an admission was the evidence leaders needed to discharge gay soldiers.

The Don't Ask Don't Tell (DADT) policy under the Clinton administration was issued in 1994 as a directive that military applicants were not to be asked about their sexual orientation. It wasn't until six years after I retired from the Army that President Obama and the 111th Congress signed the Repeal of DADT - allowing gays, lesbian, trans, and bisexual troops to serve openly in the Armed Forces. In Hawaii by then, I silently celebrated with gratitude for the changing military.

I hated having to "hide" my relationship with Linda. It went against everything my gramma taught us. It was the equivalent to lying, which disturbed my inner peace. I was now living a lie. This was such a contradiction for me, but I knew I could not share my personal relationship outside our safe circle of family and friends. Linda, not as concerned, understood. I had two innocent, young daughters to protect. And in a way, my two daughters protected me, giving me some cover from suspicion since I'm a mom.

As the mission in Berlin ended, Linda worked to get her extension in Berlin withdrawn. She wanted to leave too. She worked to get an assignment anywhere close to Ft. Meade, where I was going. She was determined and persistent. It crossed my mind that I could leave Berlin and this lifestyle behind. None would be the wiser, but I couldn't. Linda was quickly becoming my best friend. Our relationship provided a support system I needed the longer I stayed in the Army, and my girls adored her.

My mother returned to New Jersey with the girls about a month before I started to out process to leave. It would be easier to pack, clear quarters, and meet them on the other side of the pond, aka the Atlantic Ocean.

This time, everyone had their respective passports. I left Berlin just a few weeks before Linda. I checked into my new unit, 704th Military Intelligence Brigade (704th MI Bde) and started in-processing. Linda flew home to Long Island, NY a few weeks later. I drove up from Ft. Meade to meet her parents and siblings.

Instantly, her parents felt like they were my parents – and they loved their daughters unconditionally. They were so welcoming to me and my daughters. Over the next 15 years or so, I bonded with Linda's mother. She reminded me so much of my loving grandmother Novella. At the end of the short visit, we picked-up the girls in Newark and relocated to Maryland as a family.

Back to Ft. Meade

When we settled-in a 2-bedroom apartment in Severn, MD, Linda got busy trying to get the Army to station her at or near Ft. Meade, of course. This isn't easy unless you're Linda. The Army sends soldiers where the Army wants, not where a soldier wants. In true Linda fashion, she negotiated a special assignment at the Pentagon, with the help of the Training NCO I replaced when I started work. I was impressed and committed. No turning back now, I thought.

Linda commuted to the Pentagon for over 4 years, working in their massive telecommunications center for the Joint Chiefs. I was just thankful I got a day job in training and not a rotating shift at NSA. With Linda commuting, I don't know what I would have done with the girls.

Training Non-commissioned Officer (NCO)

For the first time, I was assigned to the 704th MI Bde, in support of, and walking distance to, NSA headquarters. The 704th became my home on and off or almost ten years. I started my journey in HHC, 704th MI Bde, as the Company's Training NCO. I was responsible for developing and maintaining personnel training records. I also scheduled, monitored, and resourced the Army Physical Fitness Test (APFT), weapons qualifications, land navigation training, and other required quarterly, semi-annual, and annual training requirements.

Alongside the 1SG, the Training NCO prepares soldiers to attend service and leadership schools, deployment training and plans, and executes unit mobilization plans. The knowledge and experience I gained as a Training NCO were vital when I became 1SG.

Platoon Sergeant (PSG)

I worked as a Training NCO for about 2 years before I interviewed for a Platoon Sergeant (PSG) position with A Company, 742nd MI Bn. This is one of three subordinate battalions under 704th MI Bde, co-located with the Brigade. To be competitive for Sergeant First Class (SFC)/E-7, I needed a PSG job. It is the logical next step after being a Squad Leader. Regardless of your MOS, time as a PSG is seen across promotion boards as essential and a steppingstone to E-7 and E-8. Without this position and experience, 1SGs struggle to connect, to build comradery, and build trust with soldiers.

After interviewing with A Company's 1SG Laffey, I left feeling nervous and unsure if I had shown him, I was ready for the job. I had the interview and job jiggers. Was this the right move – now? Would I have to spend longer hours at work and less with my family? Would this man respect, mentor, and treat my platoon and me fairly? Was PSG over my head and my strategic-only assignments? - I hadn't had a tactical assignment yet.

I was selected to be the PSG for 1st Platoon. This job, in my opinion, is the closest position to being a 1SG. I worked-up close and personal with soldiers in my platoon, monitoring their training, health, and welfare, and sometimes, that of their families, especially during deployments/TDYs.

The PSG teaches, coaches, and mentors' junior soldiers to be successful at work/MOS, in training, and at physical fitness. As a PSG, I advised the 1SG on personnel/soldiers in all matters with my platoon. All matters, such as when soldiers had their last dental exam. The last thing a PSG wants is a soldier deemed Category 4, non-deployable Cat 4, due to their dental health or any other preventable condition.

Not long after I started as a PSG, 1SG Laffey conducted his initial one-on-one counseling session with me. The session was primarily about my new role as PSG. He quickly noticed my personnel file indicated I now had 103 college credit hours. I completed 3 or 4 college courses, over 10 credits, in Worms and Berlin. He asked me when I was graduating. I was shocked. I wasn't in school. I told him I was taking a short break and that the last college course I completed was Speech in Berlin. Continuing his direct and rapid-fire inquiry, he point-blank said, *"You need to get your bachelor's degree!"*

1SG's questions became more and more personal. Now, he was asking about my finances. Really. Since I was a relatively new PSG and wanted to keep my job and the peace, I continued to answer his questions, smiling appropriately. He offered a solution to getting my degree. And he got me to commit my upcoming re-enlistment bonus to pay the application fees for an official evaluation with University of the State of New York, aka Excelsior College.

Since Ft. Meade is literally 20 minutes from UMBC's campus, I took a lunch period to drive on campus to pay my balance and get an official transcript. Talk about nostalgic. I walked tall across UMBC's quad in uniform, heading for the Registrars and Administration building, feeling completely out of place. With all my credits, now on record with Excelsior, and my military training evaluated, Excelsior confirmed my Bachelor of Science degree in June of 1993 without me having to take another course!

1SG became one of my biggest fans – as his PSG, now mentee, and as a Brigade women's softball player. He stopped those evening golf course runs when the Lady Cobras of the 704th MI Bde played ball. I played short-stop back then, and I loved to catch and throw on the run to 1st base. We were the best women's intramural softball team on Ft. Meade for years.

Year after year we dominated. Unit teams at Ft. Meade salivated at the thought of beating us. We were good and every position was covered by a woman who either played softball in college or should have played. We slid, dove, did splits, caught-tucked-and-rolled, and threw people out at home plate; exciting softball, I tell you.

In the 90's, military community members/families would come out to support, watch, talk smack, and root us on – 1SG Laffey included. He loved watching us in action and being our unofficial mascot. I got him as involved as I possibly could. He was right there when we won the Post championship - gripping and grinning with our first-place trophy.

At work, 1SG knew I worked hard, and it paid off. After serving as a PSG for two-years, I was selected for promotion to Sergeant First Class (SFC)/E-7. Having a bachelor's degree and being a PSG set me apart from most of my peers. I was so ready. This meant I needed to move to another job so that another E-6 could be a PSG and possibly get promoted.

New Family, New Life

Michael and I divorced in December 1994, a couple of years after we returned to Maryland from Berlin, and he from Korea. It was truly uneventful and unemotional. He had returned from Korea with a girlfriend as well. He seemed oblivious to my new lifestyle when picking-up and dropping-off Tierra and Shara from weekend visits; he wasn't concerned at all.

I asked Linda to accompany me to serve as a witness to the amount of time we were apart; separated. We met Michael at the courthouse in Annapolis, MD at the designated time. This wasn't the first time Michael had been around Linda, so everyone was cordial – we ended up having lunch together when the judge decided to recess for lunch before our case was called. He had to know what was going on with Linda and me. When duty and life-events prevented me from being with them, she was – not him. She was helping me raise his daughters.

At work, I filled an open military billet at the National Cryptologic School (NCS) as a new Systems Training Manager and Adjunct Faculty member. I began to love working at the school located away from headquarters and work drama. It was cool seeing all the wacky educators in the school. They even contributed rubber duckies, and the like, to the large water fountain just outside the school's lobby. There were dozens of ducks and a stand-alone, green, alligator in there. The faculty and staff dressed-up for Halloween, Thanksgiving, and Christmas. You name it, any excuse to create some fun.

As a training manager, I had a lot of different responsibilities. I partnered with contractors, military, and NSA project managers to identify training deficiencies and recommend solutions and options to users and training developers. For example, we advised system developers to identify the appropriate type of training for users during the design phase and not after development. This was not always done, and new systems would be rolled out without instructions or training for operators to use the new system.

In my spare time, I took NCS courses in acquisition, resource management, and integrated logistical support. Additionally, I achieved certification to teach as an NCS Adjunct Faculty member. As an SFC now, I taught two courses, Delivering Structured-On-the-Job Training (SOJT) and the 2-week, Training Methods for Cryptologic Instructors. My civilian supervisor was ecstatic. I was the perfect example of a fully integrated military person, contributing to NSA's mission.

Teaching for the NCS helped to ignite my passion and purpose – to train and teach! I was good at it, and it felt good. The feeling and sense of accomplishment at the end of a course when you know students are leaving your classroom more skilled/trained than when they walked in was a major runner's high for me. I felt like I contributed to the mission, to their careers, and to American lives. Everything I learned about teaching adults was so contradictory from everything I'd experienced in H.S., college, and Army courses. The fact that there are adult learning principles and deliberate techniques to engage students, was eye opening. I loved the content of the courses I was now certified to teach.

My personal life became more and more challenging. My mother moved in with Linda, the girls and me, in our first house in the Provinces in Severn, MD. It was a cute, three-bedroom, one car garage, split-level home, in a community of mostly military, federal employees, and retirees from both groups. She left New Jersey for good, around 1995, after a stint in drug rehab, and now needed a place to stay. I felt for her and welcomed her into my home, once again.

Remember, initially, my mother wasn't very accepting of my relationship with Linda. She thought I was going through a phase, prompted by the divorce from Michael. I felt pushed and pulled. I loved them both, but this time I knew my mother was running from her demons and needed help, and I couldn't say no. She came with clothes in hand. And in typical Wheezy fashion, began to take over.

After being a family for close to five years, my relationship with Linda wasn't in the best shape either – a lack of trust on both of our parts had damaged our relationship and certainly our friendship. I knew my mother being there wasn't helping. Hell, I wanted and needed an escape.

I called my assignment manager and asked him for orders out of Ft. Meade. It was time. I had been there for almost 4 years. My mother was smothering, and to preserve the little friendship Linda and I had left, I needed to leave. I received orders to Georgia – Ft Gordon. My mother had a reliable job now and had talked me into getting her a "hoop-dee"– a little, black, Honda CRV. She'd been with us over a year. It was time for her to find a place of her own.

Linda and I considered what to do with the house. It was put on the market and quickly removed when a softball teammate, a sailor and friend, asked us if she and her husband could rent it. Absolutely. Linda wasn't interested in leaving the area immediately. She would find a place of her own to allow our new renters to move-in. Before I knew it, she was on assignment for Korea. Her second trip to the land of the kimchi squat.

NSA-Georgia (NSA-GA)
Ft. Gordon, GA (1996-1998)

NCOIC, Signal Development Center (SDC)

When I arrived at NSA-GA, I was placed in charge of the non-existent Signal Development Center (SDC). I was to stand-up the operations from designing the layout of the furniture as well as the placement of collection and analysis equipment. It was an empty room with a raised floor for cabling and air circulation. I devised the shift-work schedules for the military analysts who worked there. I supervised a team of 10-

154

12 Signals Analyst from all four services. NSA-GA and its supervisors/NCOICs, had what is referred to as operational authority and supervision. Their services and respective units were responsible for their "care and feeding" or administrative authority.

A civilian analyst from headquarters, Ginny, joined us as the Chief of the SDC to get the mission off the ground. I was the Non-commissioned Officer-in-Charge (NCOIC) with zero interest in this type of work. As soon as I heard another E-7 was coming in with extensive analyst experience, I started engaging the Joint Training office for a job. I was so relieved to stand beside Ginny and NSA-GA's Commander at the new SDC ribbon-cutting ceremony. The work was done and as soon as the new NCOIC arrived, I was out. Of course, the move came with conditions.

Since the new NSA-GA was the latest NSA facility to open, the creation of Job Qualifications Standards (JQS) were essential to certify operators and analysts at the site were qualified to stand watch, the majority of which were military. The simplest way to describe a JQS – they are considered a detailed roadmap to bring a novice/new analyst and collector from apprentice to expert performance level. A JQS outlines every step to every task in a specific job.

JQS are displayed in the form of learning objectives with documented references and training aids such as needed tools, equipment, or technology. Each task description specifies steps to take and how accurately a task is to be performed. This is called the standard, which can be measured in time, speed, quality, or minimum required information. My prior NCS and instructor experience set me up for success. I knew how to conduct on-the-job training and understood adult learning principles needed to create a comprehensive JQS program.

Somehow, because I authored the JQS for the SDC, I became the site's resident expert. *Who knew?* The NSA-GA Training office needed my help since they were now responsible to lead the effort and mentor teams, organizational representatives from across every mission element at NSA-GA, in creating their own unique JQSs. A huge endeavor.

Joint Training Department, NCOIC

We completed the JQS and certifications of over 75% of every position at the site, including some civilian positions. This was a major achievement considering the agency was/is notorious for NOT specifying performance standards for employees. We made the *Daily NSA* news, an internal communications system for NSA employees around the world. We were so proud. And so was the site Commander and the Director of Training at NSA-GA.

It was at NSA-GA that I met the first woman promoted to a three-star General in the Army's history, Lieutenant General Claudia Kennedy. She was serving as the Deputy, Chief of Staff (D/CoS) for Intelligence. She was there to visit the newest NSA center to become operationally acceptable.

Rarely did I hear positive remarks or sentiments of admiration for high-ranking female officers. It seemed as if the higher their rank, the less respect female officers received from their colleagues and superiors. Before leaving Berlin, I heard officers rumbling and discussing the last Commander there, a female Colonel. Then I noticed, being in protocol, she left the site without as much as an "Auf Wiedersehen." Not sure if this is an IC thing, or even broader.

Anticipating General Claudia Kennedy's visit, I paid close attention to how the leadership team announced and prepared for a female three star. Would NSA-GA roll out the red carpet like they did when the Army's Intelligence and Security Command (INSCOM) Commander visited or the Director of NSA.

My supervisor, the Deputy Chief of Training, Master Sergeant (MSG) Mary Lee, and you MUST say both her first and last name, knew the General, personally from a previous assignment. Every indication was they knew each other well, based on the conversation I overheard sitting in the same office as the Mary Lee.

The general wasn't scheduled to visit the Training office that day, but somehow, she made her way there to see the MSG Lee. If you've ever met Mary Lee, you would know it. She's unforgettable - from her funny laugh to the caring way she took care of her troops. Even though Mary Lee and I, had a leader – subordinate relationship at work. Outside of work, we became friends. To this day, she's my sister from another mother.

Somehow the General was able to escape her entourage. She walked into our office alone and closed the door behind her as Mary Lee and I jumped to attention. She asked, "Mary Lee, what in the hell are you doing here?" They laughed and chuckled. General Kennedy looked at me, stilling standing, and waved her hand down towards the floor for me to take a seat. I sat down at my desk.

Mary Lee told her how she got to Ft. Gordon from her previous assignment, and that her husband, Carlton, retired after serving as a 1SG. He was at the NSA-GA too. General Kennedy listened, then told us she was briefed on the site's JQSs and operational acceptance status. She said she was impressed and knew "Mary Lee" had something to do with it.

MSG Mary Lee with her weird ass laugh, was blowing out of her mouth, snickering, and laughing, all at the same time. When she stopped, she said, "It was me and the high-speed Sergeant First Class right there!" MSG pointed at me. I smiled. Proudly. The general took a couple of steps toward my desk. I stood again. Locked-up at the position of attention. She shook my hand and placed a challenge coin in it, while shaking. I said, "Thank you ma'am...thank you so much." She looked me in the eyes and said, "No, thank you!"

In 1999, General Kennedy made international news, but not for getting promoted to four-star – she made the news regarding a sexual harassment claim against another General. She claimed he groped her. *Damn. A General?* In her memoir, she said she decided to handle it quietly and thought she had, but three years later, the same officer was selected for a position in charge of sexual assault investigations.

She felt compelled to speak up. What happened after that seemed retaliatory.

General Kennedy was apparently accused of ethical violations because of her position as a board member of three companies associated with a controversial democratic person, while she was still on active duty. She claimed she did not profit from her position, so she didn't report her association with them on her financial disclosure statements. Interesting.

As civil servants, we are required to disclose financial affiliations to eliminate conflicts of interest. I'm awfully familiar with this annual reporting requirement. For years, I personally had to complete them. They're a pain in the ass, but they are more of a drill of integrity than anything else. And just because an employee is not profiting from any stocks doesn't mean they don't have to report owning them. She faded away well before I retired from the Army.

In Augusta, GA, I worked hard and played hard. SFC pay in this low-cost of living town was surprisingly good. I loved the southern twang of this little city. The emphasis on sweet tea and soul-food was familiar. The then Chief of Training, Bruce, Mary Lee, and I were hosting visitors from Ft Meade or the "Fort" for short. It was typical for us to take the group out to dinner in quaint downtown, near Augusta's "little" river walk; and I do mean little in comparison to San Antonio's river walk.

We were just finishing up when the door to the restaurant opened and in walked the Godfather of

Soul. Our mouths flew open, it was James Brown. He and three or four people walked past our table heading toward the back of the restaurant. He looked over at us and said in his distinctive, raspy, country accent, *"How yawl doing?"*

We couldn't believe it. We all replied with *"Hey! Hello, sir. Hi, Mr. Brown!"* What a story the visitors had to tell when they returned to headquarters. In the late 90s, there were no personal cell phones. No selfies or sneaked shots as proof. I had a pager but that was so my sitter could reach me.

My time at NSA Georgia went-by quickly; it was like a whirlwind. I taught as much as possible. The first recognizable accomplishment I created was a two-hour module on the "Intelligence Community and its Customers" to include in Orientation to help junior military members identify their place and mission in this huge conglomerate of INTs as in SIGINT, HUMINT, MASINT, COMINT, and the other INTs.

Tierra and Shara were growing like weeds by now. Tierra was 10 and Shara 7. They navigated the Augusta school system well. Shara, the creative one of the two, hated the structure of school and needed more of my time and attention with homework and projects than Tierra.

They made neighborhood friends in the cul-de-sac where I rented a 3-bedroom rancher, just outside the gate on Tobacco Rd. We had our dog Woody with us, and the girls had a pet turtle we found crossing a street in the neighborhood. They named him Donatella after the Ninja turtle.

I moved to Augusta feeling like I needed space to breathe. I needed space from my mother and my heart was broken, and I felt partially responsible for its damage. I was beginning to understand who I was and what I wanted in life and in a relationship. I enjoyed my short two-year assignment at NSA-GA. It was exactly what I needed at the time. I loved laid-back Augusta, and its proximity to bustling, hot Atlanta.

Standing in front of Back Hall at NSA-GA, Ft. Gordon, GA.

Award ceremony where I received my Joint Commendation award from the NCS, after I PCSed to Fort Gordon.

704th MI Bde (1998-1999)
Ft. Meade, MD
Senior Enlisted Leader

Back to the Fort

I left Augusta when Linda returned to Maryland from Korea. She decided to get out of the Army. She was never a morning person and the early morning demands of senior leaders can't be denied. It can be tough; besides, the Army was offering bonuses for early separations from active duty. We were over strength and the services needed to "right-size."

With some encouragement and the peace of mind that I had a partner and friend to support my career and help raise my girls, I moved back to MD—back into the house we were renting to a friend, and back to supporting NSA. My mother had her own place in Baltimore now – *thank goodness.*

When I PCSed back to the Ft. Meade, I was assigned to the agency as a Senior Enlisted Leader (SEL) for the Technology Directorate (TD). There were representatives from all the services in this office. We were responsible for assigning military personnel to a billet or position, based on their service member's MOS. We mentored and coached junior military personnel and their new civilian supervisors on their first assignment, service requirements like performance counseling, and annual evaluations for NCOs working in the agency.

I was still a SFC with little mission/collection experience at NSA. This SEL job was very low-key and not very challenging at all. Most days, the other service SELs and I were counting the hours until it was time to go home. When we got sleepy from boredom, we'd walk the halls, go to one of the Cafés, or check out the drug store in headquarters building.

As it stood, civilians welcomed military personnel if a SEL could promise the service member would work in the building for at least a full year. This was to witness a positive Return-on-Invest (ROI) from the service member once they completed time-consuming and often expensive mission. The negative ROI for training military members has always been an issue for the agency.

Mostly soldiers and marines were notorious for starting the training process in a new NSA work center, to then leave shortly after they are trained for a service-specific or leadership school that takes them away for months; not that service members have a lot of control with this and certainly not when chosen to deploy.

Operations Sergeant (1999-2000)

After working as an SEL for over a year, I started job hunting. I told my 1SG that I desired a leadership position outside the fence to remain competitive for promotion to E-8 and I didn't mind leaving my low-key job to do it.

I quickly landed a job as the 704th, Brigade's, Plans and Operations Sergeant/S-3, another "one-up" position. As the NCOIC of S-3, we conducted Command Inspections of three subordinate battalions. We managed the Command's Language program. We responded to Post tasks to supply soldiers for various events and to maintain the installations clean appearance by providing soldiers to conduct police calls, daily. It was rare to see a single piece of litter on Ft. Meade. This was the staff job I needed for promotion to E-8, and the Brigade's Command Sergeants Major (CSM) believed I was perfect for the job.

After six months on the job, I was informed the Brigade Commander, Colonel Royster, would be the president of the upcoming E-8 or Master Sergeant's promotion board. The CSM would not sit that year's board, as usual. The then S-3, a Major and my boss, was ecstatic. Her opinion of me was favorable. She thought I was the bomb and she spoke with the Brigade Commander often, especially before he headed TDY to sit the promotion board.

I didn't get promoted that year. No one in my MOS did. The Commander completed his duty for enlisted promotions and returned. His feedback to the S-3 was, "SFC Lawyer-Allen was #1. Her record and picture were outstanding. We couldn't get a single promotion for her MOS. He said he was disappointed; asked for 1 promotion from another MOS. It was denied.

We were over strength at E-8 for my MOS, therefore, "BIG Army," denied any promotions for us. This promotion system proved to be complicated, because often soldiers' qualifications, experience, or readiness for the next level isn't always the issue. It is an exercise of numbers/strength for the Army.

Farewell Duke

I was working Bde S-3 when Duke was diagnosed with lung cancer. I'll never forget. He had a premonition about it. He'd say, "It's too late for me to quit smoking, but not you. He hated that I smoked cigarettes. I was beginning to hate it too, especially now with his diagnoses. Hated I picked up the habit.

I went home to Camptown and Franklin for Christmas day. He was the picture of health and in good holiday spirit. For several years, he took his only vacation for the year, in entire month of December. He slept, ate, piddled around the house, and spent time with his buddies at his favorite shot house. He loved the holidays. We all did. His wife cooked enough for an Army...and she could burn. His nieces, nephews, and extended family would visit, and you could feel the Christmas spirit.

He turned 56 years old that February, which meant he was now eligible to retire from the Portsmouth/Norfolk Naval Shipyard. He had to retire once his health quickly declined just a few weeks after Christmas. He had over 20 years at the shipyard and the minimum retirement age for the Civil Service Retirement System, CSRS. Radiation took its toll — his hair, energy, and appetite. There was no doubt— his cancer was terminal.

Every other month, I drove to Franklin from Ft. Meade until he passed away. The final time, I was at work when I was called to come home. He wasn't breathing well. When I arrived that evening, his wife gathered my three brothers and I in the kitchen, out of earshot of Duke. She wanted us to know Duke signed a Do Not Resuscitate (DNR). The nurse didn't think he'd live much longer. His organs were shutting down.

I wasn't ready for him to leave. I was just getting comfortable having candid conversations with him, about my life and experiences in the Army. I wanted him to get to know me, and me, him. I wanted him to see me get promoted to 1SG – it was coming, I knew it. He would have been so proud; he would brag to his shipyard buddies about me like he did so often.

His granddaughters, four of them now, were young and wouldn't have Grandpa at their high school graduations, college graduations, or weddings. I realized those were all selfish thoughts. He was in so much pain. I leaned over and whispered in his ear as he took his last few breaths – *"Thank you Duke...thanks for everything."*

Noteworthy. A few months after I retired from the Army and started working at NSA, I quit smoking for good. *Thank goodness!*

Chapter 8

First Sergeants' Creed

The First Sergeant marches at the rear. To urge on those who faltered. Insuring no one falls behind. Lest the Forces strength be altered. The Commander positioned out in front has the glory. Of one who leads - but ne'er forget who's at the rear. Taking care of each Troop's needs. The Cadence comes forth loud and clear. So inspired the march won't stop. They know who's watching over them. The one they call Top!

- The First Sergeant's Creed

Critical Jobs for a 1SG
Ft. Meade, MD (2000-2002)

The next year, I waited patiently for someone to leak or share a few names of those on the E-8 promotion list. The highly guarded list was compromised every year. I started to think it had to be a Senior person (enlisted or officer), sharing it. Either way, days before the official list was publicized, I knew my name was on it. Not only did I know, but also the universe confirmed it.

One morning, I was driving into work and for some reason, I was listening to the radio and to a commercial, which was rare. Don't know why I didn't change the station like I normally do. I caught a part of it – "...if you work hard, it ought to count. And it will. Don't stop working hard." *Huh?* Only GOD knew what the commercial was about.... but when I started to listen, it was the message I was waiting to hear about getting promoted. What I was beginning to understand was a quote from Paulo Coelho, the author of The Alchemist – "When you want something, all the universe conspires in helping you to achieve it."

The Promotion Ceremony

Colonel Royster, the brigade's Commander who sat the previous year's board officiated my promotion ceremony. Col Royster was a smooth, intelligent, attractive, yet below average height brother. He spoke of my record – bachelor's degree; time as a PSG; Operation/S-3 Sergeant; PT Awards. He knew it well. And how I had waited another year. "Another year of being a great soldier and leader," he said. "That's what soldiers do. They drive on -they persevere."

I shared that message the day I got promoted in front of the entire Alpha Company, 742nd Military Intelligence Battalion (742nd MI Bn) and invited guests. One of my proudest days in the Army! My daughters, Linda, and my mom pinned on my 1SG stripes with the "diamond in the back."

Never mind the fact, right after I was pinned/promoted, I dropped the entire company for push-ups. The profiled soldiers too, like the pregnant one in the 4th squad, who looked at me like this woman is crazy. I was too excited. I didn't think about soldiers with physical limitations or medical profiles.

After a pregnant soldier at the rear of the formation with a high pitch voice, yelled, "First Sergeant!?"and pointed to her clearly showing baby bump. I yelled, "As You Were." The guests and I chuckled.

Being a 1SG required time and attention to every matter as it relates to the care and feeding of soldiers. The 130+ soldiers in Alpha Company supported the NSA. We had a variety of soldiers with multiple Military Occupational Specialties (MOSs), from Mechanics, Medics, Computer Scientist, an actual Physician, two Attorneys – they worked in more than 40 work and operations centers throughout NSA. And I was their guidepost!

As the 1SG, I was solicited for advice and direction from young Company Commanders, who are usually Captains. I had three; two of which were new Company Commanders, which meant I became an expert at Changes of Command and Responsibility ceremonies, prior to my next assignment.

My Platoon Sergeants

The company had four Platoon Sergeants (PSGs) positions. Platoon sergeants carried out the day-to-day interactions with soldiers. They worked directly for me to execute the company's training schedule and support the Company Commander. Everything from PT, Weapons Qualification, NCO Development Program (NCODP), preparation for leadership development courses, dental and health readiness - to their cryptologic mission at NSA

I ate with my PSGs. Did PT with them. I trained them and attended training with them. I gave stern feedback, and I held hands through Red Cross messages, disappointments, and tragedies. We lost two soldiers while I was in the 742nd – one to a motorcycle accident in Laurel, MD and the other had a massive heart attack during the Army's Physical Fitness Test (APFT) on the parade field, right there on Ft. Meade. They became a part of me, and I of them.

SFC Andrews was a fireball. She was my older, more experienced, PSG. The others needed PSG time to get promoted. She was already there but loved to push troops and stay out of NSA. As a soldier, you either loved NSA and its mission, or you find ways to get out of there. SFC Andrews was the most physically fit soldier female PSG in the Bde, with a heart of gold. She was a single parent of a beautiful daughter around my daughter Shara's age - eleven or twelve at the time.

SSG James, was my guy. From Houston, Texas, was/is a smart, self-reliant, natural trainer, good husband, and father. He hung on to my every word. He wanted to learn how to be the best leader he could. He observed. I think I ate chow with SSG James the most. He would stick his head in my office door and say, "Top, take a break and let's get some nourishment." Soldiers call their 1SG "Top" when there's mutual respect and admiration. He was promoted to SFC/E-7, after his time as a PSG.

SSG Guimond—what a name. I believe it's of German origin. He was the deep thinker; always offering advice on how best to accomplish something; usually because he was the first PSG to complete assigned tasks. I gave him his first knock-off Swiss Army knife. He was delighted. Guimond was also promoted to SFC. I looked for their names on the promotion lists for the next two or three cycles after I departed.

Then there was SSG Thomas and SSG Pollard – two Signal soldiers: not intelligence. Thomas and I would sneak off for an undercover cigarette of occasions. He'd ask me everything he wanted or needed in the smoke break area, without the pressure of being around his fellow PSGs. I'd quickly burn one, offer him suggestions, throw a peppermint in my mouth, and go back to work.

SSG Pollard was a smoker too. A cool, older soldier, from New York. While I was his 1SG, he lost his wife to breast cancer. I met her and their sons once or twice. His wife was pleasant. Kind. And she was brave, and so was he and his sons. How do you console a grown man who has lost his best friend?

The Power of Words

One afternoon, I was talking to SFC Andrews, walking back to my office after lunch. We were discussing planned Suicide Prevention training for the unit. It was that time of year, usually before the Christmas and holiday season. We'd solicited the brigade's Chaplain to help. She and I started talking about demographics of soldiers committing suicide on active duty. At this time, there'd been several service members who committed suicide across the services and locations, supporting NSA. It flowed out of my mouth effortlessly. I said to SFC Andrews, *"The demographics indicate minorities, particularly males, are less likely to commit suicide."*

In September 2000, I would take a well-deserved weekend trip to Atlanta for Labor Day weekend – also Black Gay Pride Atlanta. I was there to hang out with my long-time girlfriends from Berlin, who now lived in Augusta, GA. Since it was Pride weekend, one could expect the smartest, most beautiful, successful, creative, black women from across the U.S. and the Caribbean, in Atlanta — celebrities included. Atlanta did not disappoint!

It was Sunday morning, September 3, 2000. Since it was a holiday, I wasn't scheduled to return home to Maryland until Monday evening. I was still a bit hung over from the night before when the phone rang. It was the house phone. It was for me—it was Linda.

"Hey. I have to tell you something," Linda said.

"What? What's wrong? What happened?" I asked.

"Butch killed himself, Tena. Butch is dead," she said.

"What? What did you say?" I said,

She repeated herself. I couldn't comprehend what she was saying. Again, I said, "WHAT!?" I didn't know I was yelling. My best friends are now slowly rising from the floor, an air mattress, and the sofa. I yelled at the phone again.

"LINDA, WHAT DID YOU JUST SAY?"

In typical Linda fashion, she said, "TENA CALM DOWN," yet she's yelling. *"Butch shot himself, and he is dead!"*

I believed my cousins Butch, and Avon were the most resilient kids and adults, I knew. They lost both parents at such a young age, yet they persevered — I thought. They appeared to have adapted well. They had families of their own and children. I spoke with Butch just a few weeks prior. He sounded okay. I wasn't worried about him at all. We laughed and joked a bit. He told me he was toying with the idea of moving back home to Camptown/Franklin or maybe trying Maryland with me. I welcomed him – all he had to do was say the word, I'd put him up.

Oh my god Avon and Gigi! Did they know? My legs are noodles. I can't walk. What? Why? This makes no sense. I have a massive headache. I'm hungover. Damn. Oh my GOD...AVON! Oh Avon. I got to get home. GOD help us all! Those were some of the thoughts running through my head. On the ride to the Atlanta Airport that morning, just like that, I was reminded of my conversation with SFC Andrews. Demographics bullshit! Wow. I shook my head. Oh my GOD. I would never imagine in my wildest dreams that Butch could be suicidal. NEVER in my wildest dreams.

Butch in his U.S. Army uniform. He was a tank repairman.

Butch modeling in California.

September 11, 2001

A memory I will never forget. I was the acting Bn Command Sergeant Major (CSM). It was Tuesday, September 11, 2001, and it was business as usual that morning. PT, then recovery via the 3 Ss (quickly shit, shower & shave), and return to work. It was a beautiful, sunny, warm fall day in Maryland. The sky was so blue and clear. No one could imagine what lie ahead. Then it happened.

SSG Pollard, 4th PSG ran into my office. Pollard, being from NY, yelled before he got to my door,

"Top...Top! A plane just flew into the World Trade Center!"

"What? For real?" I said.

I stood and walked briskly to the CQ/duty desk to watch the TV. It was usually on CNN. Pollard was right behind me, lock step. We were watching. Listening to commentary from the news anchor. The first tower — the attack was captured on TV?! Processing. *Was this a mistake or accident?*

The 2nd plane came in the camera's view and what seemed like slow-motion, we watched as it crashed into the second tower. Pollard and about three or four other soldiers coming from PT recovery, watched, in amazement. This was a deliberate attack. Oh shit. Now what? A 3rd plane into the Pentagon. The 4th crashed in a field in Pennsylvania. Rumors. Were we/NSA, next? Soldiers came into the battalion area. Eyes wide open looking for direction.

A soldier ran through the doors, "1SG, we heard NSA is next! Civilians are running out of the buildings."

After speaking with Bde S-3, I summoned the other two other 1SGs from Headquarters and Operations Company (HOC) and Bravo Company to the CSM's office. I told them Bde S-3 called. Here's what we must do and quick!"

I immediately focused on the accountability of our troops. 100% accountability. Anyone at the pentagon? Who was on leave in NYC? In the state of NY? We had two soldiers in the air at the precise time of the attack, on their way to then Primary Leadership and Development Course (PLDC) at Ft. Campbell in Kentucky. What was their route? Did they have to change planes anywhere? Were they there yet? Safe? Were they stuck in an airport somewhere? Would we have to drive to pick them up?

Back to my 1SG role, I yelled in the Alpha Company's PSG's office that we would hold an accountability formation. "Everyone outside in 10 minutes!"

I tried to be cool and collected. Don't be overly excited, I thought. I started without emotions. Just the facts, I thought. "First, we had to account for every soldier, I told them. We must secure the perimeters around our buildings. Move your vehicle to the parking lot in front of Four Hats Dining facility. Post will move dumpsters away from barracks."

Just as I was about to command, "fall out," I was interrupted by the sound of jets that I would later learn had taken off from Andrews AFB in a kamikaze mission to interrupt Flight 93, heading to PA, or any other potential attacks from air. They were extremely loud. I couldn't talk over them. I paused...an eerie silence crossed the entire company, which allowed for a moment for reality to set in for most of us. We realized our world and mission had changed. Silence. Reflection.

Once I could be heard, I told them once we sent the Accountability Report for the Bn to Bde, they could go home. "Find your loved ones. Hug your children, your spouses, your significant others. Stay there with them until you hear from your PSG, I said. When you fallout, report to your PSG for your assignment to secure the AO (Area of Operation) or find unaccounted soldiers. Fallout!"

I tried to be useful that day. I tried to not focus on daughters in school and what they might be thinking and feeling. Were they afraid? I would call them once they got home from school. Linda, like most parents, said she was picking the girls up from school early that day. They would feel safer with her. My drive home that evening/night was long — longer than normal. What are we to do tomorrow? Should I send the girls to school tomorrow? Is it safe? When will it be safe to return to our normal lives? I don't know _ IDK!

In the days following, you got a sense that America was united. People held doors. They smiled at each other. They made small talk. As a soldier, I could sense a change in how helpful the public were to soldiers. Stores near Ft. Meade ran out of flags within hours. I displayed a small one on my vehicle's dashboard.

As soldiers, we were ready to defend. Tell us where you need us to go. We were one. You f* with one of us, you f* with all of us, was the attitude. We're ready. That's how we would end 2001. A year and events that we thought couldn't possibly be topped.

501st Military Intelligence Brigade (501st MI Bde), Seoul, South Korea (2002-2003)

In January 2002, I was on a 747 bound for Seoul, Korea. It was either Seoul or Ft. Hood. I had managed to avoid a tactical assignment for 18 years. Call me fortunate or smart. Why would an over 40-year-old woman want to become a gung-ho, hardcore, tactical soldier, bound to lead troops into Iraq? GOD blessed those that did. Grateful.

I know quite a few soldiers/colleagues who did and did so successfully, but again, a tactical assignment was not "a need" in my mind. There's no doubt, had I been stationed at Ft. Bragg, Ft. Hood or with the 2nd Infantry Division in Korea, I would have adapted and persevered. I adapted when I arrived at the 501st MI Bde in Yongsan, a suburb of Seoul, to a new culture and climate.

Korea is cold as shit and in January, it's extra frigid. My buddies tried to warn me, but no one can accurately describe how cold it is in Korea unless they've sat your ass on an ice bench in an Icehouse

Bar for 30 minutes, without a coat. It was minus 3 degrees Celsius or 23 degrees Fahrenheit. We got off the bus from the airport at 0200hrs local time, at the building beside the Dragon Inn Armed Forces Resort on South Post. We were at the 2nd Infantry Division (2nd ID) Reception & Integration Center.

The under-bus doors swung opened exposing our bags. Several "Joes," aka soldiers, slung duffle bags and suitcases in a big cluster on the ground. We milled around, gathering our bags. The SFC on duty came out with a clipboard and yelled, "Grab your bags, fall-in. Gimme 4 squads." I thought, *Is he kidding. A formation. Out here!*

Without talking, we managed to shuffle into some resemblance of a formation. It was 4 squads. We got in, where we fit in, without regard to rank, the unit we believed we were going to, or gender. We were locked-up or at the position of attention for what I thought was several minutes too long for this SFC. He better get started and started soon! We could form-up in that building he just walked out of. It was fully lit and looked warm. There were seats like an auditorium. Yes!

He said, "When I call your name, get your bags, and file into the building and take a seat. He started, "Acosta, Bearman..." it was alphabetical. At this point, I was shaking. My ears felt like if plucked, they would fall off and hit the pavement like crystals. Lawyer-Allen is just before the middle of the alphabet - I can make it. *Come on Sergeant!* My damn teeth are chattering. Whew Jesus! It's just January. It's after

0200hrs. Will I make it through February and March? Lord help. "1SG Lawyer-Allen!" he finally called my name. *"Hooah, Sergeant."*

I did the duffel bag drag to the door. Let go of my suitcase and tried to swing the door open - I pulled with way too much force. It didn't open any wider. It was one of those slow automatic doors used for both disabled and non-disabled, with a push button. I almost pulled the door into my face. I stumbled over my bags. *Damn, Top.* I was freezing and exhausted from the long flights.

Operations Sergeant Major

Being stationed in Korea for a year, unaccompanied, went by quickly. Linda agreed to keep Shara and Tierra, after their father was offered the job first. He declined. The tour can be summed up in cycles or Operational Planning Phases. It applied to my job/position as the acting Operations Sergeant Major, an E-9 position, and then the Operations NCOIC. But first I was asked to attend the INSCOM highly covenant Sergeants Major (SGM) conference at Ft. Huachuca, Arizona in February to represent the Brigade. So, back on a plane for a long, flight back to the mainland.

President George W. Bush would visit the DMZ and U.S. troops in South Korea in late February 2002. I was right there, standing behind the barricaded-off sidewalk, across the street from the Dragon Inn, when the Commander-in-Chief's motorcade with him waving out of the back window as they drove past me. I waved my hand-held flag that was passed out a few minutes before his drive-by. I smiled. Felt proud. I always felt proud to be an American...especially when serving abroad.

Before that visit, President Bush would call North Korea, Iran, and Iraq the "Axis of Evil." He was in a war of words with the North Korean leader, Kim Jong-Il. There were daily demonstrations and protest outside the South gate in Yongsan. When I arrived, the entire United States Forces South Korea (USFSK) was on a curfew. We were required to be in our barracks or apartments by 2100hrs unless traveling to/from duty. This tension didn't ease until the summer. There were reports of Americans being assaulted and harassed, especially out on the economy and on commuter trains.

The first phase of my assignment/duties required immediate attention — orient self and assume role as the Plans & Operations Sergeant Major during Reception Staging, Onward Movement, and Integration (RSO&I) in March without the loss of personnel and or equipment. The brigade was "in the field" at Camp Humphreys, participating in a Peninsula-wide exercise called RSOI or Foal Eagle.

Once I in processed and was ready to work, I joined them. This was an annual US-ROK Combined Military Exercise simulation. I met my subordinates and my boss, the Brigade's S-3, in the field.

In early June, I led the brigade in its preparation for a new Commander – a Colonel/0-6. As the Operations SGM, I was in-charge of the Change of Command practice, the actual ceremony, to include a

Brigade run that the then INSCOM Commander, General Keith B. Alexander, who reenlisted SSG Guimond, requested. He wanted to run with the troops. This is the General Alexander that would become the Director of NSA years later.

I was responsible for all of logistics to include the parade field layout, and needed medics, vehicles, road guards, water points, straggler control, etc. After which, I took mid-tour for rest and relaxation (R&R) at home with my family in MD, in early July. Only to return to quickly prepare for the biggest training exercise of the year — Ulchi Focus Lens 2002, aka the infamous, UFL in August.

In Korea, I befriended four women who were all Senior NCOs who worked primarily in Brigade headquarters with me. We explored Korea together. There was MSG Rose from the Philippines who worked in the S-1 (Personnel/Administration). Beverly or 1SG Bev, she was our unit's 1SG. Bev is from the mid-west, somewhere. Tall in stature, Bev made the best stews and desserts, all from scratch. SFC Tiffany, a black soldier from FL, who was an Imagery Analyst. Tiff was the baby of the bunch. SFC Flo, a smooth Puerto Rican lesbian from New York, worked in the Brigade's S-4 (Logistics/Supply). Flo loved to play the slot machines at the Dragon Inn.

A soldier who worked in the Brigade S-2 (Security), affectionately called us the "Rainbow Coalition," and how appropriate! I'd like to think of us more like the Golden Girls. All of us were in our late thirties or early forties with families at home. If we were not participating in an exercise, we were on a bus going somewhere!

We shopped all over South Korea and mailed boxes home. We visited Post Exchanges (PXs,) at unfamiliar Camps filled with American Joes and Jills, up north and down South. We also partied – golden girls' style; we enjoyed Karaoke at a Korean BBQ Restaurant in Itaewon often – the popular tourist spot. Itaewon is the party and club area, just outside the American gate. On occasions, to see what the soldiers were up to, we'd go "up the hill" in Itaewon, where prostitutes displayed themselves in windows, waving to fat-pocket Joes. We'd stop in the popular dancing spots for a plastic liter bottle of Soju punch that tasted like unsweetened Kool-Aid but would knock you on your tail.

We went white water rafting which was exciting and fun until our Korean guide accidentally hit me in the jaw with his boat oar. Luckily, I didn't lose any teeth. We took a tour to the Demilitarized Zone (DMZ) in our Class B uniforms with our last names removed from our jackets. It was bizarre to be so close to North Korea. We looked through high-powered telescopes to see their propaganda city, which with a close eye, looks like cardboard cutouts. We walked inside the building that stands on both the north and south of the DMZ. As more seasoned female soldiers, we had each other as a support system to get through this year without our loved ones.

With my encouragement, we started a tradition while there called "Dinner & a Movie," to be held

Sunday evenings when our training schedule allowed. I was first, probably, because I wanted to model the behavior for Sundays to come. I remember making a big pot of seafood and sausage Gumbo and a dozen corn meal muffins that tasted like sweet cake. Rose, who reminded us of Betty White for real, asked if I was Creole, or from Louisiana. "Girl, this gumbo came out of a box from the commissary. I added fresh seafood and sausage," I told her.

We agreed whoever hosted dinner could pick the movie we would watch. I had two movies in mind. We'd decide based on who'd seen them. We settled on Spike Lee's Malcolm X. The historical content was worth sharing with the girls. We ate and they watched intently. Rose asked a few Rose questions, but she got the gist. We finished this three-hour movie, right after we fixed dessert – Apple Pie.

For the Christmas holidays, I invited the Staff of S-3 element of the Brigade, who worked for me, to my hooch/apartment, for dinner. It was 4 young males who lived in the barracks; they all showed-up. So did our Officer-in-Charge (OIC), a Major. I made my huge Maryland crab pot of Gumbo again. The pot was left empty except for the roux that stuck to the bottom. They loved it! I made mini sweet potato pies for them to take back to the barracks.

When the Operations SGM arrived five months later, I was moved to the Operations NCOIC position. This position is very similar in nature to the SGM's responsibilities, although more worker bee than queen bee. I responded to daily, real-world activities on the

Korean Peninsula from September until my replacement arrived in late December. My final tasks were to sponsor and train my replacement in preparation of my PCS to Ft. Belvoir, VA. The year was over. Done son!

Back to the Fort to Retire!

I returned from Korea in January 2003. I made the decision while in Korea to retire one year after I returned. It was time. Tierra would be going into her senior year of high school and Shara would be starting high school. I didn't want to leave them again. I wanted to stay in place while they attended college. I couldn't picture myself on an assignment abroad, or having to deploy while they were in college in the U.S. They had sacrificed enough for me.

I didn't take a new official photograph for my record, and I declined a review for promotion to E-9 at the next board. It was time. I could have stayed in the Army longer, but 20 years was long enough. With one course left for my Masters' degree and having served in an E-9 position already, I was certainly positioned to get promoted and achieve the rank of Sergeant Major (E-9), but that would come with a cost – I just knew it.

I was able to get an assignment with the Information Dominance Center (IDC) at Ft. Belvoir, VA with duty at NSA, as a return assignment from Korea. I "dropped my paperwork" to retire from the Army in January 2004 – it was approved. The final year was spent preparing for retirement with the mandatory

Army briefing, physical examinations, resume writing courses, VA claims, etc.

The Retirement Ceremony

In October of 2003, before my transitional leave started, Uncle Teensy, my mother, family from Franklin, Sylvia, Linda & the girls, were at my retirement ceremony at Ft. Myers in Northern VA. The ceremony was professionally done with the impressive Old Guard and their famous Bugle Corps, complete with traditional white wigs.

The Military District of Washington (MDW) hosted these monthly, retirement ceremonies for Army Retirees. It was a way for the Guard and Corp to practice. It was/is by far, the best retirement ceremony in the MDW area. Some of my unclassified accomplishments were highlighted in the award citation read at the ceremony.

My family was so proud — they beamed. They finally had a glimpse into what I was doing for over 20 years. It was hard to wrap my brain around what I kept hearing as a huge accomplishment. It wasn't a big deal while you're soldiering. I just prayed I made a difference in a soldiers' life. I had survived; I know soldiers who did not. I achieved my goal completed 20 years. *I thanked GOD, my family, Linda, and friends – who without their support, I could not have successful retired with honors.*

Part III – The "Agency"

Chapter 9

Introduction to the Agency

Feeling confident – or pretending that you feel confident – is necessary to reach for opportunities. It's a cliché but opportunities are rarely offered; they're seized.

- Sheryl Sandberg, Facebook COO

Headquarters NSA, Ft. Meade MD (2004-2006)

My actual retirement date from the Army wasn't until 31 January 2004. So, I bummed around the house for a couple of months like a housewife, watching TV, planning dinner meals, waiting for the girls to return from school and work. I had successfully served for 20 years, 3 months and 13 days.

In early January or February 2004, I was notified that the NSA wanted to interview me for a position. The position, a Strategic/Performance Consultant, was in the school, the NCS — where I had served before as a Training Manager and Adjunct Instructor. Going back to work as a civilian with the federal government and working in Education and Training (E&T) was exciting and a huge blessing.

Tierra was starting her freshman year in college and Shara started high school as a freshman. My goals with whatever job I landed was it had to be a good fit and allow me to support my daughters financially through college. This meant earning a decent starting salary, being prepared for hard work, and seeking upward mobility or promotions. It's never been in my nature to remain stagnated or slack off. I always had to be up to something. Another minor goal was to keep my "good government job" by NOT breaking a single rule, infraction, or violation. At 42, I was still young and could work another 15-20 years.

Of course, getting an interview and eventually a job offer from NSA *"was not all my doings,"* as my gramma would say. I had a co-worker and dear friend named Tessa who I reached out to with my resume shortly before I retired from the Army. She and I had managed to stay in touch after I left Ft. Meade in 1996; probably because of our mutual tradecraft — E&T. Tessa was one of the guests in Augusta when Mr. James Brown — the King of Soul — walked in the restaurant. I am forever grateful for her recommendation and confidence in me. She became an early advocate and mentor.

NSA has its headquarters at Ft. Meade in Maryland. The agency is the largest of 17 organizations in the IC, that work both independently and together to collect, analyze, and disseminate information in the interest of protecting U.S. national security.

According to NSA's unclassified website, its mission is to "NSA leads the U.S. Government in cryptology that encompasses both Signals Intelligence (SIGINT) and information assurance (now referred to as Cybersecurity) products and services and enables Computer Network Operations (CNO) in order to gain a decisive advantage for the Nation and our allies under all circumstances."[7]

Some employees of NSA use a quirky comparison and reference to NSA being the Star Trek Enterprise with headquarters at Ft. Meade, known as the "Mothership." The Mothership is all-powerful with all authority. To augment the Mothership, there are Cryptologic Centers or "mini-NSAs" in Colorado, Georgia, Hawaii, and Texas, known as the Enterprise.

Additionally, there are other field assignments across the globe and NSA employees forward deployed in other intelligence agencies, and with partners around the world – all of which comprise the global Enterprise. The Enterprise follows directions from headquarters and is granted certain authorities to work portions of NSA's mission with the Mothership's blessing.

NSA has a notorious reputation for being reluctant or cautious, about sharing information with other agencies, as well as supposedly "listening" into everyday American citizens' cellular conversations. Back in December 1995, when I was working in the NCS as a soldier, the Baltimore Sun Newspaper released a series of six articles about NSA entitled "No Such Agency. Secretive NSA: Obscure, Global Eavesdropper at Ft. Meade is Largest State Employer."

In the six-part series, Sun reporters offered a detailed, some say, often too close to accurate, descriptions of NSA ever published. I, like other

---

[7] www.nsa.gov. Mission Statement

service members and NSA civilians working there at that time, collected all of them. Gathering multiple copies each week, we looked forward to each article, impatiently reading to see if our mission, targets, class, or if the U.S. Army Intelligence soldiers would be mentioned. We excitedly read to see if the article revealed any secrets. There was a weird sense of pride from your mission being mentioned.

I was hired to work in NSA's school. The NCS is NSA's school which celebrated its 50th anniversary in 2015. "The NCS provides NSA's workforce and its Intelligence partners, highly specialized cryptologic training in analysis, cryptology, cyber, leadership, professional development, and over 40 foreign languages."[8] In essence, the school was founded to provide job training, when and where, specialized vendor or commercial training, does not exist.

I received a conditional job offer via snail mail (USPS) around March of 2004, and started the agency's hiring process, complete with yet another background check, and this time, a full scope, "lifestyle polygraph." Even though I possessed a Top-Secret clearance in the Army, clearances by law, do not transfer. I heard all kinds of tales about the questions asked during a lifestyle poly, so I was curious to see for myself. I wasn't at all concerned about them asking about my private life. It wasn't up for discussion beyond my roommate's full name.

My new civilian job also required access to Sensitive Compartmented Information (SCI), which is

---

[8] www.nsa.gov, Nov. 4, 2015

a type of <u>classified information</u> derived from sensitive intelligence sources, methods, or analytical processes. [9] My neighbors everywhere I/we lived became accustomed to someone knocking on their door, showing them a badge, and asking them if they knew about the 'goings-on' at my home and other questions like, "Do they have a lot of guests? Do they party? Are they loud? Do you socialize with them?"

I could not avoid what should be called "NSA's Hiring Abyss." This can be a long process. It becomes a matter of whether the potential external hire has the stamina and pocketbook to sustain themselves while wading through NSA's hiring ordeal, or not. Fortunately for me, I kind of knew what to expect. I secured a contractor position for about five months to keep my pocketbook weight up until I could return to the agency as a civilian. Plus, I had my Army retirement pay. I could wait.

I accepted NSA's final job offer to start as a Government Grade, GG-13, Step 3. *Not bad*, I thought. With Tierra heading to college, it was a no brainer. Plus, Linda and I had purchased our second home together. We had outgrown the house in the Provinces; literally and figuratively. The girls were teens now and sharing rooms and one bathroom wasn't cutting it for four females.

In six years, the old house in the Provinces had earned a fair amount of value and equity. It was a "sellers' market." We got an offer the first day we showed the house. It allowed for a decent down

---

9 Wikipedia contributors. (2018, September 4).

payment and more furniture for a three-level, four-bedroom house that we eventually converted to five bedrooms, using a large storage space in the basement.

The home was complete with a formal living, dining room, and a comfortable family room – none of which we had in the house in the Provinces. The basement had its own full bath with a double shower. We added a real oak bar and mini refrigerator down there and decent speakers. Boy, did we throw some great house parties and family gatherings in that basement!

Single-term Directors

Unlike the FBI, where the President can appoint a single Director for a 10-year term with confirmation by the Senate, the position of the Director of the NSA, or DIRNSA for short, is temporary and rotational. The position rotates among our primary services—the Army, Air Force, Navy and Marine Corps.

During my tenure with NSA, I witnessed the leadership of six Directors, beginning with Admiral John M. McConnell and ending with the first virtual Change of Command I had attended, when Admiral Mike Rogers passed the baton to U.S. Army, Major General Paul M. Nakasone. Of note, in NSA's almost 70 years of existence, it has never had a female DIRNSA. Two women were Deputy Directors, which is a civilian position but never a female, military, Director.

Of all the Directors, I was quite fond of General Keith Alexander and Admiral Mike Rogers. General

Alexander because as the former Commander of INSCOM, I personally met him in Korea and at Ft. Meade. He was gracious enough to re-enlist one of my PSG, SSG Guimond, at the flagpole outside of 704th MI Bde headquarters.

Having the INSCOM Commander and future DIRNSA re-enlist you is a high honor and a big deal. As Guimond's 1SG, the General and I chatted briefly about the Staff Sergeant's stellar performance before he provided comments and the oath of enlistment. General Alexander came across as a cyber intelligent, soft spoken, General with a quirky, techy, sense of humor. I found him very down-to-earth and personable.

I also found Admiral Rogers refreshingly honest. I loved his use of profanity. Yes. like a good sailor, he knew how to swear. I'm sure he offended employees when he did, you could see it on their faces, but I loved it. There's something genuine and authentic when the senior leader of an intelligence agency like NSA is willing to call out "Bullshit." I can't count the number of times my inside voice said the very word(s) – usually listening to excuses from managers, colleagues, and subordinates. I find using a good swear word cathartic and therapeutic. You might have noticed.

The DIRNSA sets the direction of the agency and the tenor of the joint civilian/military workforce. The workforce is highly influenced by the Director, to include the adoption and use of the DIRNSA's favorite terminology and euphemisms. It's comical. If the Director uses a new or rare phrase the workforce hasn't heard before, they adopt it, it propagates quickly, and then everyone attempts to use the phrase. A few that come to my mind – "90-day spin," "spiral development," and always odd and quirky, use of warfighter terms like "pull the trigger." It's very strange and it's so annoying when civilians attempt to use military terminology and acronyms for non-combat actions.

At NSA, DIRNSA also creates the Operational Tempo (OPS TEMPO) and provides the direction, pace, and priority focus for the agency. Like most big corporations, the Director also prescribes and directs Quality Control initiatives, HR, and Equal Opportunity (EO) campaigns, and the almost forbidden word, "REORG," aka Reorganization!

In my opinion, and based on my experience, the DIRNSA's goal is to make an impression by transforming the agency in a way that permanently changes things whether organizationally, mission alignment, work roles, or job titles, or analytical transformations. Inevitably, a new DIRSNA will shift the agency's focus once again to something important to him or his boss – the Director of the Office of the National Intelligence (ODNI). Some shifts take heart and make lasting change, many become fleeting memories.

Performance Consultant

I knew my new job with NSA was a huge opportunity. It came with professional training from the Association for Talent Development (ATD), formerly known as the American Society for Training

& Development (ASTD), courtesy of American taxpayers and a Republican presidency.

Working in the agency now as a civilian would be important, rewarding, and a relief from my prior military routine of leaving work for Army physical training, weapons qualification, Commanders Calls and extended TDY's for leadership schools. It would be especially interesting to witness the NCS shift to its newest focus on performance analysis to determine causes for performance gaps.

Performance Analysis vs. Training Solutions

Historically, when the agency uncovered performance deficiencies or gaps, leaders would immediately identify training as the solution. I agree, there will always be valid requirements for training and courses, particularly for new employees, new functionalities, and equipment. However, NSA has a history of throwing training at dysfunctional organizations, incompetent leadership, and for systemic and deep-rooted issues that training rarely impacts – like unconscious biases and civility. More about that later.

NSA is not alone in the faulty analysis that training is THE saving grace. A lot of organizations, whether government or corporations, believe training fixes everything. Well, it does not. Consequently, I and three other brand-new "Performance Consultants," were hired to change this long-standing and flawed approach. Our cohort or small intimate team included two retired military — one was me of course, and two civilians.

One of the civilians had a background in teaching and learning technologies. The other civilian, I believe was already an agency employee who had just completed her two-year probationary period in another directorate. The third member of the cohort was a retired Marine Master Sergeant (MSgt), Mick. Mick worked Marine Intel on active duty.

As a cohort of four, we successfully completed the rigorous ATD Certificate in Performance Improvement. Our combined experiences and new credentials forged a multi-talented team, the first-of-its kind for NSA. We were like an 'elite Special Forces' unit, ready to go into foreign territory, assess the landscape, and generate evidence-based solutions to improve the workplace, human performance, and close performance gaps.

Proper performance improvement efforts are complex and require serious commitment. The process includes performance analysis, cause analysis, intervention selection and implementation, change management, and evaluation of the results.

This thorough and systematic analysis requires time, leadership investment, and employee engagement. The endeavor does not conclude until after implementation and change management strategies are in place to permanently close performance gaps and measure the return-on-investment. When adopted seriously, the results can be life-changing for the employees and highly profitable for the organization.

Yet, we were headed for an uphill battle with our totally new approach and unfamiliar products. It was damn near impossible for the school and its new Performance Consultants to convince agency leaders, particularly in Operations, that their organization needed to subject itself to a serious "performance analysis study," conducted by NCS - outsiders.

Our cohort would co-locate within their organization for an unspecified period and then conduct climate surveys and sensing sessions to solicit the workforce's input as it relates to the performance gap(s) and how to close them. Think about this. What manager would allow this? It's quite invasive and threatening. Who wants to hear, "Sir, you don't have a process problem. It's a leadership problem — it's you!"

But like many new initiatives at the agency, Requirements Analysis and Performance Consulting was short-lived. After about two years, conducting thorough full-scaled performance analysis fell off NCS's plate. Primarily because the workforce was masterfully skilled at waiting-out Directors and other key leaders. Yes, waiting — delaying or stalling efforts to simply abandon the new initiative once the current DIRNSA or/other Directors are out the door.

Time was another challenge. NSA's OPS TEMPO is unforgiving. Customers need accurate and actionable intelligence in real-time, meaning "right now." The world keeps moving faster, and foreign intelligence keeps evolving. NSA must keep ahead of threats and adversaries. It doesn't always have the luxury of lengthy gap analysis. Without the continued and compelling focus from leaders at every level, organizational change dissipates.

Our special cohort enjoyed limited success despite the resistance from the "wait and see" disbelievers. We provided vital input to HR's deployment training, and we tackled a project in mid-point collection, which resulted in the removal of a large table in the center of their operations floor. This simple solution increased productivity of the collectors and satisfied the managers.

Collectors turned away from their positions to socialize during non-break and lunch periods, which, of course, appeared non-productive to managers, but it was really an indication of their boredom. They weren't being challenged. This type of collection required monitoring red and green lights. Simple as that.

Learning about performance improvement and using some of the tools we studied in training, broadened my view of potential root causes for "bad" performing employees. I also discovered that poor performance isn't always an issue of training and aptitude. There are other root causes such as a lack of information, ergonomics, motivational causes, organizational structure and processes, inadequate tools or equipment, and even office layout, can be a cause for poor employee performance. Removing the table from the operational floor would not have been considered if it weren't for our approach.

I was adjusting to my new life as a civilian well. I knew I would; I loved working a predictable 8 hours a day. I missed the transparency and honesty you get from working with soldiers, the comradery between soldiers, and feeling like I could trust soldiers around me. They became my family — my "ride or die" buddies. I still miss certain aspects of the Army, like the teamwork and exuberance you get from accomplishing a mission together is an unbelievable feeling.

As a former military person who had worked in NSA and more specifically, the halls of NCS, I communicated my thoughts and knowledge of the school and NSA with our cohort. We became work friends. I conducted my own mini orientation with them. I taught them the confusing floor, hallway, and classroom numbering schemes in the Friendship Annex (FANX). I broke down the organizational structure of the agency and NCS. I shared my perspective working there as an Adjunct Instructor and Training Manager and all the eccentric personalities they may encounter in the school.

I became work friends or closer to one of my cohort members — Rachel. I continued my peer-to-peer training with her by helping her certify to teach potential instructors the "Training Methods for Cryptologic Instructors" course. This course was essential to NCS building a cadre of Adjunct Instructors. Rachel was a natural, having taught in Baltimore County. She taught me everything she knew about personality types using the Myers-Briggs Type Indicator (MBTI) self-assessment. I taught her about NSA and the NCS. For years, I used this extensive knowledge of MBTI to teach countless new instructors' additional information on personality types, to enable them to reach/teach different types of learners, and I used it to observe personality types in my own family.

Years later, when I was back from the "enterprise," Rachel mentioned how much my "setting-the-stage" for her and the others, helped. She went-on to be selected to become a Senior Executive after completing her Doctorate using one of the agency's college programs during duty hours. I was proud of her, but I could not help but compare her career to mine since we both started as GG-13s the same month and year. She earned leadership positions within the school, educational opportunities, and seamless promotions. Rachel advanced faster and seemingly with much-less drama.

Chapter 10

Orientation to the Agency & It's Culture

Culture is what motivates and retains talented employees.

– Betty Thompson

National Cryptologic School (NCS), Ft. Meade, MD

The first week at work, I walked through the door of our division's main office for the typical in-processing office call with the Chief. I opened the door to find a middle-aged white woman sitting behind a tall-front desk. She was what the agency called an Administrative Specialist, aka "Admins."

Admins answer the phones, managed, and scheduled the conference rooms, ordered office supplies and logistics, maintained the Chiefs/Managers calendars, and do other administrative type tasks. To this day, I have never seen a male "Admin" at the agency. As an observation, when I started in 2004, black women seemed to be overrepresented in this work role while significantly underrepresented in others. Just an observation.

As soon as I walked in, I said hello and smiled. She replied, "Hi!" with a smile. Then she said, "You must be the copier repair lady," pointing to a large copier against the wall. She quickly surmised, since she did not know me, I must have been the repairperson she was expecting. Before I could interrupt, she said as she pointed, "It's right there." Was her assumption based on my timing? Why didn't I look like an NSA employee? I felt funny.

I said, "No, I'm not. I'm here to see Daisy." Daisy was the Chief of the then Requirements organization. I extended my hand – that usually caught people off-guard. I shook her hand firmly. It was from my acting SGM days.

I said, "I'm a new-hire, my name is Tena. How are you doing?" She was pale and speechless for a second. A co-worker, who'd taken part in my operational interview, heard the exchange and stood from behind a partition toward the back of the office and yelled, "Hi, Tena!" She walked toward the front door. She looked at me and smiled. She called the Admin by name, "Jae, this is one of the new Performance Consultants, Tena. She's here to see Daisy." Jae said, "Pardon me. We're waiting for someone to come fix the copier."

This was my first week. Jae and I had a very productive, respectful, relationship going forward; more than likely, because I didn't say a word about this to anyone. But this was my first experience combating stereotypes, assumptions, and unconscious and conscious biases at NSA.

My Personal Life

What I did not share with my cohort or any of my co-workers, was my private life. I wanted to exemplify what it looked like to be a smart, gainfully employed, black single mother, raising two beautiful black daughters. It could be done. I was doing it, and my daughters were good students and athletes. I bragged about all their accomplishments. Dancing. Gymnastics Meets. Modeling. Cheering. Acceptance to Salisbury University. Stand-out Field Hockey player. Acceptance at Morgan State. Little boyfriends and broken hearts.

I talked about what my cohort talked with me about — what we had in common like being parents. I never disclosed my experiences or outings from the weekends or travel, never anything personal about my family or me. I never talked about my real life with my daughters, my mother, their father, or Linda. I never wanted to show them the crazy, or for them to know I often felt "out of place" there. More appropriately, I felt like "a fly in a bowl of milk." I started to wear the popular mask that minorities often wear to work, like body armor, to protect themselves — their confidence, humility, self-esteem, egos, and pride.

I know. I know. Being a tween or teenager is difficult. I get it. Things were happening both mentally and physically, and sometimes it just makes teenagers dumb as hell. They do dumb shit. We all have. And no one's kids or teens are immune. But I acted as if my daughters' shit didn't stink...when it did. I portrayed only positive images of them and our lives. Of course, that was my choice, and it was deliberate. I put their indiscretions in a separate compartment.

I remember my sister-cousin Pat was visiting us from Camptown for a few days in late summer. She was at my house with one of my daughters, a high school student at the time. I hadn't been at work very long that morning when Pat called.

"This line is non-secure; may I help you? I answered with the customary greeting.

"Tena, this girl has crawled out of the living room window with that fast-tail friend of hers. I caught her going out a window and told her to get her tail back in the house. She looked me in my eyes, Tena, and kept going!" Pat said without saying hello first.

I was sitting there, not saying a word. No questions. The cubicle we all shared was quiet as hell. You could hear a growling stomach. I bent slightly over at the waist and whispered into the phone, "I'll be there in 10 minutes," and hung-up. I quietly announced while grabbing my bag with my car keys in one swooping motion, "I'll be back."

I didn't stop to answer questions. I didn't ask for permission or even look toward our branch chief's door. I walked out! I returned before the hour was over and before anyone noticed — everyone was back where they belonged. Shara, my youngest daughter was at home, and I was back at work. I didn't say a word as to where I'd been. I kept my personal life, to myself.

Speak for the School

Agency conferences, advisory groups, councils, and site reviews usually included training as an agenda item or topic, and the NCS wanted representation in the room. Agency directorates don't like surprises or fingers pointed in their direction, especially when they are absent from the discussion.

I often found myself attending these meetings at headquarters, as the only "Rep" from the school, and 9 times out of 10, the only black person in the room. I was quite nervous about this, and I often didn't know what I could possibly offer. *Shit.* Take good notes, I thought. Try to connect dots. Put yourself in trainee's POV.

Then there were times I would introduce myself and not a single person in the room engaged, or acknowledge my presence, sometimes for the duration of multi-day events. I would sit there – day after day taking notes to stay alert. They talked about training as if I wasn't even in the room. Why am I here again? Rhetorical.

When they did, I would interject, clearly a bit annoyed. Allow me to re-introduce myself. "Hey, I'm Tena from the school!" *Remember me...rude ass people*, I thought. I'd attempt to clear-up misconceptions and to clarify products and courses and offer a point-of-contact (POC).

Going around the room for weekly project updates and summaries at our staff meetings, I quickly learned our manager, Daisy, didn't want a representative (from my cohort) to just attend. She wanted the "new boots" to contribute to the training discussion, answer questions, and to help our customers define their perceived need/requirements. If my written and verbal summary of the event(s), did not include me speaking to the group, she was not pleased. She was disappointed.

You could see it on her face. Daisy would stop smiling and ask, "Did you tell them about Project XYZ?" "No, I didn't. I didn't know I should or all of the details of efforts," I'd say.

She asked, "Why?" Her facial expression spoke volumes. Daisy grilled each of us with a smile. I felt so inadequate. I thought to myself, *Shit, she should have gone!* As a result, I memorized as much as I could about every organization in the NCS.

I became particularly good at rattling-off which NCS organization down to two number designators, as to who "owned" which curriculum. I studied them. I took notes. I created my own "Smart Book(s)." This allowed me to at least provide contact information in the school at a drop of a dime. I became more and more comfortable speaking for the entire school. Eventually, I would be asked to speak for the Director/Commandant of the school. I knew my shit.

Representation Really Does Matter

Demographically, blacks and women have always been under-represented at NSA and across the IC. It became apparent to me, of all the agencies, highly technical (STEM fields) and highly classified NSA, may NEVER achieve the IC's diversity goals. Challenges with hiring minorities with the right skills, and the ability to be cleared with a security clearance, was tolerated, and seemingly excused away for years.

In my humble opinion, earnest efforts by the Office of the Director of National Intelligence (ODNI), to right-size demographically, really didn't begin until around 2015 with the first unclassified and published

211

"Annual Demographic Reports" (ADR), courtesy of no-nonsense, James Clapper, DNI. With this publication, peer-pressure and shame prompted more strategic, measurable, initiatives. It seemed NSA had received a pass before then.[10]

This concern, along with mandating a competitive selection process for vacant positions around the enterprise, and duly constituted promotion boards, were address by NSA and was highlighted again as shortcomings by a study during NSA21 Transformation under the People Initiative. More to share about "NSA21" later.[11]

Speaking-up when you are the one brown egg in a carton of 11 white ones, is tough. As a black person, you know you're being judged every time you open your mouth. It's human nature. Regardless of your race, our brains automatically begin to make unconscious judgements and comparisons which can get in the way of independent reasoning and logic. The unaware brain is trying its best without inquiry or questions, to validate stereotypical images in its storage, determine friend or foe, make the decision quickly, file the encounter, and move on. The faster, the better, so the brain believes. (Korn, 2021)

Feelings of being judged make most people anxious and nervous about how they are being perceived. You become a space cadet trying to control fear. You're literally dumber say cognitive experts.

---

[10] Ferry, 2021.
[11] *www.federalnewsnetwork.com*

When there isn't a single welcoming smile, just beady eyes, know that people get extremely uneasy. They are more likely to mispronounce terms, forget their own name, or be so nervous, that they are unable to complete a single thought.[12]

The stress of it all can really have you wanting to climb into a conch shell and stay for a while. I've seen this first-hand with soldiers appearing before promotion boards in front of four or five of senior NCOs. I saw it at NSA, with mostly minorities, having difficulty expressing themselves and conveying information or a logical thought in a large group. I felt for them.

Honestly, I cringed for them when they couldn't communicate clearly. I started a habit of being encouraging when anyone appeared nervous; I could tell. To help them, I'd make a lot of eye contact. Nod my head often and smile to let them know there's a friendly and understanding person in the room. Just that tiny support makes a huge difference with a nervous, anxious briefer — the more head nods, the more confidence.

This common, human challenge of being nervous speaking publicly is something I taught aspiring adjunct instructors to harness and use. I had experiences early on at NSA where I had a speaking role and felt like I was representing every black person in the agency.

---

[12] Montopoli, 2017.

Not a smiling face in the group. Several impatient attendees who'd finish your sentence or have an "I'm, so confused and I don't know what you're talking about look." I hated that bullshit look. I hated being interrupted, especially when I was asked a question. They were micro-triggers for me.

I'd want to ask, "Is it me or am I speaking French?" to the white co-worker who would tilt her head, squint her eyes and nose, in that "I don't understand you look." When I could no longer ignore it, I asked, "Am I confusing you? Did what I said make sense?" She'd look confused again like she had no control over her face. "Who? Me? No, I'm fine. I understand." *Tell your face*, I'd think.

Every mistake would belong to all of us — *in my mind.* I never wanted to validate stereotypes, but I had to learn it wasn't me confirming them. It was not my unchecked unconscious biases. I learned to harness this nervous energy by being over-prepared and focusing on content to deliver, and I stressed the same to new instructors.

This is how I feel about diversity and inclusion, and how I define it. A diverse workforce is about numbers; how many of each. Sorry to say, for those who are thinking quotas. It's the fairest way to achieve equal and exceed representation that's reflective of the general population. Again, remember I appreciate data and.

To me, inclusion is the feelings humans experience when in a minority status and/or setting. Do they feel included? Are other employees civil towards them? Is it a safe environment to be open and honest? Are they included fairly on projects? Do other employees communicate with them and vice versa? Know what I mean — it's about feeling like a part of the team and being in the lineup.

Culture of the Agency

A completely independent phenom at work at the agency, regardless of the Director, is its strong culture and ethos of the agency. It is one of the strongest I am aware of, and I have several suitable comparisons like the U.S. military services culture(s), sororities, fraternities, and black culture. The culture of NSA, particularly at headquarters, appears almost impenetrable. As a soldier, I didn't give a lot of thought/care to the agency's culture. I knew my assignment/time there was temporary, and if I stayed outside the wire, I didn't have to worry about it.

As a civilian, I've seen glimpses of cultural changes. Little pockets or small groups of people whose positive and recognizable changes address the character and value the agency espouses to be.

But, in my humble opinion, and from years of observation, NSA has a long-standing culture and a workforce that could be described as, antiquated (in fashion too!), mostly white, snobbish or bougie, hyper-competitive, highly-paranoid, overly confident, passive-aggressive, male dominated, and misogynistic. Whew! Did you get all of that? I have over generalized, intentional.

I quickly discovered how to navigate the cultural landmines and entrenched mindsets. I circumvented this complex and tough cultural environment for 13 years. It is not for the faint of heart. I, like other minorities who've experienced this type of environment, learn to adapt.

I was constantly aware of how I may be perceived and portrayed. I minimized the chances of managers, subordinates, and co-workers believing I could be aggressive by remaining deliberately calm. I lowered and softened my voice and stature to appear non-threatening.

I worked harder than the persons to my right and left, constantly trying to prove I was qualified for every position I held. I turned skepticism and doubt into respect and a reputation for getting the job done. I sought learning and leading opportunities. I was there to work/produce, period. No handouts for me. I earned every promotion, award, and recognition I received. I kept my mouth shut and my head to the grind. I believed if I adapted, I would fare well in this strange, mostly white intelligence agency with this a strong culture.

First, let me define what I am referring to when I say "culture." According to Merriam-Webster (2002), the culture of an organization consists of its values, beliefs, attitudes, and the shared behaviors of the workforce. It includes and refers to the "acceptable way people interact, collaborate, and work, within an organization." Culture is believed to drive decisions, actions, and overall performance of organizations (Rogel, 2014).

Keep in mind, I was hired in 2004 and there has been a sizable increase in different generations, like Millennials, Generations X, Y, and a small sprinkling of young Z (or Zoomers) in the workplace. All of which interrelate completely differently than the more seasoned Baby Boomer employees. Will they positively influence or change the culture of the agency? I truly hope so (Corrington 2019).

Lack of Civility

At NSA, common courtesies are not common. Do not expect people you recognize to interact or say the greeting of the day. A lot of employees can attest to this experience. When walking the halls of NSA, or across the parking lot, or even in the Café, and particularly at headquarters, most of the employees do not make eye contact or speak. This means, if you sat beside someone in a meeting the day before and even had an exchange about a topic, the next day they might not say hello. They just don't. So, do not expect a hi, hello, hey there, or good seeing you!

Ironically, black employees at NSA, like black people on the street, greet each other whether we know each other or not. I recall making eye contact and saying hello to a black gentleman in passing. I was walking with a white colleague from the school. She asked if I knew the person. She seemed surprised that I spoke to him. *"No, we were just speaking,"* Apparently the black gentleman was an impressive Senior Executive, who she knew by position only. In my mind, this is just what we do. We were raised to speak to each other. Not speaking seems a bit rude to me.

Along the same lines of civility, is the inability for "some" white employees to be able to distinguish between and/or identify black employees - as in facial recognition. Maybe this is one reason employees don't give the greeting of the day or say hello. This occurs way to often especially with black females. All too often, two black women are mistaken and called the wrong name. This happened to me more times than I can count. I usually knew who the person thought I was, just based on very broad similarities and work proximity.

Generally, not speaking to colleagues contributes to the lack of civility at the agency, particularly when leaders model this negative behavior and fail to build rapport with the workforce. So much so, there was an Equal Opportunity (EO) campaign, focused on increasing Civility across the agency. Oh yes - Civility Matters Campaign!

Now this is the civility that my gramma described as being courteous, like holding doors for each other, again, saying hello, and speaking with respect to each person. Things you learn at home and in kindergarten about being polite. I'll share more later about the agency's training to increase civility during my time at NSA-Texas (NSA-TX).

Passive-Aggressive Behavior

There seems to be a wide-spread culture of passive-aggressive behavior and communications. These folks are passive in person while indirectly, behind closed doors and with distance, aggressive. Some, like a young lady who worked for me in HI, often exhibited resistance to assignments or tasks. She would intentionally procrastinate and wait until the exact suspense date to ask clarifying questions or to acknowledge the tasks.

Passive-aggressive emails are quite common, especially when sent to a wide audience. On one occasion, when an aggressive email was sent to a relatively new contractor who worked for me, I responded.

Given the way the email was written and the respective audience, she could not respond. She would have been chastised or worse — fired. I did not care that she was a contractor — she was a human first and deserved to be treated with respect. The challenges presented in the email were not the contractors doings, she was being used as a scapegoat for a grumpy, NSA employee, who wanted to vent publicly before she retired. She didn't know I felt the need to vent too.

There were incidents in which I was challenged to fix whatever woes the training organization, department or curriculum was experiencing before I was selected to take charge. After being promoted/selected to a new leadership position, I was aggressively challenged, verbally and publicly, by subordinates to fix the problems because I had been selected to lead, therefore, the expectation was to get in here and fix things, quick.

Everyone Wants to be a Comedian

I witnessed a prevalent culture of sarcasm at the agency, and it's so annoying. This behavior is also passive-aggressive in nature. It's like white males, especially in group settings, want to be comedians but none are funny. I noticed this heavily with people in leadership positions/managers. Don't know if they believed it's cool or a way for people in the room to relate to them. This behavior by-far, was/is a micro-trigger for me. It grated *my a*** to witness this, whether I was the brunt of the sarcasm or not. Just being honest.

Passive sarcasm is designed to be humorous yet can have a negative impact unintentionally. While aggressive sarcasm, which I believe I witnessed in HI, is designed intentionally to be belittling – like it was to the NCS and me. I've been in the presence of agency leaders, particularly in mission, who point out all the challenges of providing relevant, current, training, and instructors, without offering solutions or subject matter experts to improve the training, and ultimately, performance. Unfortunately, this leadership example of bad-mouthing the school is propagated down and throughout to the workforce.

Limited Diversity of Thought

I believe like-mindedness, and a lack of courage to go against the grain, limits the agency's ability to prosecute its mission in new, more efficient ways. Being open to diversity of thought, teaches us to welcome/solicit, and fairly consider different opinions. Diverse thinking leads to mission solutions while valuing the entire workforce. But the only way to ensure true diversity of thought, is to have a diverse workforce at headquarters and around the Enterprise.

For the Good of the Corporation

NSA believes in supporting its decision-makers and their decisions. Once a senior leader decides on a direction, good, bad, or indifferent, employees are expected to salute and execute. I rarely observed convergent and/or divergent thinking. Negative outcomes and opinions about the agency, like its failures and demographics, are perceived as internal issues and are handled within the walls of NSA. The internal challenges are not divulged externally, at least not freely or willingly.

Condescending and Patronizing

Now, imagine a site Commander who enjoyed correcting your every word. This happened to me often at NSA-TX, by the same guy. If I said "Enablers," he would correct me publicly and say, "you mean, Mission Enablers." I couldn't say *shit* around him. I desperately wanted to ask him if he interrupted and corrected others, like his spouse, maybe, or mother, the way he did me.

Intelligence Air Force Colonels who led NSA-TX were usually selected for Brigadier General (1-star), right after being the Commander of NSA-TX. He checked the block and got promoted. He was the same Commander who didn't believe diversity of people is as important as "diversity of thought," he declared. Huh. Now, how exactly is diverse thinking achieved without diverse people, sir? Rhetorical, of course.

Culture of Secrecy vs. Transparency

I know this is an oxymoron when considering transparency and the most secretive of all intelligence agencies. Unfortunately, this is not an NSA unique challenge though; it is across the IC. You would think after the 911 Study slammed the IC for NOT sharing critical intelligence to fold the attacks, the IC would overshare. This remains a challenge, so much so, that in 2016, a public record indicated the ODNI, created yet another Intelligence Transparency Council (ITC), with membership/representation from each of the 17 IC elements to break through hoard intelligence.[13]

"Cover-Your-Ass (CYA)"

The CYA culture at NSA isn't atypical. Other intelligence agencies, corporations, and even the political environment are all examples of CYA cultures. NSA has a wide-spread population of employees who feel like they must cover their asses. Experts say a CYA work environment manifests out of fear of being wrong and/or admitting mistakes (Horwitz, 2016).

Well, there's been a great deal of long-standing fear across the IC since it famously failed to predict the attack on Pearl Harbor. I believe CYA is a form of self and agency preservation. The inherent culture of fear causes information withholding and mistrust.

---

[13] "Principals of Intelligence Transparency," 2021.

As a way of protection, some NSA employees and managers keep records, particularly as it relates to employees' performance. I know I did. Hell, I learned from my Army days to document poor performance but because I did not trust the system, I personally felt the need to keep such records/e-mails too.

I kept notes of accomplishments, old "to do lists," and I saved outgoing e-mails to include replies to incoming e-mails, by quarter, and then by Fiscal Year (FY). I documented telephone conversations and follow-up conversations with summaries of items discussed and agreed upon. NSA's HR and managers' fear of legal ramifications, usually stemming from poor performance, ties the hands of managers with subpar employees. This fear keeps the CYA culture firmly in place.

The negative effects of this strong-hold culture are obvious. You only need to spend a few days in the agency to feel it. Negative cultures are costly and breed paranoia, distrust, and poor performance. I believe this strangely odd and negative culture causes employees to become disengaged and lack productivity. Some of which is caused by the agency's risk adverse nature and disengaged managers — managers unaware that do not dedicate the time and attention to the humans/people performing the mission.

Finally, ROAD Scholars

Because the agency is so large, it is easy for some employees to Retire on Active Duty or ROAD, as we call it. They do the bare minimum and only what they

223

are asked, specifically to do. Zero initiative. They have completely checked out. They arrive to work with a breakfast and lunch, a daily paper, and a list of "to dos" for the unclassified internet. I've seen them.

To complicate matters, a small pool of key performers, who are intrinsically motivated, do most of the work. This is across Directorates. The key performers (the 20%), do the bulk of the agency's work. Living proof that 20% of the people, do 80% of the work theory is legit.

In the chapters that follow, are an examination of my work assignments, leadership positions, experiences, and interactions with fellow NSA employees across the global enterprise. I share a timeline of personal stories, career highlights and a few disappointing experiences with leaders in positions of power. In 2016, I found myself reevaluating everything, particularly my career with NSA.

Chapter 11

Time for a Change: A Permanent Change of Station (PCS)

"The first step towards getting somewhere is to decide that you are not going to stay where you are."

-   *Chauncey Depew*

Deputy Chief, Cryptologic Training System (CTS) Office - (2006-2008)

Headquarters, Ft. Meade

After two years and two Branch Chiefs, the NCS created yet another organization that absorbed performance analysis, training requirements, and the military Cryptologic Training System (CTS) Support office. The Performance Analysis cohorts appeared to be dismantled, however, no one ever said so formally. We began to seek or be sought for other jobs. Three of us managed to keep in touch over the years. My marine buddy Mick moved onto a position to transform intelligence analysis. Rachel and I were sought-out to assume positions within the school.

I was asked to move to the CTS office, which was right up my alley. I was comfortable being around troops and this branch was slightly over 50% senior military (E-7 and E-9). Little did I know, the training I attended in Pensacola after boot camp, NSA had a significant amount of input on the content of the in the form of learning objectives or standards. By DoD policy, the Commandant of the NCS is also the

Training Director for the military Services' cryptologic and cyber training. The relationship the Services have with this NSA office is a complicated and complimentary one.

The Services believe they oversee their training, yet NSA's reputation of having "excess funds" made the relationship more appealing. While I worked there, the Services had their hands out like soup bowls for NSA to fill with cash.

I heard from my colleagues that in past years, the Services felt like NSA had abandoned its responsibility to the CTS. The schools were sorely outdated with legacy training equipment that had reached its life cycle. In some cases, troops were being trained using analytic tools that they would never see or use once they began their cryptologic missions. Corry Station was in desperate need of fiber optic cabling across the entire base to modernize intelligence training there.

On the other hand, colleagues who had worked with CTS schools in years prior to my arrival, were concerned that the Services were doing their own thing without a mechanism for NSA to stop them. If a service decided to pull out of joint language training at an Air Force base, neither NSA nor the Air Force could stop them.

The Navy packed-up and did just that. This frustrated NSA and the other Services to no end, and there were talks of retaliatory actions like pulling the Air Force out of Corry Station. All the drama with the Services had NSA, specifically NCS, entertaining the idea of divorcing itself from its Training Director role, and rewriting the original charter and DoD policy to focus solely on cryptologic training within the wall of the NSA only – so I was told.

Between 2006-2008, the new Commandant of the NCS and the new DIRNSA, General Alexander, recognized this deficiency in support and cooperation. So, the CTS Support office was refreshed with added civilian employees and a new Chief. A new Commandant of the NCS welcomed her role as Training Director. She committed the NCS to ensuring relevant and current training across the Services and began to provide funding to update the three military schoolhouses (Army, Navy, and Air Force), host joint training councils, and conduct courtesy visits to the schools.

To paint a picture of this multi-service group, the CTS is a council of Colonels/0-6, from each Service, service training managers, training evaluation experts and trainers/instructors from all five Services. Yes, the U.S. Coast Guard is included and was quite vociferous. They met virtually every quarter and in-person annually, with each Service taking turns to host the conference at their respective schoolhouse. The goal was to mutually agree on the training standards to teach in joint courses for soldiers, sailors, airmen, marines, and coast guardsmen — one standard, regardless of service.

The CTS Support Office was charged by DIRNSA to "revolutionize" the long-standing Cryptologic Training Advisory Group (CTAG) process which is in essence a curriculum review. Conducting these reviews every two years wasn't working. If we consider changes in communication technology in the past 15 years, social media, cloud technology, and artificial intelligence has radically changed our lives. iPads, smartwatches, fitness trackers, and wireless earphones — the list of innovations and impact is a long one.

The competition between what each service needed and wanted trained, and what NSA and the IC needed included, posed a formidable tug-of-war contest. To compound this challenge and make it more complex, there were multiple contributing factors such as the initial training restrictions enforced on each service, such as time – as in how many weeks a military school can keep a troop, the available funding from different budgets, and the cadre needed to support each service's fiscal through-put. It's a kabuki dance that demands a bit of negotiating, agreement from all parties, and a give and take attitude — easier said than done.

This group negotiates ferociously with each other until agreements are reached on what is included or excluded in the joint training curricula. You can imagine the "healthy" disagreements among the Services to achieve agreement. The group's decisions had direct impact on each Service's ability to perform their assigned missions.

I was still working in the CTS Support office when I was approached by my friend and early advocate Tessa, to attend a meeting to share my experience in authoring Job Qualification Standards (JQS) at NSA

GA. At the meeting, I explained our process at NSA-GA to develop duties and tasks for every position across the entire NSA-GA operation.

For the next year or so, I and two gentlemen who worked with me in the CTS office, developed a draft policy and outlined processes for the adoption of the JQS program for the entire NSA workforce — both military and civilians. We proved that a JQS could be developed for any position — mission and non-mission positions included.

In 12 months, we developed and collected a repository of thousands of JQS tasks we called Reusable Objectives to share across the enterprise. This comprehensive and cohesive approach would revolutionize the development and performance standards of the joint workforce.

This project fell flat. NSA's Human Resources (HR) could not fathom what they would do if a civilian failed to qualify. If a civilian didn't qualify for the position they were currently performing, what would the repercussions be? How would they handle this in a non-punitive way and convince civilian employees they needed to participate in the agency's JQS training program?

The Policy Office had the same concern as HR. After we briefed what seemed like every organization in the agency, we were halted at the Policy Office. During the time, Mr. Blake, led the policy organization. I wondered if he'd remember me from my PSG days in Alpha Company when he was the Bn Commander of 742nd MI Bn.

In June 2007, after performing as the Consultant on the JQS effort and the agency's new Deployment (DEPL) curriculum and training, I was promoted to GG-14. I was delighted. I was then approached to assume the Deputy Chief position for the CTS. Additionally, we got a new Chief for the organization, name Patience.

She was a GG-15 with limited experience in training and with the military Services. Patience moved to the NCS from Security. The CTS may have been her second job in the school. Patience's previous role was in a customer service organization that NCS attempted to model after Walt Disney. They provided customer service efforts and learning facilitation services. After a short while, it too fell flat, or it fell victim to budget cuts. I'm not certain.

Patience, without prior military service and limited experience engaging with field grade and senior non-commissioned officers, had an uphill climb for this leadership position. Experience in or with military intelligence was essential for this position and not just for knowing about the military customs and courtesies.

This strong federation of senior military members focused on troop training, would eat you alive. They were no non-sense when it came to ensuring training was to standards. They took their responsibility seriously – which is to ensure, when the nation goes to war or engages in conflicts, the Services are trained and equipped to accomplish their individual and collective strategic, operational, and tactical missions.

Period. Today's conflicts and wars do not discriminate or distinguish between intelligence assets and tactical assets on the battlefield.

Patience had a huge knowledge gap and wanted me at her hip at every turn, every TDY, every council meeting, and every executive session with high-level service training representatives. Most of these Training Command Commanders are demanding, curt, and have little time to waste with NSA civilians.

Patience, in turn, helped me transition from my military style of writing performance reviews to the agency/civilian way with complete and thorough sentences and paragraphs that highlighted subordinates' accomplishments and their impact on the agency, the DoD, and the IC—which isn't always apparent.

Patience wasn't all bad. I liked the way she carried herself — very professional, demanded respect, and knew her entitlements, like leave, for instance. She taught me a tool to manage up and down by providing projected annual leave dates to her supervisor well in advance. She forecasted her annual leave sometimes a year out.

In her defense, she had a timeshare that she took full advantage of. I liked this long-term look, naturally, but her strategy meant we needed to plan CTS events/conferences around her schedule instead of vice versa. As her Deputy, I had to schedule my leave based on hers. She wanted me at work if she was on leave unless I was TDY with her. Patience did not want anyone else in the CTS to attend NCS staff meetings or other required discussions to speak for her, even though we had a very capable GG15 working in the CTS. She wanted to hold one person accountable – me.

Time to Move On

After working in the CTS Support office for 2 and a half years, I applied and interviewed for a Permanent Change of Station (PCS) to HI. There were two E&T positions in HI with impending openings, and I knew with a bit of train-up, I could perform. Would there be a mission/location learning curve? Absolutely.

At home, my mother was working and living in Baltimore now. She'd moved around a couple of times but seemed to be learning Baltimore City and didn't ask to move back to Severn. I was relieved, honestly. We'd see her on weekends, birthdays, holidays, and BBQs. I knew she was still using. I could tell from her appearance and her finances. Her skin was darker, and she always needed one of us to meet her at BWI to give her $20 for "bus fare to get to work for the week." After getting the requested funds, she'd get back on the train and head back to Baltimore.

In September of 2007, I hadn't been working in the CTS office long. She was hospitalized at Johns Hopkins in Baltimore; she had her first stroke. I knew it was drug-use related. Of course, she has never admitted that. I heard one of her attending physicians tell her she had to quit smoking.... everything! She laughed uncomfortably.

After recovering with us in Severn, she returned to her apartment in Baltimore. Of all of life's challenges, I compartmentalized my mother's addiction, our fragile relationship, and my anxiety about her, the most. I lived by the saying, "out of sight, out of mind."

Tierra graduated in May 2008 from Salisbury University, and Shara graduated from Old Mill High School. Tierra achieved a bachelor's degree in Math and a teaching certificate in 4 years, even as a transfer student from University of Maryland Baltimore County (UMBC). She had her first teaching job in Annapolis at a middle school. I was so proud of her.

I was equally proud of Shara. Shara was accepted to Morgan State University – an Historical Black College/University (HBCU) in Baltimore. I was surprised she wanted to go to college. When Shara started H.S., she began to dislike school, and she started doing just enough for passing grades, mostly Cs. I was happy she had turned a corner. I was enthusiastic about experiencing an HBCU for the first time with her. Go Bears!

Linda and I had become roommates with mutual interests, like the girls, friends, family, our home, sports, and our careers. Try as we might, we could not recover from the damage that infidelity, and dishonesty about infidelity, caused our friendship — on both parts. It was after we bought our second house, it became apparent our romantic relationship was over. As hard as we tried, we were surviving off history. It would never be the same. Linda moved to the bedroom in the basement. I exhaled upstairs with the girls.

A year later into this new situation, I had an epiphany. A Permanent Change of Station or PCS was just what I needed; hell, we both needed. Like my PCS to Ft. Gordon, I ran. I knew this was the only way we could move forward in other relationships, and I sensed Linda was ready. We couldn't live in the same house and date, that would be way too awkward. I felt like I was holding my breath at home, waiting for her to say the things I had already concluded. It didn't happen.

As for my mother, she needed to figure out her own life. She'd been to rehab in New Jersey — she knew what she needed to do. She needed to go back to rehab and quit for good. I could no longer hang around, listen to the denial, the excuses, give her money, and watch her slowly kill herself.

I was selected to be the Regional Education & Training Director-Pacific (RETD-Pacific). Sounds fancy and important, right? Well...more to come about that. I was moving to HI. I would focus on my civilian career and navigate the single life for the first time in over 20 years – over 4800 miles away. My PCS was a fresh start...again.

Executive Assistant to the Commandant

Shortly after I got the official notification from HR of my selection to move to HI, I was summoned to the CTS Chief's office. She informed me the school's new Commandant and Director of Training for all of NSA, who I refer to as Judy, Madame Commandant, wanted me to act as her Executive Officer/Assistant (Exec) before PCSing/departing. What? Why? Can I say No thanks? I knew I could not!

I was informed Judy's actual Exec needed to take an extended leave — at least 60 days, maybe longer. This timeframe was during the annual CTS conference my office sponsored with a host site. This year it at was to be at Goodfellow AFB in Texas. Judy, as the Training Director of NSA and the services' intelligence training, she planned to attend the entire conference. She thought the timing was perfect for me to accompany her too Goodfellow, as Acting Exec, and in preparation for my PCS to HI. That's how it was "packaged to me." In a few weeks, I high-tailed to the front office of the NCS to cross-train with Judy's Exec.

I made the best of it. I worked the same hours as Judy and earned a ton of credit hours that I could not take fast enough. I attended meetings with her to record action items and take notes. I read her e-mails, sorted them, printed pertinent correspondence, and then sorted into classified and unclassified — we're talking hundreds of daily e-mails. The unclassified folder went home with her nightly.

The next morning, I sorted and distributed tasks handwritten on the top of hardcopy e-mails, to the College Deans. I acted as a "go-between" Judy and her Deans, clarifying questions for them, listening to their frustrations, sometimes calming them down so they could focus and understand Judy's hand-written "love notes." They began to trust me...so did Judy. I felt special.

Judy was mandating that data support everything we do in the school. She was data-driven which made perfect sense to me. Like researcher Dr. Brene' Brown,

I too believe if it can't be measured, it does not exist. Judy was also driving the NCS into the 21st Century with technology. We were a bit behind the virtual learning curve if you ask me. It was now 2009, I completed my master's degree completely online before NCS' offered its first virtual offering. Additionally, course offerings and schedules needed to be driven by requirements or needs. No requirement/need, no seat. Not enough requirements, no local course. Simple.

Judy seemed to have a steel-trap mind. She didn't forget taskers that took way too long for a response. Her staff and deans respected me in my role. My goal was to not piss off Judy. So, I'd ask her questions for clarification to help me communicate what she wanted. Soon, I was able to predict what she wanted and when. Her OPS TEMPO resembled a General in the Army. Judy was tough, especially for an NSA civilian leader. I admired her honesty and straight-forwardness. Not everyone got her, though. I marveled at her involvement in every aspect of the school.

I saw her make an employee cry...on the employee's birthday. *No Shit!* She was completely unaware she hurt the lady's feelings – she felt horrible and looked awkward apologizing.

I was highly organized. I had to be. I travelled with her to Texas after providing her my handy, personal packing list to use at home which she found hilariously organized. I drove the rental car during our trip. Remember, I drove the INSCOM Commander around Germany when I was stationed in Worms.

Working in Protocol of Field Station Berlin, made me comfortable around seniors. I grabbed her bags and made sure she was at the head of the conference tables. Those previous experiences paid dividends. I knew how to open car doors, where to stand, and how to drive.

On our way home from San Antonio, I literally bumped into DJ Michael in the San Antonio Airport. He was heading home to MD after being there on business with the government, he said. He hadn't changed much — he appeared taller and slightly rounder. I recognized him right away. I walked right-up to him and called his entire name, "Michael... what are you doing in San Antonio?" He smiled. A quick hug. He explained what he was doing — he owned his own business and was there to work with the Army on a project. His flight was later than ours. He gave me his business card. I said I'd call to catch-up. I wasn't sure if I would or not.

NSA-Pacific (NCPAC), 2008 – 2012
Regional Education & Training Director – Pacific (RETD-Pac)

New Life in HI

I woke up early the morning I was to leave for Honolulu. I was so excited to start a new life. As my dependent, Shara travelled with me to HI and would return mid-August in time for school. I tried again to convince Shara to transfer to HI Pacific University and stay in Oahu with me. She wasn't remotely interested. She was dating someone she met at Morgan and wanted to stay put. I got it, but I was not feeling her little boyfriend. I smelled trouble. Tierra would meet us in Honolulu. She was celebrating her graduation from college in Atlanta with her cousins and would fly from there to Oahu to help me find a home and get settled. Tierra has always been very helpful.

Was I worried about the distance from my daughters? Absolutely. But I felt comfortable in knowing they had their father nearby. Michael lived in Prince George's County, MD and Linda was still in the house in Sever. I knew she'd be there for them. I've probably taken advantage of her friendship and her connection with my daughters in this way, but they know her and rely on like another mom or aunt – or so I like to tell myself. She has an independent relationship with them.

We arrived in Honolulu safely after an unexpected night in LA. We ended up spending the night with my sister-cousin Avon and her daughter Claire after we missed our connecting flight out of LA. Claire picked us up from LAX. We went out for Sushi at the restaurant co-owned by Ashton Kushner and caught-up. Claire was gracious enough to get us back to the airport for an early flight from LA to Honolulu. I got to spend some needed time with Avon. I missed her. It worked out perfectly.

My life in HI was starting out great. I loved the house I was renting in Waikele. The landlord was accommodating and prompt. It was walking distance from a public golf course and a small outlet mall with a couple of options for sit down dining. The first two months there, I focused on my new job and losing a few pounds. I was heavier than I'd ever been...and it happened so gradually. No P.T.! After work, I'd walk 4 or 5 days a week and cut carbs from my meals and dropped 10 pounds. I loved walking and hiking in HI. It was so picturesque, and I didn't miss a single-colored Hibiscus or rainbow. *Hello GOD...I see you!*

My best friend Mitzi was stationed there but was deployed to Iraq when I arrived. When she returned at the end of October, I helped her celebrate her safe return and my arrival to the island. We couldn't believe it. We lived on a tropical island. *No shit.* Years earlier, Mitzi and I talked about where we wanted to live after we retired or hit the lottery. HI offered lots to do and when you don't want to do anything, there's always the beach to just chill. I didn't feel alone there. I met Mitzi's soldiers, and we all hung out together. I went to Mitzi's famous BBQs, game nights, and girls' night out. At almost 47 years old, I felt young again hanging out with the never-a-dull moment soldiers!

Concerns about the high cost of living in HI were addressed and tapered when I learned I would get a Cost-of-Living Allowance (COLA). The COLA in HI and Alaska (AK) was more appealing, especially to junior grade, federal employees. Yes, HI is awfully expensive, but doable. Tales of junior soldiers and young agency employees having roommates were not uncommon. Lucky for me, I had an Army retiree ID card and privileges to use the Commissaries, Post Exchanges, and AFEES gas stations across the island – a significant savings on groceries and gas.

New RETD-Pac

In this new role, I was tasked to lead E&T services supporting both the NCPAC office and 10 or so small, remote NSA sites with NCS Education & Training Program Managers (ETPM), across the Pacific theater. This position came with a huge geography and an enormous budget cut imposed throughout the entire NCS. I embraced the challenge of rebalancing priorities with limited resources.

When I first arrived, I seemed to have credibility with the NCPAC's Site Chief; he listened to me. Regrettably, he PCSed shortly after my arrival. The new NCPAC Chief who replaced him was a face from the past, Mr. Blake. My old battalion Commander and the Chief of the Policy Office at headquarters who I briefed on the JQS effort. There seemed to be a shift.

Mr. Blake was like a dark cloud that appeared and hovered over Camp Smith, especially for those who wanted to extend and stay in paradise for as long as possible. Briefing him at his first daily NCPAC Stand-up, I wondered if he remembered me — the JQS briefing. He flatly said no. That clearly indicated he would not remember me from my Platoon Sergeant days either.

When I settled-in at work, I knew exactly what Judy's thoughts and expectations were regarding every aspect of the NCS and its priorities, having worked so closely and spent so much time with her. I was required to attend daily stand-ups to brief training highlights, schedules, and anything on the horizon.

During the first week of the new NCPAC Site Chief, I noticed he had something sarcastic to say after every office's update, especially training. *What the hell is that about?* Then other leaders from across NCPAC offices started doing the same to each other. Each morning, it was a race to see who could be the most sarcastic and obnoxious. They'd all laugh like these cats were comedians. I wanted to say, *"Homey, you don't know me like that,"* to be joking around at 0800hrs.

After training updates, I'd usually hear... *"I can teach that!"* I'd just smiled at these passive-aggressive, cynical leaders. It took everything in me to not reply with, *"Well, get certified and teach it then!"* A lot of knowledgeable and confident people believe they can teach until they must teach. I've seen them "fall flat," to keep it mildly.

After several months of experiencing this with my manager, NCPAC's CoS, who attended stand-up too, I decided I would only attend when I had something to share in detail about training. And besides, the CoS was there. *Couldn't she pass along what was happening in training?* I didn't return to a stand-up until I was the acting NCPAC CoS.

The RETD office was authorized two billets — the Director's position (my job) and a Customer Service Representative (CSR), who worked directly for me. This was a GG11/12 position, and the young lady was selected by the NCPAC prior to my arrival. Her name is Carrie. She got there a few weeks after I did, again with limited training or NCS experience. Her only experience was from a student's perspective.

I called this type of learning curve the "Road to Hana (on the island of Maui)" — with over 100 hairpin turns! I did my best to train Carrie on everything I knew. From our new learning management systems, clean and clear course announcements, enrollments, and different types of withdrawals, the whole kit and caboodle.

After months of frustration and patience, she operated independently of me. Carrie had, in fact, caught on quickly. She established relationships with key points of contact in the school and at NSA-Hawaii (NSA-HI) who in essence, provided most of the courses we needed in the Pacific region.

The first two quarters at NCPAC was spent managing expectations. I was the bearer of really bad news. In past years, the sites in the region were accustomed to getting a decent lump of allocated training funds to attend training, that seemingly could be spent at will. Our budget for the upcoming Fiscal Year 2010 (FY10) was nothing like previous years – it was reduced by Judy dramatically.

Judy, via me, emphasized getting the right training to right people at the right time. No fluff or nice-to-have training. No training for the 'supposedly already trained' employees. And we must take full advantage of the agency's training, which is a lot less expensive than external vendor training. Judy encouraged us to acquire technology necessary to push online and virtual training the region. The huge budget cut shocked the region's ETPMs and their Site Chiefs. They received a detailed e-mail explanation from me, as way of introducing myself and the news about the cuts.

The RETD's budget was shared sites around the Pacific Region, which from here on out, required detailed spend/budget plans. We needed to account for every penny. To do that, we created a massive 10-12 tabbed Excel spreadsheet. Surgical execution of this budget increased the strength of our justification for additional dollars that we needed for unfunded equipment — and we got it.

Judy knew we had valid requirements and would not waste funds – and most importantly, she trusted me. The region secured and executed over $100K to upgrade classrooms, computer labs, install video teleconference systems. We advocated for the delivery of virtual courses piped to HI at pacific-friendly hours, which saved over $300K in travel cost.

Leadership Training in the Region

As a military veteran, I was used to leadership training that corresponded with your level of responsibility and position. So, when the agency announced four levels of leadership training and stood-up a Leadership Directorate, it made sense. However, leadership training being external to the school/NCS made zero sense for obvious reasons. If you have another entity of the agency delivering training, you now must duplicate resources. Duplication of any kind cost all of us.

In the Pacific region, new and evolving supervisors/managers were allowed to attend and complete the Pacific Leadership Academy (PLA) in Honolulu at an estimated cost of 60K per FY, for three to five, agency employees — expensive training, especially to TDY students to Honolulu for 2-4 weeks. I also became aware that in previous years, the NCPAC Chief and his Deputy, required employees in the region to submit a locally created application to attend PLA, for NCPAC's leaders to make selections.

Using skills and formulas learned as a Performance Consultant, I had to show the Site Chiefs and ETPMs in the region the negative ROI in funding PLA, especially now that the agency had its own leadership development program. I knew the field sites in the region wouldn't be happy with the results. This was an unpopular change but fiscally prudent. The field sites liked the perk of attending the 'prestigious PLA!

I asked the new Leadership Directorate at headquarters via e-mail to take a stance on whether agency employees *should* attend external leadership programs or the agency's new leadership development program. They sheepishly responded with, "we highly encourage agency employees to attend our training." That did not help. That was not what Judy, or I wanted to hear.

Now I had to defend this position with the all the Pacific Site Chiefs aka, the Wolf Pack. They were already calling Mr. Blake, complaining about the budget cuts. Once I revealed with Judy how much the agency would save each year by NOT participating in PLA, she made the unpopular decision to pull the plug, but I communicated her decision with the Wolves via their ETPMs and attached my ROI worksheet to my e-mail. You can't argue with numbers — $ saved.

I pushed through this early period at NCPAC and began advocating for more funding and seat allocations for the agency's contracted leadership courses as the RETD. I was getting into a routine. We met with the ETPMs around the region via VTC, monthly.

Early on, connecting to over 10 sites was sketchy and hit or miss — bandwidth limitation caused sites to drop frequently. We'd try to send slides, rush through our agenda, all to accommodate a 30-minute meeting. So, collectively we decided to make an innovative change. We started using NCS' very own e-Class system and called it e-Meetings. We eliminated bandwidth issue, and as Educators, "we ate our own dog food" by using our own tool.

In 2011, the government announced an initiative called NAREA — Non-foreign Area Retirement Equity Assurance Act, to reduce the Cost-of-Living Allocations (COLA), which augment federal salaries(non-taxable) for high-cost of living states like HI and AK. The initiative would replace COLA eventually, with locality pay which is taxable.

The justification for the change and new program seemed fair and employee focused. Locality pay would be used to calculate employees high-3 salaries (in years and dollars), to determine their retirement annuities. COLA, being non-taxable, could not be used toward retirement.

NAREA was quite complicated on just how the agency would step down COLA payments using a Tier system, while simultaneously increasing locality pay. So much so that the Chief of HR and her training team travelled to AK and HI to introduce the program. *Okay. Do your thing HR and Finance.* I didn't give this change much thought. I trusted that what needed to happen with my pay, would happen. Since I moved to HI, my bi-weekly pay amount was never predictable or the same. This HR and Finance driven change, would come back to *bite me in the a** and leave a bad taste in my mouth!*

Chapter 12

Living in Paradise; Working in Hell

If your value your integrity, then be prepared to take a beating from those who have none.

-Lars Lau Thygesen

NSA-Pacific (2008-2012) Continued

As part of my RETD orientation and on-the-job training, Judy approved a travel budget for me to conduct staff visits to multiple sites in the Pacific region which I would oversee. For some reason, Judy approved other staff members from headquarters to accompany me. Not sure why. I didn't really mind the company — I prefer to travel internationally with a buddy.

Japan and Korea

My first site visit took place in June 2010 to Japan and South Korea. Site Visit agendas are Standard Operating Procedure (SOP). When visiting each location, after the usual introductory pleasantries, one has a formal office call with the Commander or Site Chief, a site mission/operation briefing, and tour of operations to include their training space(s). As the RETD, I provided an overview of the RETD's Role, NCS strategies, training priorities, and developmental plans. We responded to the site's training questions, took action items/notes to provide to the appropriate POCs when we returned, and provided advice and assistance while on-site. Most often, we shared points of contacts (POCs) at the NCS to quickly resolve training issues.

The NCS' Chief of Staff (CoS), Petra, and the Registrar, Melissa, joined me. We met-up in one of the terminals in Narita, Tokyo's International Airport. At our very first stop in Japan, I didn't know what to expect. The new ETPM, Martha, had just arrived at the site to replace Helen. Helen and her family were PCSing back to headquarters in a few months. I'd had an interesting discussion with Martha, who headed to Japan around the same time I PCSed to HI. She and I attended NCS' Pre-PCS Orientation Training together before leaving headquarters. I had no idea we would have such a terse conversation so soon. I was curious how she would respond to me visiting.

I disapproved her spend plan because she wanted to use over 50% of their annual allocation to attend an E&T conference in Atlanta, Georgia. Yes. She would fly from Japan to Atlanta. Attend a four-day conference. Take leave. Fly back to Japan. *Are you shitting me!* She PCSed to Japan right around the same time I moved to HI – less than 6 months. She straight up asked me if I disapproved their site's spend plan or did Judy? I told her I did. I didn't need to ask Judy. I knew she wouldn't approve any ETPM to attend this conference shortly after taking an E&T position for which you are allegedly already qualified and certified, to perform. She told me in previous years, their site determined when and how to use NCS' budget and not the RETD. She was under the impression the funds were for her professional development.

Over the phone, I slowly and clearly told her that ultimately, the decision was Judy's and that I'd gladly tee this up for the Commandant. There was silence on the phone. She said nothing. I said nothing, waiting on her decision. She finally said, "Okay. I'll let our CoS (in Japan) know. I'll just discuss it with her because she approved my spend plan."

Well, Martha was not there for our visit. She was TDY and on leave. She was, in fact, attending the instructor conference in Atlanta she wanted NCS to fund. I later learned this site had an additional training budget provided to them by their mission element at headquarters. Employees were, in fact, getting opportunities for training without the NCS' piddly money. I concluded, in previous years, Piper used NCS' gifted funds for the site's ETPM's, professional development without resistance. I had interrupted a pattern. Interesting.

At the end of the day and the agenda, we started packing-up to head back to lodging for the night. We had a full day ahead of us the next day. Piper asked Petra to remain behind in her office for minute. The rest of us walked out. They closed the door quickly. I didn't think anything of it. Piper had mentioned her impending PCS back to headquarters, so I thought it was "CoS to CoS" kinda thang — may be job shopping. I was just hoping she wasn't interested in working in the NCS.

Returning to post lodging at the end of the day, Petra quietly and unemotionally told me, "They are NOT too happy with you." They did not like having to ask for my approval on their spend plan. Piper claimed that I had not specified changes from NCS' budget guidance from previous fiscal years. She went on to say that I didn't host monthly enterprise meetings nor communicate "well" with the region, which was the primary means in which they received information from the RETD's office. I did not communicate with them frequently enough. They were unaware of NCS' budget cuts and expect the same amount. I shook my head. I couldn't believe what I was hearing. Perhaps Martha twisted reality with Piper.

I promised to share notes and dates of our VTCs with Petra when I returned to Hawaii. She seemed okay with waiting for our visits to conclude. I reminded Petra of the e-mail I sent introducing myself to the "Wolves in the Pacific"- a self-proclaimed name of the Site Chiefs. I explained our reduced budget and the need to prioritize requirements. I reinforced that they use NCS funds for their mission essential training needs. I hated having to explain myself like that. I knew Petra would inform Judy — she had to. I was prepared and unafraid. I knew Judy would support me after hearing the entire story — spend plan and all. *Okay...game on.*

While serving as her Exec, Judy taught me to keep every stinking e-mail I sent and received. I organized my e-mail folders just like hers — by quarter and FY, then In and Out. I maintained e-mail folders for the rest of my NSA career. The next day, I played it cool, respectful, yet still business. That evening, the site's leadership team invited us to join them at the Community Club's Monthly Right-Arm night. A Right-

Arm Night is a designated happy hour for managers to treat their subordinates with pub food and drinks. It's popular overseas.

We all attended and considered this event a good place to get some dinner. The Site's Chief, Mr. Christopher, attended along with about six or seven other site leaders and us. We had a long table. I was sure to sit some distance from Piper. An English-speaking waitress took our drink orders and gave us clearance to enjoy the buffet. It was cool.

Everyone was chatting it up. I was seated beside Mr. Christopher. So, I was coming up with small talk to not come off as awkward. I preferred just sitting there, enjoying my dinner and a Japanese beer. We ate, drank, and socialized for about an hour and a half or so. Folks were moving around a table, changing seats, talking about everything. When Mr. Christopher announced he was leaving, we all agreed it was time. We were heading to Tokyo early the next morning.

Mr. Christopher reached out for a handshake and casually said, "thanks for visiting." I returned a thank you. Mona and Petra were saying farewell to Piper and Helen. They were exchanging hugs. I headed toward them since I was sitting down the table a bit. I said good-bye. Exchanged typical "call me if you need anything" to Helen, the ETPM. I wished her well on her next assignment. It was a pleasant exchange.

I moved toward Piper, slowly. I waited until she stopped talking. It was now my turn to say goodbye to her. I said, "thank you for having us," and went in to hug her. Just as I went in, Piper quickly put her arm across her chest and gave me a stiff-arm. I stumble back, off guard. I was speechless. All I could muster was *"Okay,"* as she sarcastically with a smirk said, "Have a safe tripppp."

Our next stop was north of Tokyo. It was a quick over-nighter. There, I experienced my first Earthquake ever! After work, we returned to the hotel room on post to chill before heading out to dinner. I'm not sure what my co-workers did, but I took a nap. I was exhausted. I fell asleep within minutes.

I woke up to what I thought was someone banging on my door non-stop. It startled me. I yelled... "who is it?" I couldn't focus. I was still kind of out of it. The knocking didn't stop. I sat-up and as soon as I put my feet on the floor, no one was knocking on the door. I staggered to the living room and kitchenette. The cabinet doors were tapping and the front door shaking. I stood there, holding on to the kitchen counter while the shaking slowed down...to a trickle and then stopped. Oh Shit. That was an Earthquake.

Our colleague there told us when we went out to dinner that "small earthquakes" like those were the norm. What an experience. It was less than 2 years later (March 2011) that northern Japan suffered a major earthquake and subsequent tsunami known as the Great Sendai Earthquake – it was devastating.

After a day in Tokyo, we were on our way to Korea...my old stomping ground. I knew exactly where to find our NSA compadres. We stayed at the Dragon Inn, the same military resort hotel where I stayed in 2002. Life does bring you full circle sometimes. I couldn't believe it. I had a list of items to pick-up while shopping. I couldn't wait. Thank goodness it was early summer in Korea.

The site visit was uneventful. The ETPM was a retired Army Major- an officer, so we got each other. He knew I was a former 1SG. I was straightforward, no chaser. I knew his game as well. I was honest with him, and he knew it. If his requirements were valid, they would be submitted as unfunded requirements or UFRs. As the Pacific region, we'd had great success the previous FY with getting learning technology funded via UFRs.

Alaska and the Pacific Northwest

The next two RETD site visits took me to the Pacific Northwest in April 2011. Again, a senior person from headquarters; this time with my supportive co-worker, Tessa. I understood her role and her participation in site visits. It made sense as she was the Enterprise Liaison. She acted as the point of contract at headquarters to assist with unique "field challenges," especially when an enterprise site couldn't get traction with the NCS departments or colleges. I didn't mind her company at all. We were both introverts, highly organized, and way too hard on ourselves.

Alaska was beautiful. The snow-covered mountain and lakes in Anchorage are post-card worthy. During our off time there, we explored the area. After work, we took off to a ski resort for a lift ride to the top of a mountain for good view of Anchorage. It was gorgeous.

I saw my first brown bear and bald eagles up-close and personal; in captivity, of course.

Both Northwest site visits went well. Our constituents were pleased to see us. We left with multiple action items to help them navigate hurdles. They felt heard and appreciated by the RETD and our headquarters. The ETPM in the Pacific Northwest arranged an-after work visit to a winery. It was beautiful to see grapevines on hilly acres upon acres. The wine was okay, but we had the best chocolates I've ever had, made by local monks. I've had some good chocolates in Europe, but these dark, rich, bonbons, had me ordering them from Hawaii. *Hope they won't melt. Shit.*

In June 2011, I, along with the NCS' Partner Training Liaison, traveled to Canberra, Australia, with a follow-on site visit planned for New Zealand. To say I was bubbling with excitement to travel to two places on my bucket list, was an understatement. We spent three days with customers and partners in the Australian Security Intelligence Organization (ASIO) in the picturesque national capital of Australia, Canberra.

After work, the ETPM in Canberra acted as our tour guide. She provided an educational and thrilling tour that included seeing hundreds of kangaroos and their joeys. We got out of the car for close-up photos. There was an especially playful joey jumping in and out of its mother's pouch, sometimes headfirst, leaving his feet exposed above her perfect pouch.

While driving through this park, kangaroos dashed across the road in front of us. It was scary. The ETPM said they cause damage and even vehicle accidents like deer at home. It reminded me of having to look out for deer driving rural roads at night in VA. We shopped for art and selected boomerangs in Canberra for family and friends.

I also witnessed the indigenous people of Australia camped outside of the country's Capitol, in makeshift tents. They refused to occupy the indoor offices provided to them along with representation in the Australian government. Instead, they preferred to stay outside in rebellion of the government and their status as a people. Regardless of where I've travelled in the world, I've seen people who have been marginalized to the degree that they feel disenfranchised.

As a black woman, I empathized with them. Even though it was June, it was their winter. Their seasons are opposite of North and South America. They burned large drum barrels of something to keep warm and to cook meals. Our guide informed us that they are outside regardless of the weather. When asked, and they had been repeatedly, they refused to go inside and participate in a government they believed pilfered their land and way of life.

Regrettably, our travel plans to Christchurch, New Zealand were cancelled. All flights in and out of New Zealand were terminated due to the Eyjafjallajokull volcano eruption in Iceland. The ash from the eruption caused serious ash clouds which caused disruption to air travel to 20 countries. The airspace around New

Zealand was closed. We quickly made plans for our return home, praying Australia's airspace was not next.

When we learned New Zealand was out, we flew to Sydney for an overnight and a day to explore before leaving for Honolulu and Baltimore, respectively. In one day, we saw most of the city's sightseeing highlights via a tourist bus called, "Hop-On, Hop Off." We explored the Sydney Opera House, Bondi Beach, North Beach, Hyde Park, Chinatown, and we found a festive German restaurant for dinner. Yes, schnitzel and pomme frites in Sydney.

After returning to Hawaii, Judy came out to visit during a Regional Conference for all the Pacific Site Chiefs. She personally briefed them and entertained all their training inquiries. It was refreshing to hear Judy repeat everything I told them about curriculum strategies and a new individual requirement gathering process rolling out soon, all while 'singing my praises. I got the sense Judy was pleased with my job performance.

A New Year - Free to Love!

In January of 2009, I started dating a senior enlisted soldier in the Army, stationed at Schofield Barracks, there on the island of Oahu. For the first time in a long time, I felt free to love. Let's just call him SGM. SGM was infantry, a jump master (airborne), air assault, and a path finder; not to mention, Ranger qualified. I hadn't been around hardcore soldiers like SGM, since attending leadership training in Bad Tölz, Germany in 1987.

When I wasn't with my friend Mitzi on weekends, I was with SGM. Having arrived just a few months before me in 2008, we explored the Hawaiian Islands together – all of them. He loved golf. I was learning to play golf, so we played a *shit load.*

We played on five of the eight beautiful Hawaiian Islands courses. We played at the Marine's Kaneohe Klipper on Oahu right after President Obama and his entourage finished hitting the greens during one of his holiday visits to Oahu. We bumped in front of George Lopez playing at Manele Bay at the Four Seasons Resort on Lanai — the most beautiful golf course I've ever played. The ocean in the backdrop, cliffs, and black rock against the bluest water. George told us we could play through. He had three guys with him and didn't want to hold-up a two-some.

Not very long after I met SGM, he informed me his unit was scheduled to deploy to Iraq in June of that year. We were doing well with mutual interests, and he wanted to continue to communicate and get to know each other virtually. I agreed. He left for his deployment to Iraq while I was TDY in Japan. I wasn't in HI to say good-bye.

SGM and I used Skye then the way people use Zoom now. He e-mailed almost daily: poetry, love letters, songs, and notes. I mean, he "love bombed" like no other. I could set an alarm by his calls. He was attentive, and I wasn't interested in looking elsewhere. While he was away, I lost another 10 pounds or so and felt better than I'd felt physically in years. I was getting my "hot girl" beach body on!

This was the beginning of me waiting for SGM or traveling to see SGM. This became my life. He was as motivated and reliable as ever. I could feel the "so-called love" from afar. And he seemed too always be away. M finished his deployment to Iraq in June 2011. I beat him back to Oahu by about a week. It was great having him back. I had gotten used to life alone in Oahu. It was gorgeous — truly living in paradise. He seemed delighted to be back with me. We had a great visit. He was affectionate, kind, persistent, and was financially secure. Plus, he was a soldier. I understood and love soldiers!

Remember Carrie was selected prior to my arrival in HI. We began to have an arm-distance relationship. We barely spoke. Some mornings, she'd arrive and not say good morning. Some days, she sighed and blew air from her mouth all day because of tasks I had her do. In all fairness, she suffered numerous tragedies and bad breaks in three years, but that was no justification or excuse for some of her behavior.

I noticed Carrie giggling with male customers and being very snippy with women. This was later confirmed when a female employee told me how she avoided Carrie. They'd rather ask me questions about training. She was rude, condescending, and impatient with them. The one thing I knew for sure, she would work as hard as I was, and would be polite to ALL customers.

We had a lot going on. We were transitioning to a new learning management system to gather individual training requirements, across the entire region. She would help me roll that process out. It was her job. To complicate and add to our plates, Carrie and I had to temporarily relocate to historic Ford Island while NCPAC was being renovated. We packed-up a huge walk-in closet and a copier room full of supplies, holiday decorations, and copy paper. We sweated for days trying to neatly pack, destroy tons of old course materials and books, and pack our own desks and things for Ford Island.

It was one of those days that we were just humping and not communicating at all. When I finally said, "Good morning, Carrie, today we have to......" as I laid a document on her desk. She snatched it up and spun her chair around, showing me her back. I asked calmly and quietly, "Please don't turn your back while I'm talking to you. It's rude and disrespectful, Carrie." She spun around and said, "Ohh...kay," along with a sarcastic smile. Was I in a time warp or some shit? Why on earth did she think it was okay to behave that way? I shook my head and walked back around the partition to my desk.

Later that afternoon, I heard her talking on the phone to one of her friends at headquarters. She was snickering and laughing as if nothing happened that morning. I was still scratching my head, trying to figure out what was happening. What had I done to her? Then I heard her say, *Angry Black Bird (ABB)....*" Then, *"Like always. Angry for no apparent reason."* More laughing. Oh yes. I knew exactly who she was talking about on the other side of the partition.

I immediately walked out of the office down the hall to Security. I needed someone to talk me off the ledge. *Did she call someone — me — an ABB. Get out of here!* I talked to the Security Chief, Phoebe. She and I were friends. Soldiers. She was retired from the Reserves. And I trusted her. I told her what I heard. Phoebe calmed me down and reminded me that even if I heard what I thought I heard, Carrie would not admit to saying that. It would be my word against Carrie's. I had no proof she was talking about me. Phoebe was right. I was eavesdropping; she wasn't speaking to me. I realized if I complained, I would definitely look like a ABB. I knew it.

She slipped-up again months later, when she accidentally, pretending to be joking, referred to my lunch walking group with my friend the front office and Phoebe, as "Biddies," She asked, "Did you Biddies go for your lunchtime walk around Camp Smith today?" Biddies, really?

I had a huge challenging job corralling 10 or so, remote ETPMs, called the Pacific Cadre. I represented the NCS' Commandant and the NCPAC Site Chief, which required keen competence and sharp political savvy! This job would normally come with a team of 3-4. I had one unmotivated, and certainly not trustworthy, direct report!

An Opportunity to Lead in Hawaii

I got a call from Judy in late April or early May 2012. She asked if I was interested in extending in HI for another year or so. Before I could answer, she went on to say, Ken, the current Chief of Training at NSA-

HI, the larger site north of NCPAC, was selected to attend the Air Force's WAR College. Judy needed a quick fill in just a few months. Judy said I could think about it and call her Executive back with my decision. I didn't need to. I wasn't ready to go back to Ft. Meade or Maryland for that matter. The challenges there (work or personal or both?) were better from afar — out of sight, out of mind. I knew I could lead a training office at a Cryptologic Center, and this was my opportunity to prove it. I needed to if I wanted to get promoted to GG15. I told her yes, right away. I was willing to extend.

I asked when she needed me to replace Ken. She said, "I want you to start cross training with him now. Maybe spend a couple of days a week up there. Carrie can handle the NCPAC office." She told me she would call Mr. Blake and share the plan. She expressed discontent with Ken for not informing her that he applied. It was after his selection that she became aware. This really ticked her off! Ken and the previous Director of Training were curtailed for shorter assignments in Hawaii than expected.

My NCPAC assignment in HI was coming to an end in August, and honestly, if I could leave earlier, I was game. SGM had another year on-island. We had moved in together when he returned from Iraq. I felt like he wanted to ask me to marry him. He inquired and hinted and asked if I was ready whenever we heard the Alicia Keys song with the same title. *Shit. Was I?* What I learned was all the pre-proposals were to ensure he would not be rejected. The last thing he wanted/needed was rejection.

As part of this transition, Judy tasked me along with Petra, NCS' CoS, to develop and implement the Asia-Pacific Education & Training Regionalization Strategy. This strategy needed to 1) align scarce resources aka reduce billet 2) maximize customer service and 3) increase course offerings in the region. It sounded almost impossible! I acknowledged. I knew where this was heading. Judy asked me a few months after I took over as the RETD if I thought a GG-15 and GG-11 were needed at NCPAC. She had her eyes on billets and a strategy that saved resources.

The next day, Judy called and spoke with Mr. Griswold, the Deputy Chief of NCPAC. He walked down to the training office and confirmed the new plan for my extension in his usual emotionless way. Not a thank you. I wish you well. Nada! He was matter of fact, chewing on a bag of baby carrots, which he did often, walking down the single hallway at NCPAC, farting. Amazing how different people are raised. On a golf outing, he told us he attended UMBC for undergrad – no way, I thought.

Petra took care of the coordination with HR, NSA-HI, and NCPAC for my extension. A Staff Processing Form (SPF) needed to coordinate the direct nomination — typical government paperwork. HR approved the reassignment, the extension, and changed my rotation date in the system. I assumed HR would also update my NAREA or COLA Tier or status in the system. I could not.

If I had wanted to extend at NCPAC, I couldn't. Mr. Blake declared shortly after he arrived in HI that he would not approve extensions for anyone unless it was mission essential, and no one in his opinion was mission essential. Mr. Blake claimed to be following DIRNSA's guidance to rotate employees in and out of the field/enterprise assignments. "Field Rats" needed to return to the headquarters.

I quickly packed-up my belongings for my impending move to NSA-HI. I reported in mid-June 2011. NSA-HI's CoS, who we will call Donita, and the training team, welcomed me excitedly, especially the military and contractors who had worked with Carrie and I to offer course seats to NCPAC employees. They knew us well and appreciated our work ethic at NCPAC. If they needed people to fill seats, we would shake the bushes. We were able to enroll non-agency personnel from Pacific Command (PACOM), who possessed a Top-Secret security clearance and desperately needed NCS training.

Carrie remained at NCPAC to provide support from there until her rotation of September 2011. I was relieved to get away from her and the leadership team there, who had truly little use for NCS training. I felt so unappreciated and invisible. Not to mention, this was the space I needed from Carrie. It had gotten to a point where we would go all week without talking about anything except for work.

I grabbed my box on a Friday to report to the NSA-HI, or the tunnel as it's called, on Monday. I returned to NCPAC just twice thereafter. Once, I returned to dispute my rating for my Annual Employee Evaluation (AEE). Mr. Griswold was my reviewer since Marissa was my rater. I had to appeal to him and plead my case (prove) as to why I disagreed with my direct supervisor's rating of # on a 5-point scale. My Rater didn't seem to mind my non-concurrence at all – she encouraged it. I returned with documented accomplishments that Carrie and I achieved, along with performance review sessions that indicated a preliminary rating of 4s on all objectives from Marissa.

After talking through my accomplishments and showing him summaries of performance reviews, to do lists, and positive customer feedback, he changed my scores to reflect what I earned - over 4.0.

It was the right thing to do. I had every intention of filing an official dispute had he not changed it. He was clueless as to what we had accomplished. Mr. Griswold's main concern was normalizing ratings to get a desirable/clear cut line, based on who he and the Chief believed should get a bonus. With this new, higher score, and for the first in my three years there, I would finally get one.

Mr. Griswold wrote on the top of a copy of my AEE, "Gag Order." I asked him why? He clearly wanted me to see his scribbled note. He looked directly at me and asked if the Commandant had asked me to not reveal the plan to move both training billets to NSA-HI. He wasn't aware of the Regionalization plan — I didn't believe it was my place to inform him. I'm not sure why he didn't express his concern with Judy when they spoke on the phone. I told him no. She never asked me to hide anything. But clearly there was no need for a GG-15 position at NCPAC and one at NSA-HI, as I outlined in my RETD Regionalization strategy. A gag order? Was he serious?

I understood his concern — removing billets or personnel is threatening to leaders' power base and status as a Chief, but I assured him there was no gag order. However, the fact that he believed Judy had convinced/manipulated me into "a gag order" was insane and spoke volumes about his thoughts about me. We're talking the Department of Defense employees and a gag order...really?

Chapter 13

Too Little, Too Late!

The wisest of people in this world are those that admit when they are wrong.

- *Unknown*

Chief of Training, NSA-Hawaii (NSA-HI) (June 2011 to May 2012)

NSA contractor, Edward Snowden, became a household name in 2013 after he gave classified documents to the Guardian, the Washington Post, and other publications. The public probably learned more than they cared to about NSA and its facility in Hawaii - which again is one of four regional centers spread across the United States. I left the facility on/about 01 June 2013, before the Director christened Edward Snowden and his name as, "he who shall not be named."

I'm certain I passed Edward a few times in the almost mile-long tunnel walk, once you enter NSA-HI's facility. Or I passed him in a hallway of one of the three floors built below a pineapple field adjacent to Schofield Barracks. I rarely forget a face whether that of an NSA contractor, civilian, service member, or otherwise. I suppose I have NCS training in facial recognition to thank.

I find Edward Snowden's circumstances and case intriguing. On the one hand, I understand concerns regarding civil liberties. As a black woman, I can't help

266

but empathize with anyone who feels their rights as a citizen are violated. On the other hand, as a member of the IC, the significance of Snowden's brazen betrayal and departure was shocking among NSA employees; contractors included. There's an understanding that we're to keep our opinions internally. This is reinforced by a signed agreement/contract that holds employees criminally liable for revealing and sharing secrets, especially to the world.

As Judy's direct nomination to the Chief of Training position, I by-passed the usual application, interview, and selection process. As the new leader of the E&T organization, I led a staff of over 90 military, civilians, contractors, and multi-cultural language instructor. I managed all the E&T programs and oversaw the delivery of a wide range of NCS courses all in support of NSA-HI and the region's cryptologic and cyber security missions.

Divide and Conquer

Shortly after I arrived, I met with the entire team — the Training Department's civilians, military, and contractors. I wanted to address the blaring questions in their minds like, "why her?" and reduce uncertainties. I told the staff about my education, training background, and experience, and my leadership philosophy to include my time in uniform since there were a sizable number of military members in the department, I knew they'd get it.

I needed to share my credentials and establish credibility right away. I expected there would be the usual skepticism and resistance because I'm black, a woman, and this group had changed leaders twice in the past two years. I would win them over with my hard work, honesty, and professionalism, like I'd done many times before.

I also wanted the team to understand my goals and intentions for the Department, which included increased customer service and focus, increased satisfaction rate(s) of training requirements, delivery of the new computer network courses, and specifying adequate requirements for the tunnel's renovation project (space, technology, and furniture); the department, like NCPAC was moving to new spaces in the tunnel.

When I moved to NSA-HI, they were right in the middle of a huge tunnel renovation effort. I couldn't seem to get away from building/floor renovations. I talked swim lanes to clarify expectations. The Deputy who now worked for me, with little NCS or training experience, would focus on the tunnel renovation, logistics and space — divide and conquer. I would work everything NCS — training, instructor/adjuncts, students, curricula, and dealing with site's leadership.

I relaxed. I talked about my military background, my daughters, and my impending nuptials. I promised that even though I was "temporary," I'd work hard to enable them to succeed. By the end of the short 30-minute gathering, I saw smiles. There were more questions. Some wanted to talk to me one-on-one. I could feel them – they exhaled and relaxed with me.

Over the years and especially as an NCO in the Army, I learned setting aside time as a new leader to speak with my team(s) has been huge in managing expectations, articulating vision and focus areas, while allowing them to get to know me a bit. After I talked through about 4 planned PowerPoint slides, I sat on a tabletop in the front of the group to answer their questions.

A few days later, I met with the CoS for NSA-HI, Donita, shortly after I started at the tunnel. She was a beautiful, tall, model-looking, black woman. I remembered her from her brief visit to NCPAC. She played basketball in college and had served in the Air Force. We had much in common.

Donita was respectful, kind, and strangely calm. She created a totally different atmosphere than that of NCPAC. I felt welcomed and wanted. She told me she would be my first-line supervisor — made sense, I worked for Marissa, the CoS at NCPAC.

Donita's leadership style was to allow her Chiefs (Training, HR, Security, and Logistics) under her purview to do their jobs, and she merely reported-up. That simple. Any questions, she called for clarification or asked us to send her an e-mail with details. Our achievements were hers and ours, of course. If there were projects or tasks to be completed, she was the point of contact person, and we were her "go to team!" I was impressed. I admired any leader who was able to stay out of the trenches with their employees. Well, not completely but, she was a masterful tasker.

Donita and I got each other. I was doing my thing upstairs in training, and she didn't have to worry about it. Again, I only had 11-12 months on the job. I was either going to set the next Chief of Training up for success, or I could sit back and not get my hands dirty. Between work, life, and personal events, I worked my ass-off. Literally.

Weekly staff meetings and my one-on-ones with Donita indicated I was focused on the right things. We were putting up numbers — satisfying training requirements and delivering new Cyber courses. We were leading the enterprise in getting this training to site and setting-up teams. I could sense Judy was pleased as well. Whatever we asked for, both Judy and Donita were supportive.

Just as I was settling-in, Petra, NCS' CoS, sent me an e-mail and asked, "How are you coming along with Pacific Regionalization Strategy?" *What? How am I coming along?* (Inside Voice) My response, "Working on it now. Will send a draft via email to you for your review, first?" I created a groundbreaking plan that was eventually approved by each of the site Chiefs in the Pacific region, complete with a signed Staff Processing Form (SPF).

The Chosen One

The plan resulted in four NCS hubs in the region, reallocating billets to locations with larger populations for employees, which in turn resulted in increased course completions. The strategy was implemented by my successor after I departed, however, billets were reallocated prior. I was told this enormous and risky undertaking was "a testament of Judy's level of trust" in me. Was It? Really?

I felt like I could do no wrong. As gramma would say, "I was smelling myself." My instincts, or common-sense approach to leading NSA-HI Training department, were spot-on. The organization and I were receiving almost weekly accolades from Donita and our mission customers. We were consistently advancing the NCS' goals and the NSA-HI command's priorities as well; akin to serving two competing masters—NCS and your local site leaders.

NSA-HI's Training Department didn't use resource constraints as an excuse. We explored options like delivering courses on the unpopular swings/evening shift. We funded travel for instructors to come to Hawaii to teach high-priority cyber courses. At this point, contracted instructors delivered cyber courses — military and government instructors were not yet trained. We set up the first cyber labs in the enterprise, which were used as test beds for the rest of the NCS satellite schools.

Donita was pleased. It was obvious. She enjoyed spending time with us — for luncheons, holiday celebrations, and of course, visits to see our language instructors off-site. They were the real heroes of the group. Their accomplishments helped the site win a prestigious annual mission award.

Donita enjoyed the attention she got from the Training staff. We/I treated her special and with respect; rightly so. We invited her to our events, like hail and farewell, annual BBQs, and award presentations. I made sure I announced her as the Chief of Staff; she deserved it. She earned it. She beamed with pride about the newly revised Site Orientation, complete with a NATGEO video about NSA and a site tour.

Donita bragged to the Site Commander, a Navy Captain, when we designated an entire day to recognize and say thank you to NSA-HI's Adjunct Faculty members. The event was held in mission spaces, so it was well attended. Besides, we offered them free lunch.

As the Chief of Training, I opened the Adjunct event, sharing comments about my experience as an Adjunct Instructor while in the Army. I attested to the sacrifice it was to prepare yourself to give your best when teaching — particularly on weekends because your course starts at 0800 Monday morning. It's a commitment and a sacrifice that not everyone is willing to make. Being an Adjunct does not relieve you of your normal job or duties.

I shared with fellow adjuncts, that as an introvert, teaching required a lot of personal energy to engage students all day in the classroom. However, I taught because I believed our NCS courses were critical to develop the skills of our workforce. So important, that I was willing, as an introvert instructor, to be uncomfortable. I saw Donita out of the corner of my eye. Smiling. Head nodding. She was proud as Shit.

Just shy of 3 months in position, Donita told me the Chief of HR, Lillie, would now be my first-line supervisor and my rater. This was incredibly odd to have HR supervise the Chief of Training. I had never worked for HR before, and I didn't believe any other E&T assets worked for HR. As usual, I said little — saluted and executed. At this point, I wasn't worried. I was cooking with Crisco. My AEE would take care of itself. I believe I had only one face-to-face, performance review with HR before Lillie went on extended sick leave; she was out at least six to eight weeks. Her absence coincided with the stressful period of the annual promotion cycle. Lillie returned the day after I missed the deadline to submit a promotion packet. A day I'll always remember.

A Death/A Birth/A Wedding

At home, SGM moved in with me when he returned from Iraq. I had moved to beautiful Ko'Olina Resort, in a 3-bedroom condo with a view of the ocean. No shit, it was spectacular! The community had a golf course where the LPGA played the Lotte Championship annually, three-manmade lagoons, a couple of restaurants, a Hawaiian ABC store, and the new Disney property Aulani.

We were adjusting to living together well. He was very affectionate and helpful with everything. He cooked, cleaned, and did his share of couch surfing. We were both counting the months and weeks before we did the "unthinkable." Unthinkable was right, especially at our age, I thought.

I was planning our beach wedding in Maui. It would be beautiful. We decided to do it without invited guests. Traveling and lodging in Maui can be expensive, especially for our children and parents. I was cool with that. We weren't spring chickens. I didn't need an audience. My feelings were real, mature, goal-based, and wasn't because I felt desperate or didn't have other offers. I legitimately thought we were both mature and in love. I knew I was. I had matured. I forgave and overlooked things, imperfections, the absence of his close family members, and his need for constant gratitude.

Farewell Uncle Teensy

I was at work one early December morning, going through the 100s of e-mails I'd get daily. My work phone would ring. It was my uncle's daughter, Lynzee. She never called me at work. Considering the time difference between Hawaii and the east coast, something was wrong. Uncle Teensy had a heart attack at his home and died. Just like that. Just...like...that. I was floored. *What?* I could not breathe. *What?*

After having one of his legs amputated, he'd recovered at the VA hospital in Atlanta and had finally moved to his dream retirement location — Tampa, FL. He was healing well and awaiting his prosthetic leg from the Tampa VA hospital. He hadn't been in Fl six months before he passed away suddenly. I was heartbroken. I felt sick to my stomach.

I closed my office door and sent an e-mail to my department leads and the SEL, advising them that I was rescheduling our morning meeting to the next day. I couldn't talk without choking on every word that came up and out. I couldn't leave work to just ball and sulk in my grief. My deputy, Elvin, was out that day on sick leave. I walked out the mile-long tunnel to my car, trying to hold it together. I had to call my mother and tell her that her youngest brother, and last remaining sibling, was dead. Later that day, when I got home, SGM held me all evening and night. I could not believe that my uncle – my brother. He was doing so well in FL. He seemed happy. Now he's gone. *Keep it together!*

With the date of my uncle's service up in the air, I couldn't go home. I was getting married in less than 2 weeks in Maui; his funeral arrangements had not been made at that point, and Shara's baby was due in 3 weeks, early January. I knew Uncle Teensy would understand. He was happy for me. He wanted to "meet the joker," he said, when we came back to the mainland. I kept hearing my Uncle Teensy tell me, "It's okay, Skinny." He wasn't much for a funeral anyway. Oh, how I wish he'd met SGM. Damn.

The Wedding

Time flew-by. Before I knew it, I was hand carrying my beautiful wedding gown, selected by me and my closest and dear work friend in HI, onto Hawaiian Airlines for the short hop over to Maui. I was nervous, yet happy. I was getting married, again. As the saying goes, "Never say never, right?" The day before the wedding, SGM and I went whale watching. It was that time of year when pods of Humpback Whales migrate to the warm Hawaiian waters to mate. They thrashed and splashed showing their male prowess.

After whale watching, we headed to the spa for a tranquil couple's massage. When my phone rang, we were getting dressed in warm robes in the locker room. It was Shara and Linda. Linda was at Ft. Bragg with Shara. We had already planned that we would tag team. I was scheduled to be there in about a week for the delivery. Well, Shara was in labor. She wasn't due until the 7th of January or so. In typical Noah fashion, he came early; he was ready. Before we got back to hotel room from the spa, she had delivered Noah, without complications. *Thank you, GOD,*

On December 31, 2012, I stepped out of a white limousine onto Secret Beach. I felt like the most beautiful woman in the world. Besides the wedding planner, photographer, harpist, and Hawaiian Minister, there was a couple in lawn chairs, just watching weddings and sipping wine. Everyone looked at us as SGM led me down a steep step to the sand. A gasp was audible – the smiles. Another couple was finishing up photos on the large black rocks off to the left side of the beach. My heart fluttered. He held my hand as we walked across the sand. I was shaking. I was getting married.

The wedding was beautiful. His vows. The black rocks. The sand. My vows. The sunset. The crystal blue ocean was picture perfect. The butterflies. The harp. Our Hawaiian minister exhibited his caring manners and prayers. My heart fluttered again walking to the rocks to the left to take the last of our photographs before heading to Mama's Fish House in Paia.

We'd been to Mama's before. The first time there, we were just dating. We saw a wedding couple there having dinner with guests, apparently after their own wedding. We loved Mama's ambience and their food. So, we made it a point to go back for our wedding night dinner with our own limo. Just the two of us. It was very romantic and the crusted, macadamia nut Mahi Mahi was on point.

Since it was New Year's Eve, the fireworks and parties were jumping on Maui. When we got back to the hotel, we changed clothes and went out by the pool to watch fireworks all over the island. Low-and-behold, Aerosmith was the guest band for the hotel's NYE party, complete with lead singer Steven Tyler. We got the best, free, wedding concert ever. They played inside the hotel while a group of us jammed by the pool. *Walk This Way! Talk this Way!*

"The Missed Promotion"

Just back from getting married and welcoming my first grandson, January was a blur. Elvin and I conducted our weekly staff meetings with Donita, our department Chiefs, and with the NCS leadership via Video-Teleconference. At more than one weekly meeting with our civilian staff, we discussed the 2012 Promotion Cycle and Timeline. I asked who would be submitting packets, and of their subordinates, who intended to do so. I knew I would be asked, and I needed to gauge my own level of effort and time.

Three of us were GG-14s and eligible for GG-15 — Mick, the retired Marine from our cohort at headquarters and now Chief of Cryptologic training at NSA-HI; Elvin, my deputy; and me. Mick expressed his discontent with the whole process. He had no intentions of ever submitting a promotion packet. Interesting. Elvin and I said we would. At this point, I believed, and convinced Elvin, that the date for submission for us (GG-14 to GG-15), was later than lower grades. Besides, per the promotion process, he would need to submit it to me, and I would forward without prejudice, because we were the same grade.

Again, in my mind, the e-mail sent to the workforce from the Acting HR lead, Oliver, specified two deadlines. Now remember, Lillie was on sick leave. One deadline specified for "GG-14 and below," and another for "GG-14s submitting packets for GG-15." In my mind, I saw that as separate and distinct. All I kept telling myself was the process for promotion to GG-15 is different than the lower grades. I remember a colleague emphasizing that when she was promoted to GG-15 at headquarters. It stuck in my head. It's different. Different due dates. I believed that. So, when I missed the deadline for submission, so did Elvin. Shiiiiit!

It was early February 2012. My sister-cousin Avon was in Los Angles visiting her daughter Claire. During a one-on-one with Donita, I asked if I could take a long weekend. I wanted Friday and Monday off to see my sister in Los Angeles. She said, "Of course." It was approved. We didn't discuss the upcoming promotion deadlines, which would occur on that Monday when I was on leave. SGM tagged along. We had a great time exploring Hollywood with them. I would return to work Tuesday morning. Again, the deadline for submissions was Monday by (NLT) 2000hrs

I always got to work before Elvin. When Elvin walked in the office that Tuesday morning, the first thing he said was, "We missed the deadline to submit our promotion packets." I asked him what he meant. He said, "The deadline was yesterday, wasn't it?" I tried to quickly find the e-mail from HR buried in a shit load of e-mails I needed to go through.

What's that child's name down in HR? Oliver! Oliver sent the e-mails. He was the Acting HR while Lillie was out. Found it. I read it again. Shit! Out loud. *Shit Shit Shit!* I picked up the phone and called Oliver. He confirmed the deadline for "ALL packets WAS due last night by 2000hrs," using his usual, slow, sassy, voice.

I left the office. I jogged down one flight of stairs to Donita's office. She had someone in with her. I stood by her door indicating that I could wait. I needed to wait. When they left, she walked toward me. She was shaking her head. I started to explain. *"I misinterpreted the e-mail. The damn e-mail, and I don't know why the deadline NEVER came up in any conversations we had. I thought packets to 15 was the later date."*

Donita said, "I thought you knew." I said, "No. I went on leave. I would never have gone on leave." She told me the acting HR lead had called headquarters. Donita asked why I hadn't called her first. She looked disappointed and sad. I was holding back tears. I felt so incompetent. How could I? Why didn't I ask a single soul? Donita told me she would confer with her boss, the Deputy Commander of the site — the civilian position, one down from the Commander. He was, in essence, the site's senior NSA, civilian promotion authority.

I tucked my tail, went back upstairs, and feverishly reviewed, edited, and put my promotion packet together. It was ready by 1700hrs when I made the last copy and closed the file folder to hand to Donita. I had been waiting for her call all day. She didn't call.

Elvin worked on his too. He gave me his packet before he left for the day. I quickly checked the box to forward to the next level, which I assumed was the Chief of HR, Lillie. *Was she back from sick leave?* By 2000hrs, both of our packets were stacked and ready. I went home. I prayed all day that Donita would be allowed to accept our packets or possibly grant an extension because I was on leave and so was my rater. It also crossed my mind that everyone at site could be given another 24 hours, to make it fair for all.

I left work. I prayed all night. Every time I woke up, and I woke up a lot, I prayed. The next morning, Donita walked in my office and closed the door. Elvin had not arrived yet. She spoke with the Deputy Commander — she said he supported "whatever she wanted to do." Then, she said, but the acting HR lead had called HR at headquarters to weigh-in, based on my call to him. HR at headquarters, advised him to enforce the deadline and not allow managers to accept any packets passed the due date in the email.

Of course, one would say promotions are not guaranteed nor promised. No, they are not. I get that.

But what if a promotion is implied? So, why did I believe I missed getting promoted to GG-15 that year? First and most importantly, others and I knew I deserved a promotion. I sensed, if I submitted a packet, both Judy and Donita would support it in merit and with funds. I had proven my worth. I had taken heat rounds from the Wolves in the Pacific for Judy. I overcame resistance from disgruntled colleagues. And since the most recent Performance Evaluation is used in the promotion packet, I had to meet with Mr. Griswold, Deputy Chief of NCPAC, for a fair evaluation that reflected what Carrie, the CSR, and I had accomplished.

Donita initially thought I was, a GG15 – she flat out asked me. She said NSA-TX was looking for a new CoS, and since I was heading there, she thought I would be perfect for the job. She said I came to mind when some colleagues were discussing the opening. Once I told her I was a GG-14, she asked if I planned to submit a packet for promotion. I told her emphatically, yes! I had every intention of submitting a packet. Donita said something quick like, "you better," and we got off the phone.

We never discussed dates or how to submit. Just that I would submit a packet was the conversation. I knew I was ready. I knew the time was right. Promotions to grade 15 are rare and even rarer in the field, especially with people in support roles. Like the Army, the higher the promotion, the lower the percentage of employees at that level, creating a pyramid of grades from the lower level, mid-level to GG-15s and Seniors at the peak. I was in a leadership position, managing a large department and solving difficult problems. I knew the 'stars were aligned' in my favor.

I knew from conversations and the hints from both Donita and Judy regarding cost-sharing promotions, I was highly supported by the two people I needed to confirm my worthiness. I had earned it. It had been a long time since I was only responsible for my job, and not two or three overlapping positions. Judy was clear, if enterprise sites were asking to help in funding NCS position promotion, to contact NCS as early as possible. I had high expectations.

Donita said she called NCS and spoke with Judy. She told her what happened and asked Judy if my packet could go directly to NCS and its board at headquarters. Of course, that was not permissible. I was assigned to NSA-HI. She felt terrible.

When Lillie, my now HR supervisor arrived at my office that afternoon. I hadn't spoken with her about any of this. I was quite surprised when she walked in my office and closed the door. Lillie was empathetic. She tried to reassure me that I would still be highly competitive next year when I arrived at NSA-TX.

She felt sure that the Chief of Training at NSA-TX, would recognize my blunder as a person who worked hard for others and didn't take care of herself. Lillie was sure of it. I would have an advocate and a highly persuasive manager at there. I asked if she could take Elvin's packet since it went to me first. It was 48 hours after the deadline. She said she couldn't. I felt worse now, not just for me but for Elvin, and I knew what this meant for the both of us.

I told her it wouldn't be that easy since I would be relocating. I believed and still do, that promotions and opportunities are a bit more complicated for a black person and there's data to support this claim. I knew I would have an uphill battle, yet again, to prove my worth to a whole new group of people who didn't know me. My previous accomplishments would not be enough. NSA-TX would likely have a Janet Jackson "What Have You Done for Me Lately," attitude.

Additionally, I wouldn't be in a leadership position. I wouldn't be on a billet/authorized position as a spousal accommodation or a Married Agency Employee (MAE), at all. SGM was on orders for Ft. Hood. NSA-TX, 160 miles away, was the closest I could be assigned as an agency employee, to Ft Hood – ergo the accommodation. Of course, I was right. *The sun doesn't shine on the same dog's ass always.*

On my way home that day, I called Linda and told her the entire story. She got it. I thought *my shit didn't* stink. The chosen "one." She knew I was beating myself up. I couldn't help it. It was completely my fault. I accepted full responsibility, and I still do. I didn't go to work the next day. I couldn't. I needed a mental health day. I felt inept as a leader. I couldn't believe it. I felt so sure about this promotion. I felt all I had to do was submit a packet. I was embarrassed. This mistake shamed and humbled me.

Chapter 14

The Last Hoorah...Texas Bound.

Compartmentalizing is used to avoid mental discomfort and anxiety caused by a person's having conflicting values, emotions, and beliefs.

Psychology Today

NSA in Texas (NSA-TX) (2013-2017)

SGM and I arrived in San Antonio, TX after a short stop and tour of the AT&T Stadium, home of the Dallas Cowboys in Arlington, TX – not that I'm a Cowboys' fan but their stadium is impressive. As the stadium with the highest seat capacity in the NFL and a mechanical marvel with its retractable roof, it was worth the tour.

After picking-up SGM's car, shipped months earlier to Dallas, we headed south on I-35. On our way south, we stopped in Killeen to get SGM's boxes from my friend Stacey. Yes, the same one. Stacey retired from the Army at Ft. Hood and stayed in Killeen, TX; she loves it there. She lent a hand, like she had so many times before.

She was shocked to hear I got married again. I could hear it in her voice over the phone. She knew Michael from Worms and had met Linda in Maryland during a visit. Since SGM would be stationed at Ft. Hood, he asked, via me, if he could ship a few boxes to her home to keep until he arrived. Of course, she obliged.

Stacey surprised us with dinner, and it was delicious. I missed her country cooking. We had baked rosemary chicken, rice, turnip greens, with fried corn bread (as in fried in a cast iron skillet), on top of the stove. She sent us on our way fat and happy. Luckily, we were only about an hour and half away from our temporary lodging.

We stayed in an Extended Stay hotel for a couple of months. It took us way too long to decide where to live in San Antonio – typical for SGM. He often suffered from what I call, analysis paralysis. Initially, we were going to rent an apartment. Then, I introduced the idea of buying. If we stayed in San Antonio for at least three years, and the market remained unchanged, we'd make a sizeable profit from purchasing and then selling. That's all SGM needed to hear – make money with little effort. He was all in.

SGM was primarily concerned about where he would stay in Killeen. The plan was for him to spend the work week in Killeen and weekends in San Antonio with me in our new, 4-bedroom home in Stone Oak, 20 minutes or so, north of downtown San Antonio. He found a cheap studio that suited him and his needs. It started out with him driving every weekend, then to me offering to alternate the drive which he declined, to me not seeing my husband for 2 or 3 weeks. He came up with a written schedule of when we could "visit." We would see each other on long weekends, holidays, and planned vacations.

Once settled at home, my new work assignment began to shape-up. I looked forward to finally observing, and working for NCS-TX's Chief of Training, Dr. Casey, affectionately known as Dr. C. I was familiar with Dr. C. I'd met her in person at one of NCS' Annual Enterprise conferences, at headquarters.

She introduced herself with a smile. I was preparing for my PCS to HI. She was kind, welcoming, and encouraging about the position. Throughout my time at NCPAC and NSA-HI, Dr. C was helpful and accommodating. She and her TX team had a reputation for getting things done and keeping data to prove the ROI. They were good at statistics. I loved it.

At the conference, she offered me suggestions on places to live in Oahu and told me if I had any questions about my job, the RETD position and its history, or Oahu, to call or email her. She'd previously held the RETD-Pacific role. But much had changed, she admitted, since she left. Wow! Impressive. I would learn she really was encouraging, motivating, supportive, yet she empowered her subordinates to lead; without her taking credit. I started observing Dr. C's every move and her leadership style, on Day 1 at NSA-TX.

With Judy's endorsement, NSA-TX made an "accommodation" for me without having an open billet in NCS-TX, since San Antonio was the closest to SGM's assignment at Ft. Hood. I became the Curriculum Manager (CM) for the high-demand Analytical Skills (ANSK) curriculum at NSA-TX; several of the courses were operational/mission mandated. From an organization perspective, this was a good job and one NCS-TX greatly needed help with, yet it was three levels down from my position in Hawaii.

Married Agency Employee (MAE)

As a MAE, I freed-up my new supervisor Theodore, aka Theo, a fellow GG-14, to lead our team in the delivery of all cryptologic and cyber courses. Expectations were clear. I was to complete multiple Analysis Skills (ANSK) courses, get certified to teach high priority ANSK courses, recruit, and certify a cadre of additional ANSK adjunct instructors, while managing the curriculum, with a contracted Learning Facilitator. Say less! I went to work. As an MAE, I filled a 'need' vice a real position. There are very few leadership positions available to MAEs.

Trouble from Paradise

Remember the new program in Hawaii that reduced COLA? Well, shortly after I started working at NSA-TX, HR notified me that I needed to meet with them and the Finance/Payroll office back at headquarters. I was summoned over to local HR for a VTC. Once connected, Finance/Payroll informed me that while in HI, I had been overpaid in error, COLA or Nonforeign Area Cost-of-Living Allowance (NAREA), it wasn't clear which, to the tune of almost $7K. I needed to pay the agency/government back. What? I was surprised this was what the VTC was about. I didn't have a clue.

Apparently, I wasn't the only employee in this situation; the agency was notifying all of us. A friend and agency employee at NCPAC informed me that the same thing happened with her; she paid it back without question. Come to find out, there were around 10 agency employees in both HI and Alaska, who were overpaid through no fault of their own, and now the agency was trying to collect.

I was advised I could repay over months any amount that was comfortable for me. Or I had the option to submit a rebuttal or request, which other employees had decided to do, on the grounds that there no way employees/I could have known they were over paid, and the error occurred due to no fault of employees.

First, the decision would be decided by and agency authority. NSA-TX HR Rep's and a HR Rep at headquarters (actual employee that briefed us at NCPAC), seemed to believe if Finance/Payroll made this mistake, then they should be liable to correct it. They supported me submitting the request to eliminate repayment. So, I did. I was indifferent, really. I felt and sensed that the agency was doing a CYA and its 10 or so employees were to blame.

I drafted a compelling argument as to why employees could not identify overpayment of COLA or NAREA. I sent copies of my Leave and Earnings Statements. None of which showed a consistent amount for entitlements, nor did it specify what financial Tier I was on, or what Tier I amount in entitlements was supposed to be. Hell, I didn't know. The agency's mistake drugged on for about 6 months without a word.   felt like my rebuttal had a fair chance. If not, I would allow them to take it back.

The agency's "authority" or decision maker in this case, finally sent everyone an e-mail that said, "...you were aware. You were advised by the Commander of AMOC (Alaska) along with HR on a certain date, in AK, to expect a reduction in COLA." *What?* I wasn't stationed in Alaska. I don't know the Commander of AMOC. What?

The response looked like a "canned letter" used for several employees at AMOC. It looked and sounded like an admission that finance messed-up, but you pay. I sent my second rebuttal. *What da hell?* I was in it to win it, at this point. The next letter of rebuttal was supposed to go somewhere in Washington, DC; I imagine an element in the Office of Personnel Management/OPM. I waited patiently. I wasn't going anywhere. The agency knew where to find me.

Exceeding Expectations in Texas

While going through the certification process for a 40-hour ANSK course, I created reusable lesson plans for aspirant Adjuncts like me. I needed a basic script, so did other instructors. I revamped the course syllabus to put foundational knowledge up-front in the schedule, allowing practical application, exercises, and the capstone, later in the week. I recruited students with potential to get certified to teach this course. My goal was to identify at least two standout students. Boy, how that would make their chest swell.

I organized the course materials with a "grab and go" folder and binder, both softcopies (electronic) and hardcopies (paper) for our Adjunct instructors who worked in mission. I taught a portion of almost every offering. If I wasn't teaching, I was in the back of the classroom, taking copious notes to share actionable feedback with new instructors.

As the CM, I knew I needed to create repeatable processes to advertise, solicit instructors, prepare them for delivery, and to make my job easier and predictable. In FY14, I satisfied over 450 mission requirements, meaning 450 students completed the courses I managed. Theo asked me to share my successful approach to course management with other CMs in our department during our tradecraft development sessions.

I was then asked to act as Program Manager (PM) for the IC driven, Instructor Quality Program or IQP. This Under Secretary of Defense for Intelligence (USDI) mandate, required instructors to be observed by trained observers annually to ensure quality instruction and instructions. I kicked off the IQP without a hitch. Instructor observations were quickly and easily scheduled, and feedback sessions provided to all our instructors.

The first full quarter in San Antonio, I was chosen as NSA-TX's Civilian Enabler of the Quarter (4th Qtr./FY13)– *a rare recognition for our E&T team.* This award was for quickly assuming the critical Course Manager (CM) role during a surge of high priority requirements. My efforts enabled the site to achieve its goal of providing critical thinking skills to 100% of its new analysts.

Beginning of 2014, after nine months at NSA-TX, the promotion cycle was rolling around again. My first packet submission at NSA-TX was submitted well before the suspense date to my same-grade supervisor. Theo quickly forwarded it to my Reviewer, or next level, the Deputy, NCS-TX. I didn't hear anything. It was now late March or early April. I asked him if he received feedback on my packet. Theo hemmed and hawed until he finally suggested we meet with Deputy Chief of Training, Raymond my reviewer.

Raymond, Theo, and I went into the conference room. Most of the staff were leaving for the day since it was after 1600 when I finished teaching. It was quiet. Raymond first asked if I had heard from the Chief of Training, Dr. C, or NSA-TX's CoS, Brad. I said no. I was a bit confused; thought that was why we were in the conference room. So, Raymond admitted he knew my packet had not been forwarded from the site.

For me to be selected, the nomination needed to go from NSA-TX's promotion authority, back to the Headquarters for approval. Raymond said he wasn't sure why I hadn't been given feedback to that effect, but he'd help me arrange a meeting. My eyes began to water. I was speechless. I felt the lump developing in my thought. *Oh no Tena...don't you cry. Don't f...'in cry in front of them.*

I held up one finger and asked them to give me a minute, please. They graciously left the conference room. I stood up and paced the conference room. I knew it. I would not get a fair look — no way. I paced.

Tears streamed. I paced. So, what kinda feedback would this be — oh I know...forget everything you've accomplished and contributed to this point. You're an MAE now! Bullshit. If I needed to break my back, shuffling around, doing everything no one else wanted *to f'ing do*, to get promoted, then that's what I would do. I called Linda on the way home.

I sulked — woulda, coulda, shoulda for a few days. Tucked my tail and went back to work. I didn't solicit promotion feedback from Brad until about 8 months later, in preparation for the next cycle. To make matters worse, the GG-14 that replaced me as Chief of Training at NSA-HI, got promoted (supported by Donita), her first cycle there. I couldn't talk to anyone about how I was feeling — It was too raw. I needed to chill. When we met, Brad said exactly what I thought he would. "I was an MAE and not on a billet. Blah, blah, blah. The people who were promoted to GG-15 at NSA-TX were on billets." Paraphrased here.

Competition Among Us

There seemed to be an unspoken competitiveness amongst or with "some" black women in the small circles I transverse. I noticed or sensed this comp more at headquarters, but I never imagined I would witness it first-hand. I have never viewed other black woman as competition. I envisioned two or more of us as a powerful force for any change, but apparently, I was competing with another black woman in our department — an instructor in the field of computer networks. I don't understand what drives this competition. It's like we believe there's only room for one of us. It's like we're pushing, clawing, and shoving to be on top — to be the one and only, productive, smart, likeable, black woman. It's silly!

We both PCSed from Hawaii to Texas. I concurred/supported her promotion package from GG-13 to GG-14 even after I learned I could not compete. Ironically, NCS agreed to cost-share her promotion with NSA-HI that year. We were now the same grade — GG-14s. She and her spouse stayed at the same extended stay hotel as SGM and I, before finding our long-term homes in San Antonio. We, I mean I, drove us to work from the hotel daily. After riding as a passenger with Wilma, I would never let her drive me again. We joked about her poor driving. Wilma knew it was horrible and scary. I really thought we were establishing a good relationship outside of work. Hell, she's my homegirl.

I had noticed Wilma was questioning a lot of things I was doing, especially after the tradecraft session on how I organized and managed the ANSK curriculum. Well, she revealed herself totally one day in the office when a colleague, we will call Eduardo, a language instructor, sitting nearby asked what I had planned for the weekend. Wilma was directly across from me — back-to-back, yet a good 6 feet apart. I could hear her conversations when Wilma wasn't whispering to her husband, and she could hear mine. I heard Wilma spin around her chair to face the middle of our little pod.

I told my Eduardo that I didn't have any real plans. SGM was scheduled to come home for the weekend, and I hoped to get some rest and relaxation (R&R).

Eduardo looked at me and then at the black women behind my back. He smiled...acknowledged by saying "good," and then he asked her, "Wilma, why did you roll your eyes at Tena?" Silence. He didn't know he had just created a social faux pas for all to see and hear — him being male and Hispanic may have had something to do with it, with him revealing what Wilma really felt about me.

I laughed. I stewed. I listened. Wilma said, *"I rolled my eyes? No, I didn't. I didn't mean to. Why would I roll my eyes at Tena?"* I didn't turn around. Eduardo, now quiet, hunched his shoulder up as if to say, I'm sorry. I didn't know she was a hater. I didn't have much to do with her after that. I had to support her from a leadership perspective when I became the Deputy Chief of Training at NSA-TX, but I would never have her and her karate kid husband over for Thanksgiving dinner again...that was for sure.

Honorable Mention - Teacher of the Year

It was early 2014, 2nd quarter, and I was humping as a CM and an Instructor. The NCS's annual Learning Excellence Awards (LEA) was coming up. A call for nomination write-ups went out to the Enterprise. LEAs are considered the cream of the crop awards for everything and everyone in the agency that had anything to do with training, teaching, and/or mentoring.

I asked my rater if he was okay with me writing-up or basically nominating myself — he was fine with it. He'd won an award previously and thought I had a good shot. So, I did. It took me about 3 days to submit the final version of my nomination for "The Vera Filby — Teacher of the Year" award, citing the courses I managed, the course material I created and organized, and the students I taught, now in 6 courses.

Months later, Dr. C made a huge announcement in the conference room in front of the entire staff. I was selected as Honorable Mention for the Teacher of the Year Award. What an honor! I would attend the LEA ceremony at headquarters along with invited guests. To me, it was recognition for over 20 years of faithful service, teaching for the NCS.

Feedback from the awards board indicated that had my nomination (write-up), highlighted external customers, I would have won. I thought that was implied when the write-up mentioned me teaching from Texas, soldiers from Ft. Hood, instructors from NSA-GA and Pensacola, students from local federal agencies, and the Air Force's criminal investigators from Lackland — all of which I had a hand in supporting and/or training. Instead, a language instructor at headquarters was selected the winner.

Don't get me wrong, an LEA award is considered quite an accomplishment. Along with a plaque, your name is forever listed on NSA'S LEA internal webpage. And the opportunity to attend NCS's annual ceremony at Ft. Meade with my daughter Tierra, my Army buddy, Sylvia, and her daughter Sherae. They were so proud of me and excited for an inside look at the famous NSA school. I am very appreciative and proud of this teaching award.

Top & below: My collection of multiple plaques, awards and challenge coins.

When the promotion cycle rolled around again, I was less anxious about what the results would be. The writing was on the wall. My status as an MAE had not changed. Brad was still NSA-TX's CoS. I was expecting the same feedback but got something much more bizarre. I went to see him after my packet stopped at his level once again. Brad had a copy of my packet, and it was apparent he had just read it or perused it before I arrived at his office. He wrote on it.

Brad told me about the challenge with me was I was "excess," not on a billet — but accomplishing great things. Like free labor. He could not justify promoting me when he had other GG14s, just as competitive, on a billet. Brad joked around and said, "Let's say, hypothetically speaking, now if Dr. C or Raymond got hit by a bus — this would allow you to step-up to a leadership position." *I shit you not. A bus?* I said very slowly, "Ohhh...kay." Wasn't sure what he expected. He went on and on. I checked out and started thinking about stopping to pick-up dinner at the local H-E-B grocery store.

Opportunity to Lead in Texas

Around June/July 2015, unfortunately Raymond's health began to decline. He was on sick leave more than he was at work, and when at work, he was discussing his imminent retirement. Dr. C solicited help. She needed coverage until his formal vacancy announcement was filled. She devised a plan to rotate potential leaders to cover Raymond's position and try the job out, so to speak. Other GG-14s and I quickly volunteered. This was way too easy, and I loved Dr. C's energy and leadership style. The week went-by quickly.

I applied to be Dr. C's Deputy, and so did 10 other people across NSA-TX and from around the Enterprise. I submitted my Internal Resume online and watched as Dr. C and Chiefs scurried around to conduct a blind review of applicants. This was a new, criteria-driven approach to help reduce bias in the selection process.

Dr. C intentionally devised this process of a blind review to demonstrate to site, our Chiefs, and NSA-TX's new CoS, a more equitable way to select candidates, reduce unconscious biases, and to prevent any questions of the results, more than likely. Brad, the former CoS resigned from the agency for a more lucrative salary and to stay in San Antonio.

In August 2015, I was selected out of 10 or so candidates. I was #1. Dr. C would show strong evidence as to why she and her Chiefs selected me as the next Deputy Chief of Training, that interviews were not needed. And this was an urgent fill!

I was finally on a valid billet — supervising four front or first-level managers, providing guidance to 4 divisions, contractors, and military team members. I attended and attended/participated in weekly operational briefings, E&T leadership meetings, and everywhere else, NSA-TX's training organization had a seat. I taught and certified multiple instructors across multiple curriculums. I prepared for and executed interviews to select new candidates to work in E&T.

Chapter 15

The Decision

The credit belongs to the (wo)man who is actually in the arena, whose face is marred by dust and sweat and blood; who strives valiantly; who errs, who comes short again and again, because there is no effort without error and shortcoming...

Theodore Roosevelt

Deputy Chief of Training (D/Ch) (2015-2017)

As Deputy Chief of Training, I was working 9-10 hours a day which seemed to go by in a flash. Most days, Dr. C was the first to arrive in the mornings and I was one of the last to leave. The third year at NSA-TX, I was finally serving in a GG-15 position; now why this Deputy position was coded for GG-15 is beyond me. When I surmised Dr. C, genuinely cared about me, and the staff, I let down my guard, followed her lead, and watched her every move. She became an advocate, my biggest cheerleader, a mentor, and friend. I did whatever she asked of me.

It was February 2016, a full four years after I missed the promotion packet deadline at NSA-HI; I submitted yet another packet for promotion. The new year brought major change and churn to normal operations being driven by the NSA Director's Transformation of the agency, known as NSA21. This was an enterprise-wise endeavor to address findings from several employee surveys, sensing sessions, diversity and inclusion reports, and working groups.

NSA21 was to drive performance and mission improvement by removing inherent stovepipes, shake entrenched mindsets, realign Directorates to finally emphasize the importance of People — their professional and personal development, strategic assignments, fair competitive selections for promotions and bonuses. This agency reorganization and cultural transformation promised to be 'legit and huge.' Little did I know, I would go through my own transformation right along with NSA21.

Dr. C was a part of preliminary focus groups that supported this first *reorganization* of NSA in years; there had been many. According to plans, there would be a redistribution of resources/billets, new organizations created absorption of some organizations to reduce redundancy in missions, and renewed focus on workforce development — like more career opportunities, career coaching, and assistance in job placement.

In NCS-TX, we were hopeful that it meant finally getting needed billets to handle our already expanded role in delivering Cyber courses for both NSA and Cyber Command personnel. You know the old "do more with less," appeared to be the mentality from headquarters toward the enterprise. For years it seemed as if the workforce in the enterprise paid for being away from the headquarters, by having to perform multiple work roles to support an enterprise site, while employees at headquarters are primarily assigned one workrole.

NSA Discovers Civility Matters

Shortly before I was selected to become the Deputy Chief of Training at NSA-TX, the "Civility Matters" campaign announced by headquarters came complete with mandatory, two-hour block of Civility training.

Now, what this training revealed to some, and me, was the deep-rooted, systemic, unconscious biases of a great deal of employees in the agency. This was yet another effort to change the mindsets of agency employees, in hopes of creating a more civil and inclusive culture, with training. The NCS was tasked to help deliver training, in partnership with the EEO Directorate, to the entire workforce including the enterprise.

Honestly, this training was right-up my alley. I wanted to help develop it and teach it. At this time, I wanted desperately to say some things I had not said before, publicly.

After NSA-TX co-developed lesson plans with Equal Opportunity trainers at headquarters, we adopted a lesson plan that we believed would resonate with our 70:30 workforce ratio of military — civilians at NSA-TX. We added a short but poignant video of "The Voice of Italy" where a nun sings an Alicia Keys song and totally surprises the judges when they turned their chairs.

We used common terminology in a class exercise for both military and civilians to make hiring decisions from "contrived" portfolios, all with the same content but unique photos. Time after time, the resume with the minority was not selected for an additional interview. As a skilled instructor, I added personal stories, examples, and insights to personalize and reinforce the training. Boy, did I!

Teaching this 2-hour block of training would exhaust me, but I would sacrifice being nervous or uncomfortable as an introvert, to teach. I shared my experiences of being bused to Carrsville Elementary School which helped shape my mindset. I share I headed to an integrated school for the first time in 1969. I told them how my grandmother laid down the law and how I heard my subordinate referring to me as an ABB, basically because I was in charge, and I asked her to do work. Then, I'd jokingly say, "I don't care if you call me ABB...just call me!"

Then I relayed the story about the white male, security clearance investigator, not an agency employee, assigned to work on my five-year update, asked one of my military co-workers, who can appear to be white, if I were "ever angry or aggressive?"

The same investigator, minutes later, interviewed a black, civilian co-worker. He chose not to ask her the same line of questions. When she returned from the interview, the two compared notes there in front of me, in our small circle of desks. I couldn't believe it. I shook my head; they did too. I had to decide what to do with this. I rhetorically asked the class. Should I confront this guy? Call his supervisor? Some of the students yelled, 'hell yeah!"

They hung-on to every word I said. It was quiet as a mouse in room. I would often lower or raise my voice to emphasize important points. I also confessed that I too possessed unconscious or implicit biases. I described in detail my experience taking the Harvard's Implicit-bias Association Test (IAT), which I took twice to confirm the results. Social scientists argue most people have some degree of biases.

The IAT, introduced in 1998, is a social psychology measure designed to detect the strength of a person's automatic association between mental representations of objects or concepts in our memory. There are 15 different IATs, to measure our "preferences" associated with race, gender, age, weight, disabilities, and other categories. (Sleek, 2018).

I told the students how I reacted when the final analysis of the Race IAT stated, "You demonstrated a more positive attitude or preference toward Europeans/Caucasians than Non-whites," or something to that effect. Bull! No, I don't! I didn't believe the results. Our conscious bias stem from our natural tendency to make accusations to help us organize our social world.

The IAT is a direct illustration of our bias. The students were intrigued. Black students, mostly military members, would speak-up. They would share stories of long-standing internal racism and judgements made about how they spoke or talked. There is no way around biases — we're all biased!

I had the Amen corner rocking. By the time training was over, I was spent like I had just finished a good 2-mile run, back when I ran. You're tired as hell, but the run was so exhilarating. You're just waiting for the second or third wind to get you through the day — it always does. And you know your instructor skills were outstanding — you smoked it. You were firing on all cylinders. No lesson plan needed — completely off the dome. Mike drop.

Left on Read

It was at NSA-TX that I lost all hope of having an honest-to-GOD conversation with an influential leader about how my status as a MAE, now inhibited my ability to compete for promotion. I just needed an ear with someone outside the NCS and NSA-TX's CoS. Dr. C and I talked about it, of course. She had heard bits and pieces of the missed promotion story. I had worked rings around most of my colleagues around the globe, and everyone in the NCS knew it! It was a shame and a bad break, some probably thought.

This was my last-ditch effort to bring attention to MAEs, promotion deadlines, and the subsequent pickle I was in. I was beginning to process or really think about the emphasis placed on the date of submission — why such a hard date? Rarely are managers or first-level raters, waiting for packets to arrive. And when they do, they may sit in their inbox or queue for days before managers do their part; in most cases, managers are given weeks until the next step in the process.

My first attempt to solicit advice was with a black, female Senior Executive, who for many years was the Director of Information Assurance Directorate. Her name was Ms. Deidre. She was one of only two black Directors at the agency for years; the other was a sorority sister who led the EEO Directorate. After the NSA21's shuffle, Deidre was selected/moved to a newly created position focused on eliminating disparities in performance appraisals, promotions, and performance bonuses. I don't precisely remember her title — all I know is, she visited NSA-TX in her new role, "righting the wrongs."

Ms. Deidre held what the Army calls, Sensing Sessions or "bitch sessions" if you despise these forums. Employees are told "it's a safe environment" and they can tell her, what issues related to impartial awards and promotions needed to change. I had nothing to contribute to the group. They all knew the challenges. Documenting them again would not change a thing. At the conclusion Deidre insisted we e-mail her if we wanted to add more or had an issue we did not want to discuss in an open forum. So, I did.

I sent a thorough e-mail explaining my circumstances. I was fair in my description of what happened and how I missed a deadline and became an MAE. She stressed how easy it was for the workforce to reach her. She boasted about how the Director ensure there was a dedicated portal to collect correspondence, just for her. She told us, "I personally read and respond to every e-mail I get." *Bullshit!* Deidre completely ignored my e-mail — maybe she didn't get it.

The second senior, female leader I emailed, and asked for advice was the Deputy Director of Operations at NSA-TX. Let's say her name was Janet. She would leave NSA-TX to return to headquarters a few weeks after I sent her an e-mail for personal mentoring. No reply!

She PCSed back to an Operational leadership position at headquarters without an 'adios.' I thought of all people, I would hear from her since she volunteered to mentor the TAC's leadership. As a co-chair of the TAC, I met with Janet monthly for a year. Crickets!

What happened with Sheryl Sandberg's "Lean-In Circles" and women supporting women, crap. What does it say when a woman isn't interested in another woman's plight? I couldn't believe it. About six months after I sent my e-mail to Deidre, she retired from the agency. Gone!

It's worth mentioning here — after I missed the promotion deadline at NSA-HI, even as embarrassed as I was, I wanted to hear from Judy, the former Commandant of the NCS. Not a single email or call. I was disappointed. I admired Judy. What she had done with the school was miraculous. I would have worked in Timbuktu for her.

Judy reminded me of a good, effective, Army Colonel — say what you will about them, they got *shit* done. When you believe in your manager, you will do anything to ensure they are successful. She retired shortly after I got to NSA-TX.

Now Donita, the former CoS in HI, was at NSA-TX! Yes, as in PCSed to Texas about a year and half after I arrived. *No Shit.* We were both professional and cordial; personally, I have nothing against Donita. We interacted well. She worked in Operations/mission as their CoS.

4th Time's a Charm

Shortly after my promotion packet was sent to Dr. C, she encouraged me to accept a special assignment as the NSA-TX's lead for structure development of the new Workforce Support Activities (WSA) — a brand new Directorate. WSA would absorb the support functions previously known as "Enabler" organizations (NCS, HR, Budget/Finance, Security and Logistics).

I knew what Dr. C was doing; she wanted me visible — visibly working throughout the promotion selection process across Directorates. I knew I was taking-on extra work, but I agreed. I, along with the Enabler Chiefs and with little guidance from headquarters particularly the NCS, were to create new organizational structures/charts with required positions or billets, to support our post-NSA21, missions. This strategic "stretch" assignment proved to be demanding, complex, and important to senior leadership. NSA21 was referred to as "the Director's baby."

For the NCS, the NSA21 transformation authorized the creation of two new Colleges for the school, with a promise of increased billets in the global Enterprise. To my knowledge, the Enterprise were never authorized the "promised/expected" billets.

Right around this time, Donita, was selected for elevation/promotion to Senior Executive. With her notification, she moved from Operations to assume the Director of the newly formed NSA-TX WSA. This meant, as Deputy Chief of Training, I was now, technically working for Donita, yet again.

Anybody Can Lead Training

With NSA21 organizations and positions flushing out, we would learn Dr. C would be leaving training. She was a direct-nominate to lead NSA-TX's new Workforce Development (WD) organization. With this announcement, Dr. C began to advocate for me to assume, the Chief of Training position, her previous role.

Dr. C had first-hand knowledge of the records and resumes of at least 10 candidates who applied for the Deputy of Training positions when I was selected. No one on-site or in the enterprise that was interested in the job, came close to my E&T experience, and knowledge of the NCS.

We knew the learning curve was too great to just place anyone without recent NCS experience in this position. This was the new NCS post Transformation, now with two new Colleges — Cyber and Leadership Development and an ever, evolving requirements gathering process.

She spoke with the Commandant of NCS at headquarters, Luis, encouraging him to step-in to recommend to NSA-TX's leaders to move into her vacant position. Luis refused to intervene; he was reluctant and dead silent. NSAT-TX decided of all the position enabler position, the Chief of Training position, would be the only one advertised for competitive selection.

A competition of power occurred across the Cryptologic Centers and mission elements at the headquarters; in this case, with the NCS. Luis was resigned to the Site Commander's declaration that NSA-TX had 51% decision-making authority or "say," regarding civilian personnel fills, while the mission element at the Mothership had 49% of the decision-making power. Really? Ridiculous!

You're Getting Promoted!

For months and weeks, I watched Dr. C review stacks of promotion packages and mine was one of them. After she participated in the "Enablers" board, I waited to hear the news. When she announced to the entire staff, that I and a GG-13 to 14, were getting promoted, I exhaled. A deep sigh. Finally. I'm forever grateful for her support and advocacy; she was instrumental, as Lillie imagined.

After my promotion announcement, Dr. C and I talked about her move because of NSA21. We both agreed, it just made sense for me to replace her as the Chief of Training. I'd done it before, and I had the needed experience. And now that I was getting promoted, it was really a lateral move to another GG-15 billet. This would also open an opportunity for an emerging GG-14, to be selected as Deputy Chief, or so we thought.

I was an easy shoo-in, which would result in a seamless transition from Dr. C to me, if you asked me. Besides, to my knowledge, there was one direct nomination for the Chief of WD — Dr. C. The HR, Security and Logistics Chiefs 'kept' their jobs with different/changed, Rotation Dates or RODAs, pending on their tenure. Low and behold, site's leadership decided they would advertise the Chief of Training position for competitive selection; it was the only enabler position to advertised.

Now the question for me to consider, since the decision was made, would I apply and interview. As days went by, it became a matter of principles and morals for me — how many blazing hoops was I willing to jump through, smiling, and wagging my tail? I pondered.

A few weeks later, I headed to DC to attend an IC course for a week and a bit of leave to see my mother in Baltimore. I was relieved to get a break from making line and block charts with my SEL, an Air Force E-8, SMSgt Jay F. Jay attended meetings in my stead; he acted as the alternate structure POC and had my back.

When I returned, interviews for the Chief of Training had been conducted and a selection made — well at least that's what I was told. Dr. C predicted this outcome, informed me the Deputy Commander of NSA-TX, Mr. Dapper, wanted to know why I had not applied to become the new Chief of Training. He wanted to talk with me about this as soon as I returned. *Hmmm.... how should I respond?* With the truth!

I walked over to his office. I informed Mr. Dapper that I was not aware interviews were scheduled when I departed for DC. True. That I wasn't sure I wanted to interview since I had just been selected via competitive selection for the Deputy's Chief of Training position. Facts. He listened and told me "they" thought I would interview and if I had, I would have been selected. I viewed this as a day late and a dollar short. If they felt this way, they should have communicated this with me.

Change is Inevitable

Dr. C sensed a change in me. It was early one morning, and we were the only two in our corner. I remember her asking if I was excited about my impending promotion. I told her yes, it was all so surreal. I had waited for this promotion for so long.

I told her again and again how I appreciated her support — and I did. I knew if anyone could help advocate successfully for me to get promoted, she could. She was convincing in every way. I reminded her she could sell a bike to a blind man. She would just laugh. She knew I was struggling with something. She knew.

To tell you the truth, the closer I got to the promotion ceremony, the less it meant to me. I would finally get an overdue pay raise. My salary was already more than I had ever imagined I would make. With my Army retirement, I was making six-figures. I had earned it...and I knew it. I was becoming more and more disenfranchised. I could feel it. I dreaded work

Shortly after the WSA board finalized its promotion selections and forwarded the results for approval, I found out a fellow GG-14, a colleague, there at NSA-TX, missed the deadline to submit their packet. Ironic or what? It was noted the missed deadline was not by a day but days. The individual, after learning his/her packet for promotion was late, became irate with his/her supervisor for not informing "them" of the deadline, and ensuring he/she submitted their package.

Now, never mind the site e-mail about deadlines, which was still pinned to my desktop, was crystal clear. This employee placed the blame completely on the supervisor for not reinforcing and confirming the deadline with "them," the subordinate. They took zero responsibility. The end result — the individual was selected for promotion to GG-15, effective the same day as mine, proving the existence of different rules/strokes for different employees/folks. Very Interesting!

At home, SGM was getting ready to retire from the Army with over 30 years. He said his plan was to chill and play a ton of golf. He would be moving from Ft. Hood to San Antonio with me permanently — or so I thought. He did play golf and bummed around the house...for a hot month.

Before I knew it, SGM was working toward getting certified to substitute teach in Bexar County and apparently looking at other jobs - said he was bored. I think the reality of retirement set it; even though he would receive VA benefits, he fully realized what his retirement pay would look like after having to send HALF! (*in Eddie Murphy's voice*) to his ex-wife.

One evening after work, SGM informed me he had applied to teach Junior ROTC in FL. He talked in his usual circles about an Army buddy that encouraged him to apply. A few months later, he headed to Delray Beach, FL for an interview and tour of the high school. He returned beaming. He thought the program was a good move until he could withdraw from his TSP at 59; he was 52 years old.

Of course, he was hired. He was a recent retiree, who was infantry, a ranger, jump master/airborne, air assault, path finder, and previous medic. Hell, I'd hire him too. *"You want to yell and deal with high school students? You sure? I asked."* He was sure. From his resume, he was hooah-hooah. But he seemed to struggle to connect with soldiers and children. I noticed his soldiers didn't light-up with excitement about him being around.

Regardless, he was leaving San Antonio to move to FL to teach. I knew he preferred distance — the longest we had lived under the same roof was a year or so when we were newlyweds. His apartments at Ft. Hood and eventually in Delray Beach, gave him the freedom to be him without judgment and accountability. And he knew I wouldn't stand in the way of his career desires. If you want to leave, let me help you pack, dear.

The Promotion

In June 2016, the site's promotion ceremony was held in NSA-TX's Hitt Building. After an award, I was the first person to step-up on the stage to start promotions to GG-15. My family couldn't make the ceremony. Tierra & Shara were in Hawaii. SGM was now in Delray Beach. Dr. C, my manager and mentor, was unable to attend the ceremony, she was TDY.

There were two people standing beside me at the ceremony who knew nothing about me, nor did they give a rat's ass about my accomplishments.

When I looked out at NSA-TX's leadership team and the audience, there she was — Donita. When I could, I looked her in the eyes. She smiled. I winked. I wanted her to know it was okay. She was sitting front and center, looking like she wanted to desperately read my mind. I smiled back. She knew what that meant. "It's all-good." The colleague that submitted their package late, was promoted on the same stage that day with me.

A New Chief for Training

In late August, Dr. C moved to her new office. The newly selected and promoted Chief of Training, came from Operations, right there at NSA-TX. The strategy to fill vacancies created by NSA21 was to give priority to personnel on site, before considering an employee needing to PCS to TX.

Prior to her arrival, I withheld judgment. I'd met the new Chief years before while traveling with Judy. She had led language training experience, so she had a clue. I was resigned to letting her lead — finishing-up Transformation 21 efforts for local WSA and figuring out my next move. Rumor had it, that Donita was leaving NSA-TX within a few months. With her promotion to Senior Executive, she was looking for a new position.

My marriage to SGM was going to shit in a hand basket, and quick. Yes, I wanted to leave the agency. Yes, he gave an acceptable excuse — love and marriage. But let's be clear, I was nervous as hell about the move to FL with him. I was sure if SGM and I didn't start marriage counseling ASAP, we would divorce. Even with the distance now, we struggled to communicate.

Not Again...

Exactly one year after I got promoted in June 2017, I supported/concurred with one of our best Language instructors in our cadre, in getting submitted for promotion to GG-13. I was rooting for Dr. Perez, aka Dr. P., even though her immediate supervisor, who worked for me, was less enthusiastic. Dr. P. was the most effective and creative language instructor we had. She had crossed-trained to teach two Analytical Skills courses, which she personally incorporated relevant content into her language lessons. She was a star. Yet, she dealt with cultural challenges being an educated Latino woman working primarily with male Latino's, and their machismo.

When she was selected for promotion, Donita, asked me, and just me she said, to accompany Dr. P. to her office so she could inform her that she was selected. I said okay. Just me? Strange. Okay. I arranged for the two of us to go see Donita and her Deputy, Don.

When we arrived at her office, Donita and Don were all smiles. They shook Dr. P.'s hand and told her Congratulations, you've been selected for promotion to GG13. She beamed. She was grateful. She thanked them repeatedly. She cried. I was so proud of her. We embraced. She was by-far the most deserving.

Donita then looked at me. She extended her hand and said "And you...congratulations to you. You're getting a Quality Step Increase (QSI)" — a step increase. *A what?* I was speechless. Dr. C hadn't mentioned her recommendation for a step, and we talked extensively, daily. Was Donita trying to repay what happened in HI? What a blessing! "Wow. Thank you," I said. "I wasn't expecting this at all. Thank you so much." Donita repeated over and over... "you *deserve it.*"

A promotion and a step the very next year — unheard of. She went on and on, talking about me and my work with the NSA21 stuff. I returned to my office. Thank GOD I didn't say anything to the staff. I just went back to work, like any other busy afternoon.

That evening I felt skeptical. Something wasn't right — my gut told me. Dr. C would have had to submit me for a step, right? Wouldn't she at least know. Why was she excluded from the congratulatory announcement? She snuck one over on me. I would chat with Dr. C in the morning. I called and told Linda. She was happy for me — reminded me to "never give-up on people." Donita was sorry she could not help in HI. I told SGM. His typical response when we were talking about my career... "All right then, that's good." Yet not fully understanding.

The very next day before lunchtime, I got a call from Donita. It was on the secure phone line. After exchanging quick pleasantries, Donita said she hated to call...but had to share some news. I was not getting a step increase. She didn't have the resources ($) she was promised and wasn't aware until that morning after speaking with the site's Deputy Commander.

I said *"Okay...no worries."* My gut instinct was right. She apologized at least twice. I stopped listening. I was processing — did *she call me to her office the day before or was I dreaming?* I heard her say, I will get you a performance bonus for all the hard work you've done with NSA21. Blah, Blah, Blah. I said, "No problem. It's all good." I'm not making this up. Whiskey Tango Foxtrot (WTF)!

Ushering in a New Perspective

A few months after the new Chief of Training settled in, I announced I would retire from the agency as soon as I reached the minimum retirement age — about a year away. I had finally, after four years of personal turmoil, gotten the promotion I worked for and wanted, yet it didn't mean a hill of beans to me.

Hell, I felt sick walking into work. I could no longer stomach my job. I didn't want to work a single day past my 56th birthday on the 25th of October. According to HR, I should wait until the end of October, 2017 to align with a pay cycle, so I did.

I desperately wanted/needed to live authentically without the added burden of trying to represent my race, gender, or any other category or label placed on people for comparisons, to determine good or bad, worthy or unworthy. I could no longer appease managers that didn't deserve to be respected. I started vocalizing my discontent within earshot of my direct-reports and my new manager. I needed to chill. Most days, I left work physically but couldn't mentally. I had to apologize for being insensitive at times with my neophyte manager, who asked for what I thought was way too much help for their grade and "experience."

I finally concluded that no matter how many organizational changes, transformations, leadership changes, campaigns, call-it-what-you-like, NONE of these efforts, would/could positively affect the strong-hold culture of cowardly leaders, inconsistent rules that apply to some, partiality, and discriminatory practices. My point-of-view, of course, mine!

I saw the site Commander and civilian Deputy Commander for a Commander's challenge coin the morning of my last day. By 1400hrs on 31 October 2017, I had my security out brief, which reminded me yet again of my life-time obligations.

I walked out the building to my car. I was headed to Killeen to pick-up my best friend Mitzi. She would drive with me from San Antonio to Lake Worth, with a few pitstops along the way. We would celebrate.

I ceremoniously dropped my Temporary (T) badge in the drop box at the gate. Out the gate on Potranco Rd for the last time. I looked in my rearview mirror and I flipped the entire site a bird! I don't know what came over me. I just did it and smiled. It felt good!

Left a Bad Taste in My Mouth

I believe I was in Lake Worth for about a week when my shadowbox and encased flag that flew over the agency, on a specific date, arrived. Newly retired for about 10 days or so, I got a call from my HR

Retirement Representative, whom I'd become familiar with on a first-name basis.

She called to inform me, after waiting for four years, a decision was rendered reference my appeal to forego repayment of the over payment error for NAREA received in HI. The decision — I was responsible for the repayment and the agency took what they overpaid me from my unused, accrued, sick leave which, at retirement is typically converted to pay. I SHIT YOU NOT! She wanted to give me a heads-up; my final pay from the agency would not be as expected.

The agency took over $6,700. I couldn't believe my ears. The hundreds of sick leave hours I accrued, were gone. A bad taste came in my mouth. I swallowed hard. It stayed. I swallowed again. The bad taste is still there!

Afterword

Camptown

While I was still working for the agency and living in San Antonio, TX, I volunteered to help plan the 2016, Camptown Reunion — a three-day, community-wide event, with a Meet & Greet, a huge Community BBQ/Picnic, and an old-school dance party on Saturday night. After which, most of the community were up bright and early on Sunday morning to attend church service at Piney Grove. We've had two successful reunions with almost 300 participants at the last reunion in 2018. Working to bring the reunions to fruition made me realize, even more, how special, and how much I love my community.

Notorious Wheezy

It was a Friday afternoon. Shara and Noah had just left to go home. I love that they live close, and I can see them often. When I walked out from checking laundry, I looked across the kitchen at my red miniature chalkboard on the countertop. It's a part of my deliberately sparse décor. I love red in a black and stainless-steel kitchen. This decorative chalkboard acts as my mindfulness board. I usually write short quotes or something inspirational there in chalk — something like "Be grateful."

For months now, it said, "Love heals — Just love!" What if that was what my mother needed? Love. I pondered — why don't you just love her for who she is? Had you thought of that. Tried that. Love heals, right? That is the one thing you have been unwilling to do. Unconditionally and unapologetically let down your guarded gate with the alligator filled moat and just love her! That's the lesson for me as it relates to Wheezy. Understanding. Forgiveness. Touching. Inspiring. Supporting. "There, but for the grace of GOD."

It's now February 2021. I was headed to the washer and dryer to put my second load in — whites. I started thinking about my mother. I hadn't heard from her in a few days. Well, it is the "first of the month" as the lyrics say in Bone Thugs and Harmony's song. Typical. It's the 4th. Suddenly, it comes to me — I missed her. I have not seen my mother since the pandemic began. I knew she was high risk to contract COVID-19. I thought, why jeopardize her health with an unnecessary visit by either of us? At one point, her senior apartment in Baltimore was closed to all visitors and FL was a hot spot.

A few days later, I learned my mother was admitted to the hospital. It became apparent that she had another stroke. She's currently in a rehabilitation center in Baltimore, near the beautiful Inner Harbor. My sister-cousins Pat, Avon, and I, sped to MD to be there for her after hearing the news. She's recovering well and has made significant progress.

A Soldier for Life

When I look back on my career in the Army, it was the foundation and the beginning of who I've become. I took the U.S. Army's values to heart and tried to live them daily. Loyalty. Dedication. Respect. Selfless Service. Honesty. Integrity, and Personal Courage. I still try to live by these values. I'm proud of my service and what I was able to contribute to the defense of this great nation. I lived and visited countries/places I didn't know existed coming from Camptown. I met soldiers from all walks of life that I can never forget. Those here and those who made the ultimate sacrifice — Rest In Peace. What I know for sure is we have some of the most dedicated, intelligent, and loyal, young Americans standing watch while we sleep.

NSA

It's been 17 years since I entered-on-duty with NSA — and almost three years since I retired. Maybe the climate is different; I certainly hope so. I also hope that by sharing what I've observed and experienced during my career at NSA, it resonates with others, particularly minorities. It is my hope that leaders are held accountable for the climate they create or enable. I also hope other minorities, especially black women, feel validated.

My hope is they will feel a sense of camaraderie with other women and minorities, who can confirm, it wasn't them. They felt shit too! Just couldn't put your finger on "exactly what took place" in certain instances, but you just know something went awry. I wish I had been braver, more courageous to have stood-up against NSA's negative, deep-rooted culture and called-out its disparities and biases.

If you recall the recent political climate — it was not conducive to being a quote, unquote, "whistleblower." No ma'am! No sir! My black ass did not stand a chance up-against the Mothership — not a chance.

As a black woman, I've always known I had to work hard and sometimes harder than the person next to me because of my race and gender. I accepted that fact and did my best to do just that — work hard. I earned a reputation for following-up with tasks/projects/etc. until completion; for being fair; and knowing my tradecraft. My goal has always been to contribute and be a positive example for others to emulate. Just to be clear, as a double minority, there's a constant mindfulness of certain things or behaviors to not exhibit, like being loud, argumentative, or appearing uninterested or lazy.

SGM

Just eight months after I pulled into our new, five-bedroom house with new speckled, epoxy floors in the garage in Lake Worth, FL., I moved out. I couldn't breathe in the house that was supposed to be our retirement oasis and my sanctuary. The huge deposit for a new inground pool and outdoor kitchen was paid and lost. I left SGM and everything that reminded me of him.

It became so apparent why he and I married — I was looking for something different. He was looking for someone to make him look and feel normal, and not a major cause of his first divorce. Neither one of us could mend or supply the other with what we needed. I realized that as much as SGM and I had in common, we had an enormous number of values and "things," that were incongruent.

His behavior began to be indicative of a person with some deep-rooted issues that neither of us were equipped to help or deal with. He had absolutely zero skills in handling anything that wasn't admiration, ass kissing, and praise of him. He was often a recluse in our home. He became argumentative about everything. Moody. Highly opinionated and judgmental, as hell. I was praying he would conclude on his own that he needed therapy. He didn't. It got worse.

After deciding that divorcing SGM was my only option and chance at happiness and sanity, I filed. Not an easy decision but a needed one. I questioned how I could have been so wrong about him. I felt duped and terribly angry. I ignored large, waving, garrison-sized, red flags repeatedly. I've come to realize my gut instincts are powerful. His bait and switch behavior was narcissistic. This is not a diagnosis; it's simply based on 9 years of observation of SGM.

My Best Friends

My daughters and I have truly become best girlfriends. Our relationship deepened during the tough period after arriving in FL, where we only had each other to rely on. We pushed through! At one point, we all lived together in my one-bedroom rental in downtown West Palm Beach (WPB), FL, pending other moves. It was incredibly tight, but we managed. We had Noah to help us keep things in perspective and to keep us sane.

For the first time, I feel like my daughters feel safe being honest with me about everything. We're keeping it 100% with each other — the good, the bad, and the fabulous. We talk almost daily, usually via Facetime; often, Linda is included. We've discovered a great deal of appreciation for each other and learned what real love and support is.

Tierra moved from her job in Fort Lauderdale to a teaching position in Atlanta in December of 2019, a few months before the Pandemic. Shara and Noah moved to their own place in August 2020, just a 15-minute drive from me. It's a lovely, well-shaded and quiet, condo community. She has the perfect screened-in porch for Noah to play.

My Life

I'm finally living in my own space/condominium, on my own terms, alone. It's all mine! My life in WPB is spent with my daughter and grandson Noah or visiting Tierra in Atlanta. We enjoy the beach and doing things outside. I still play golf. I love the competition, even with myself. Before the pandemic, I was a substitute teacher for Palm Beach County — mostly substituting at Noah's elementary school so I could see and encourage him, and on occasions, have lunch with him.

As a Certified Professional Life Coach (CPC), most of the coaching work I've done has been free of charge. I can't bring myself to charge anyone for what I'm willing to share for free — life lessons! My life coaching goals are to motivate and inspire women to set and achieve realistic goals that improve their careers, relationships, and their lives.

In the process of writing this memoir, I realized for years, I've stacked traumas and disappointments on top of each other repeatedly. I built a wall and tough exterior to protect myself from difficulties in life, particularly with close family members. With my mother, I became numb to the hurt and the repeated disappointments that occur when a family member is an addict, by distancing myself from her whenever I could, by thousands of miles.

For the first time in a long time, I feel great about my life. I've accepted my flaws 'n all. I've forgiven myself for personal decisions I've made. I'm doing what is best for me. Not what looks favorable or acceptable. I no longer feel the need to impress. I have removed my armor, mask, and shield.

I set boundaries and demand adults be accountable and responsible for their actions. I say "No" without guilt. I go for long walks to the beach. I turn my phone off and take naps. I meditate. I communicate my thoughts and feelings thoroughly and honestly with family and friends — no pretense. My home is peaceful and simple. I vowed to put myself first and to finally laugh, to love, to dance, to travel (again), and to be me...authentically.

I pray I inspire someone to be courageous, to be authentic, to be themselves, to forgive (themselves and others), and know they are enough!

My grandson Noah Ryan
and me.

My dear Sister-cousins.
L-r, Avon, me, and Pat.

My youngest daughter, Shara.

Shara's boot camp photograph.

My oldest daughter, Tierra. On our way to dinner.

Tierra is a former NFL cheerleader.

Three Amigos; my best friends.

References

>   Ashkenas, Ron; "Breakthrough Your Mental Bureaucracy;" Harvard Business Review; February 28, 2012.

https://hbr.org/2012/02/break-though-your-mental-burea.html.

>   Blair, Karen; "4 Ways That Sexuality Can Be Fluid: New research explores four types of sexual fluidity in women." Psychology Today; Dec 29, 2019.

https://www.psychologytoday.com/us/blog/inclusive-insight/201912/4-ways-sexuality-can-be-fluid

>   Brown, J. (2021). Culture. In E. M. Sanchez (Ed.), Merriam-Webster.com dictionary. Merriam-Webster.

https://www.merriam-webster.com/dictionary/culture

>   Corrington, Abby; Finkelstein; Lisa, King, Eden; Thomas, Courtney; "Generational Differences at Work Are Small. Thinking They're Big Effects Our Behavior." Harvard Business Review. (2019).

https://hbr.org/2019/08/generational-differences-at-work-are-small-thinking-theyre-big-affects-our-behavior

>   Ferry, Korn. "Understanding Bias and the Brain." Briefings Magazine; Issue 23; 2021.

https://www.kornferry.com/insights/briefings-magazine/issue-23/understanding-bias-and-brain.

> Horwitz, Daron; CYA Culture and The Importance of Admitting Mistakes. Forbes; 2016

https://www.forbes.com/sites/daronhorwitz/2016/02/28/cya-culture-and-the-importance-of-admitting-mistakes/?sh=79e3e3a714a6

> Montopoli, John; "Public Speaking Anxiety and Fear of Brain Freeze." National Social Anxiety Center. (2017).

https://nationalsocialanxietycenter.com/2017/02/20/public-speaking-and-fear-of-brain-freezes/

> Rogel, Charles; "The 12 Attributes of a Strong Organizational Culture;" March 18, 2014. Talent Management & HR. The 12 Attributes of a Strong Organizational Culture – TLNT

> Sleek, Scott; "The Bias Beneath: Two Decades of Measuring Implicit Associations:" January 31, 2018. Association for Psychological Science.

> Strobel, Warren P; "Diversity Lags at Top of U.S. Spy Agencies;" Wall Street Journal; September 2020.

"https://www.wsj.com/articles/diversity-lags-at-top-of-u-s-spy-agencies-11600430401

> History of Federal Minimum Wage Rates Department of Labor(.gov). (1982).

> "Annual Demographic Report: Hiring and Retention of Minorities, Women, and Persons with Disabilities in the United States Intelligence Community." Fiscal Years (2015-2019).

https://www.dni.gov/files/documents/FY-2015 and FY-2018.

> Definition of "Culture." In Merriam-Webster.com (2011).

https://www.merriam-webster.com/dictionary/culture.

> "The Schoolhouse Museum. An African American History Museum of Public Education."

http://www.theschoolhousemuseum.org/Default.aspx.

> National Security Agency (NSA) Mission and Values Statement.
> NSA.gov www.nsa.gov
> List of U.S. Security Clearance Terms. In Wikipedia.

https://en.wikipedia.org/wiki/List_of_U.S._security_clearance_terms#:~:text=Sensitive%20compartmented%20information%20(SCI)%20is,and%20be%20granted%20SCI%20eligibility.hat is.

> Former Directors of NSA.

https://www.nsa.gov/about/leadership/forme
r-directors/.

> "DNI Affirms Commitment to
Transparency." Revised Intelligence Community
Directive Focuses on Greater IC Transparency.
The Intelligence Transparency Council (2016)

https://www.dni.gov/index.php/how-we-
work/transparency

> "Principles of Intelligence Transparency
for the Intelligence Community."

https://www.dni.gov/index.php/how-we-
work/transparency

> National Security Agency/Central
Security Service. https://www.nsa.gov

Acknowledgements

Start Each Day With a Grateful Heart

To my gorgeous best friends and daughters, Tierra and Tashara Allen – a huge thank you for being my rocks. Your advice/counsel and help during this process is so appreciated. You've taught me so much – from unconditional love to the latest and greatest technology. Your contribution to this project is yet another testament of your love & support.

To the love of my life – Noah Ryan, you are such a blessing to all who encounter you. I thank GOD for you. Hope when you're older and read this, you will know how much your Rah-Rah loves you.

For my Mother's love, thank you Ma! "There but for the grace of GOD." Your life could have been mine – I love you. You are still my girl.

To my beautiful on the inside and out, Sister-Cousins, E. Patricia Lawyer, Avon Lawyer-Skinner, Julon "Gigi" Shaw, & Carol Lynn Harvin-Robinson, whom I have endless love for. Thank you for loving me.

To my Beta Readers/1st Editors/Biggest Cheerleaders: Dr. Clare Carey, Linda Dorsey, Teart Coles, Carla Renee' Vines, Karen Bolden, and Ms. Betty "Cindy" Mahomes – Rest in Peace (RIP). I could not have done this without all of you. Your guidance, candid feedback, advice, and encouragement to "keep it real," inspired me to do just that. Humbly, I thank all of you!

My beautiful nieces by blood and/or choice: I'm so proud of the women you have become. Resheema &

baby Kristen, Bianca, Kiana R., Sheena, Claire, Julvonne, Julon (aka my Buddha Bear), Nova, Susan, Lynzee, Jaleesa & Ava J., Dana, Kiana L., Ashley, Sherae, Shelisha, Chandra, Dawn, Stephanie, Tammi, Glenia, Trisha, and Salida.

Love and respect to my amazing tribe and family: Linda Dorsey, Mitzi Edwards, Teart Coles, Anastasia "Stacey" White-Whitmore, Tinesha Mahomes, Sylvia Swinson, Aunt Cora "Sister" Burnette, Julia Justice Hegger, Della R. Stokes, Susie Blow, Nicole Alford, Sandra Renault, DeeAlice Moton, Tally Downton, Shantay Clemons, Audrey Lawyer, Mary Lee, Sandra Dorsey, Susan Crothers, Toni Long, Jan Parker, Keisha Lee, Dorothy Baker, Tina Smith, Pamela Edwards, Vonda Munden, Joyce Stewart, Denys "PH" Smith, Dr. Ana Gonzales, Paula Bennett, and Dione (last name deliberately excluded).

To my line sisters, your love and support means everything: Tina Dowhite, Lisa Shannon, Pamela Hutcherson, Phyllis C. Spencer, Gina Loving-Clash, Stephanie E. Spencer, Kim Jackson, and Isha Alexander-Farewell. Spring 81, Lambda Phi Chapter, UMBC. Skee-Wee!

To my guys, first to my brothers in heaven: Butch and Uncle Teensy, I miss you both so much. RIP SSG Robert "Bob" Kitchen.

To my three brothers: Robert aka Pop, Tony, and Kiminey, circumstances brought us together; only love can sustain us.

Thank you, gentlemen, for your love, friendship and/or support: Andy Chandler, Obren Barnes, Michael Allen, Darryl Edwards, Curtis R., T.C., Andre', Manu and Idris Alford, Tyler Long, Jamel Crouthers, Larry Skinner, Larry Skinner - II, Michael W., Tiger Lawyer, Micah Reid, Jakari Spivey, Joell Spivey, Justin Loar, Justin Loar, II, Jude Loar, John Keys, John Jennys, Guy Collinsworth, and Kelly Sherwood.

To my colleagues, who became friends, thank you for your support: Dr. G., Barb, Bernie, Camie, Carl, Clare, Dianne, Deb, Erica V., Francie, Jason F., Joyce, LaDon, LaShena, Lathen, Michele F., Mike N., Molly K., Monica, Patricia, Patrice, Patty, Rena, Reba, Sue E., Tina, Wanda D., and last but certainly not the least, Tracy.

To my editor, au du jour, Ms. Liane Larocque of Mystic Canyon Publishing, you were a godsend. I couldn't have done this without your expertise and guidance. Thank you for empowering authors and publishing dreams.

Love & gratitude to all my family & friends from the Communities of Camptown and Franklin, VA.

The (Wo)Man in the Arena

"It is not the critic who counts; not the (wo)man who points out how the strong (wo)man stumbles, or where the doer of deeds could have done them better. The credit belongs to the (wo)man who is actually in the arena, whose face is marred by dust and sweat and blood; who strives valiantly; who errs, who comes short again and again, because there is no effort without error and shortcoming; but who does actually strive to do the deeds; who knows great enthusiasms, the great devotions; who spends herself/himself in a worthy cause; who at the best knows in the end the triumph of high achievement, and who at the worst, if s/he fails, at least fails while *daring greatly*, so that her/his place shall never be with those cold and timid souls who neither know victory nor defeat."

— Theodore Roosevelt

LIST OF ABBREVIATIONS

AIT   Advanced Individual Training

AWOL   Absent Without Official Leave

CIA   Central Intelligence Agency

CTS   Cryptologic Training System

DIA   Defense Intelligence Agency

D/Ch   Deputy, Chief

DoD   Department of Defense

DIRNSA Director of NSA

FBI   Federal Bureau of Investigations

IC   Intelligence Community

JQS   Job Qualification Standard

MAE   Married Agency Employee

NCS   National Cryptologic School

NCO   Noncommissioned Officer

NGA   National Geo-Spatial Intelligence Agency

NRO   National Reconnaissance Office (NRO)

NSA   National Security Agency

NSA-GA National Security Agency - Georgia

NSA-HI National Security Agency - Hawaii

NSA-TX National Security Agency – Texas

NCPAC National Security Agency/Central
Security Service – Pacific

PCS	Permanent Change of Station
TDY	Temporary Duty
WSA Directorate	Workforce Support Activities
WD	Workforce Development
Bde	Brigade
Gp	Group
Bn	Battalion
Co	Company

Army Ranks and Positions

COL	Colonel (0-6)
LTC	Lieutenant Colonel (O-5)
CSM	Command Sergeant Major (E-9)
SGM	Sergeant Major (E-9)
1SG	First Sergeant (E-8)
SFC	Sergeant First Class (E-7)
SSG	Staff Sergeant (E-6)
SGT	Sergeant (E-5)

SPC	Specialist (E-4)
PFC	Private First Class (E-3)
DS	Drill Sergeant
NCOIC	Noncommissioned Officer in Charge
PSG	Platoon Sergeant

Air Force Rank Used

| SMSgt | Senior Master Sergeant (E-8) |

USMC Rank Used

| MSgt | Master Sergeant (E-8) |

Other Frequently Used

| SEL | Senior Enlisted Leader |
| PT | Physical Training |

About the Author

Tena Arnett Lawyer is a retired U.S. Army intelligence soldier who started her career mentoring, coaching, and training, in the Army. With over 30 years of experience in the Intelligence Community (IC) in Education and Training (E&T), Tena holds a Masters' degree in Educational Leadership and achieved Suma Cum Laude. She is a Certified Life & Career Coach and has a certificate in Human Performance Improvement (HPI) Analysis from American Training & Development (ATD).

Tena served as both a Director and Deputy Director of Education & Training departments at satellite campuses of the National Cryptologic School (NCS), for the National Security Agency (NSA), where she managed the staff of first-line managers, instructors, curriculum developers, and learning facilitators. Not only did Tena lead, but she also taught countless offerings of analytical & critical thinking skills, basic instructor training, unconscious bias training, and peer-to-peer training & development.

Currently, Tena is a certified professional life coach (C.P.C.), and now author, blogger, and substitute teacher in Palm Beach County, FL. She has two daughters: Tierra Sherelle and Tashara Burnett. Tierra teaches Math and Science in Atlanta, GA and is a former Baltimore Ravens Cheerleader. Tashara Burnett, a published author of two books, is a full-time college student and mother of Tena's only grandchild, eight-year-old, Noah Ryan.

Tena is available for book signings, book club discussions, and speaking engagements. Send serious inquiries to **AuthorTena.Lawyer@gmail.com**, with specifics of your request.